Prelude

FROM EARLY IN HIS career to the publication of his two volumes of *Systematic Theology*, Robert Jenson has described himself as a theologian of culture.[1] Jenson's every theological effort is borne out of his engagement in the conversation that the church shares with the cultures that surround her. The ensuing interface between theology and culture within Jenson's work is evident for all to see. Few contemporary theologians, if any, have made cultural considerations so central to their program. All this is part of a relentless drive towards a truly systematic theology. The gospel, according to Jenson, comprises the total story of all existence, and subsequently speaks *to* and *through* every avenue of life and history. Hence there is no area of culture that can avoid the glare of theological extrapolation and no aspect of theology that can deflect the scrutiny of cultural reflection.

In his attempt to design and construct a theological system capable of containing and conveying culture, Jenson alerts us to his own intellectual inheritance. As James J. Buckley argues, having been bold enough to build the first large scale systematic metaphysics since the collapse of Hegelianism, Karl Barth's own legacy lives on in this Norwegian American theologian of the twentieth and twenty-first centuries.[2] Commencing with his doctoral studies, published in the 1963 monograph, *Alpha and Omega: A Study in the Theology of Karl Barth,* the construction of a coherent theological system has been Jenson's lifelong labor of love.[3] With the major themes first outlined in, *Story and Promise: A Brief Theology of the Gospel about Jesus,* Jenson published his

1. Jenson, *Systematic Theology Volume One.*
2. Buckley, "Intimacy," 18.
3. Jenson, *Alpha and Omega.*

program in full some twenty-five years later in the two volumes entitled, *Systematic Theology*.[4] Although much has developed between times, the publications represent a powerful testimony to the consistency and cohesion of Jenson's thought through time.

As a theologian, Jenson is curious and courageous, dramatic and provocative. He can be prone to the most delightful, while occasionally frustrating, flight of fancy. At times, he appears the model systematician, while at others his virtuosic ability and tendency towards theological extemporization are both exhilarating and confounding. His refusal to accept the metaphysical language handed down to Western thought by Greek philosophy, and his subsequent insistence upon an alternative universal grammar rooted in the gospel, has caused some to denounce him as unsystematic.[5] However, other colleagues have applauded loudly both the courage and content of his convictions. In deciding upon Jenson as the subject of this work, I can recall two decisive discussions with my then tutor, Colin Gunton. The first concerned the lack of secondary literature devoted to Jenson's work to date. We will return to this issue at the end of the introduction. The second revolved around Jenson's ability to design and defend a theological program. "Like all great thinkers," Gunton said of his friend and colleague, "he manages to avoid falling through the holes in his own argument." In the main, the study that follows heralds the importance of Jenson's theology while occasionally reinforcing Gunton's quip. Above all, I hope to demonstrate the significant benefits that are to be derived from an in-depth engagement with this imaginative and profound figure.

While enquiries abound as to the details of his methodology, the overriding pursuit of Jenson's theology is clear, and furthermore no apology shall be given. On each and every page, in one way or another, Jenson asks, "Who is God?" Avoiding all excuses, theology begins and ends with this one question. Jenson's retort is somewhat brusque: God

4. Jenson, *Story and Promise*.

5. Labelling Jenson is easier said than done. Even in his boldest imaginings he eludes easy classification. His rejection of the metaphysics inherited by the classical tradition is a case in point. As A. N. Williams suggests, Jenson has become "increasingly sympathetic to and more deeply steeped in" those aspects of the tradition which owed most to the metaphysics of Greek philosophy. Williams, "The Parlement of Foules," 188.

RHYMING HOPE AND HISTORY

Rhyming Hope and History

THEOLOGY AND CULTURE IN THE WORK OF ROBERT JENSON

~

Russell D. Rook

PICKWICK *Publications* · Eugene, Oregon

RHYMING HOPE AND HISTORY
Theology and Culture in the Work of Robert Jenson

Pickwick Publications
A Division of Wipf and Stock Publishers
199 W. 8th Ave., Suite 3
Eugene, OR 97401

www.wipfandstock.com

ISBN 13: 978-1-60899-600-1

Cataloging-in-Publication data:

Rook, Russell D.

Rhyming hope and history : theology and culture in the work of Robert Jenson / Russell D. Rook.

xxii + 218 p. ; 23 cm. Includes bibliographical references.

ISBN 13: 978-1-60899-600-1

1. Jenson, Robert W. 2. Christianity and culture. 3. Christianity and art. 4. Music—Religious aspects. 5. Aesthetics—Religious aspects—Christianity. 6. Theology, architecture and art. I. Title.

BR115.C8 R660 2012

Manufactured in the U.S.A.

Contents

Acknowledgments

THERE IS VIRTUALLY NOTHING about writing that I find easy. That said, penning thanks and acknowledgments is among the harder tasks. While my name appears on the cover, *Rhyming Hope and History* has certainly been a community effort. For this reason, not all who deserve thanks will fit on this page. However, I hope that these few ineloquent words will honor the countless colleagues and companions who have contributed to this work. Above all, I offer these paragraphs, and all that follow, with eternal thanksgiving to the gracious God who has given me everything.

This book has its beginnings in my doctoral studies. As a result, my thanks go firstly, to Bishop Lesslie Newbigin for showing me the world-changing possibilities of theology. Lesslie all but enrolled me for post-graduate studies with Professor Colin Gunton. I am ever grateful for the theological hotbed provided by the students and faculty of King's College London and to Colin for his inspirational teaching and introduction to the person and work of Professor Robert Jenson. As the subject of my work, I am grateful to Robert Jenson for his dramatic and ever engaging body of work, gracious and patient correspondence, and for one day in Princeton that will live long in my memory.

I also owe thanks to Dr. Brian Horne for his unstinting commitment to my theological development and for not once moaning at me for being late! In recent years my work and life has been enriched immeasurably by Dr. Stephen Holmes. I value Stephen's friendship and guidance more than he'll ever know and look forward to the realization of some of those projects we have imagined over coffees and curries. I also offer my heartfelt thanks to the staff and students at St. Mary's

College of the University of St. Andrew's, the resources and support provided by the British Library and the University of South Africa.

In the time that it took to research and write *Rhyming Hope and History,* my work and ministry have taken numerous turns. Through all of these I am grateful to my family, friends, and colleagues who enable me to pursue work and study and remain patient on the many occasions when my reflection and activism don't quite rhyme. Thanks must go to The Salvation Army for investing in my theological education; the ALOVE UK team for teaching me what it means to work for and follow Jesus; to the executive of YOUTHWORK the partnership and to the Spring Harvest leadership team and theme groups for their immense friendship and encouragement. I am also ever grateful to Raynes Park Community Church for continuing to teach me what it means to be part of the body of Christ.

Last, and by no means least, I must acknowledge some of my companions in the theological journey of life. To Mark Knight, a great friend who has taught me a lot about theology and almost as much about coffee, I am eternally indebted. To Phil Wall, for his unique brand of friendship and brotherhood, it is an honor to "do life deeply" with you. For Andrew Barton, Gary Bishop, Luke Bretherton, Tania Bright-Cook, Chuck Day, Philip Garnham, Adrian Gosling, Andrew Grinnell, David Hitchcock, Johnny Laird, Ian Mayhew, Andrew and Janet Miles, Phil Needham, Dean Pallant, Geoff Ryan, Barry Sawyer, Matthew Smith, Maeve Sherlock, Chick and Margaret Yuill, and others too many to mention, thank you for sharing your lives with me. Thanks also to Bri Stynes l'Hostis for preparing the manuscript and to Dr. Robin Parry for your editorial skill and support.

I am grateful to Ma, and my in-laws in South Africa, for their hospitality during my sabbatical and for keeping Charlotte and the kids busy while I was in the library. To my family, who have invested in my education from the earliest opportunity, and who have graciously suffered the subsequent silences and stress: I owe you more than I can hope to repay. To Nonna, Dad and Sandy, Mum and Linda, Lyndall and Phil, Geoff and Patricia, I simply say "Thank you."

Finally to Charlotte, Joe and Toby, thanks for the love you afford me and the price you pay. It is a sacred honor and joy to share your hopes and history.

Russ Rook
September 2011

Abbreviations

Citations from these works by Robert W. Jenson will be referenced using the following abbreviations.

A&O   *Alpha and Omega: A Study in the Theology of Karl Barth.* New York: Thomas Nelson and Sons, 1963.

AT   *America's Theologian A Recommendation of Jonathan Edwards.* New York: Oxford University Press, 1988.

ETC   *Essays in Theology of Culture.* Grand Rapids: Eerdmans, 1995.

KOTHF   *The Knowledge of Things Hoped For: The Sense of Theological Discourse.* New York: Oxford University Press, 1969.

S&P   *Story and Promise: A Brief Theology of the Gospel about Jesus.* Philadelphia: Fortress, 1983.

ST 1:   *Systematic Theology. Volume One: The Triune God.* New York: Oxford University Press, 1997.

ST 2:   *Systematic Theology. Volume Two: The Works of God.* New York: Oxford University Press, 1999.

VW   *Visible Words: The Interpretation and Practice of Christian Sacraments.* Philadelphia: Fortress, 1978.

Citations from the underlying work will be referenced using the following abbreviation.

TTC   *Trinity, Time, and Church: A Response to the Theology of Robert W. Jenson,* edited by Colin Gunton. Grand Rapids: Eerdmans, 2000.

is "whoever raised Jesus from the dead!"[6] In this central truth, we have obtained the password to every honest investigation of theology and culture. For it is the centrality of the resurrection which provides the gospel with its seal of authority over all other realities. Furthermore, the gospel story enacted by Christ in his life, death, and resurrection, is not merely a narrative concerning God's intervention in human history, but also reveals the dramatic life and personality of the triune God. Hence, for Jenson, it is only through the trinitarian language of the gospel that humans can truly grasp creation and the creator.

Having edited and compiled an exceptional collection of essays in his honor, Colin Gunton's title provides the perfect précis of Jenson's theology. *Trinity, Time, and Church,* outlines the two foundational triumvirates of his system.[7] The first is that of the triune God himself. For Jenson, all theology is framed by a trinitarian consideration and commitment. Jenson's weightiest publications reinforce the point. *The Triune Identity: God according to the Gospel,* and the first volume of his systematics, *The Triune God,* place Jenson firmly within the twentieth-century revival of trinitarian theology.[8] For this reason, the triune God is not be confused with the god of human religion. In Jenson, the God of Israel and the church does not identify himself as an amorphous power in the sky, nor as a multitude of unreachable deities, but rather discloses the "proper name for the God of the gospel: he is called 'Jahve.'"[9] As such, God reveals himself in contradistinction to the fictitious deities and anthropocentric projections of human religion. In Christ, we meet the fullness of this revelatory God and from hereon know him and relate to him in three particular persons. He is Father, Son, and Holy Spirit, and what's more, he will brook no competitors. For Jenson, this creed comprises the one marked theological discovery of our time.

The Trinity initiates Jenson's second theological threefold formula. In this, the triune God is found alongside the concept of time and the community of the church. Jenson's treatment of time constitutes what is arguably his most significant contribution to contemporary theological

6. *ST* 1:44.

7. Gunton, *Trinity, Time, and Church.*

8. Jenson, *The Triune Identity.*

9. *S&P,* 113.

debate. For Jenson, the names Father, Son, and Spirit do not represent an inconsequential list of God's personal ingredients, but rather outline a narrative which constitutes the very life and nature of the godhead. The triune God is a timely God with a history all his own. What's more, we, his creation, have become part of this time and history. Henceforth, solicitations to God's timelessness are to be deemed a denial of the one true God and are exposed as a retreat into human religion. We will return to time in a moment and from hereon with some frequency. The finale that this timely, triune God has for his creation is wrapped up in the life and work of his church. It is in this community that God makes himself available to creation. As Buckley points out, Jenson's theology is characterized by an inseparable link between the communion of the saints and "the identity and character of the triune God, who is the beginning and middle and *telos* of human and cosmic life."[10] In the life and community of the church mankind becomes part of God's story and in this event we anticipate the climax of history.[11]

Before we frame the work ahead, one final Jensonian tendency begs our acknowledgement. While the Trinity, time, and the church comprise the major themes of Jenson's output, a word should be reserved for the one who makes this music possible in the first place. A misinformed reading of Jenson might well subjugate these subjects in favor of Jenson's Christology. However, Jenson does not exalt Christ above the triune God, nor does he promote him as the godhead's major constituent. As Gunton has pointed out, Jenson's "Trinitarianism [is] predicated on the claim, developed from Barth, that in Jesus Christ we meet God, and that Jesus is the only eternal Son that there is."[12] Along similar lines, Robert Louis Wilken recounts his response to Jenson's *Systematics*: "I was struck at how biblical it was and how at the same time Trinitarian. To some this may seem puzzling, but the . . . Bible is a book about the triune God, and . . . the God Christians worship and confess

10. Buckley, "Intimacy," 12.

11. Between 1981 and 1989, Williams asserts, Jenson's thought "is dominated by his work on the Trinity, time and divine impassibility." From 1991 onwards, Williams surmises, "he does not reject the stance of his earlier work . . . but turns to issues pressing on the contemporary church." Williams, "Parlement of Foules," 189.

12. Gunton, "Creation and Mediation in the Theology of Robert W. Jenson," 83.

is identified by the narrative of the Bible."[13] While Christ maintains a towering presence over each and every movement of Jenson's work, he does so as the maestro who conveys the music of the triune discourse to creation. Instrumental within human history, Christ conducts and calls on us to take up our part within the triune music. Hence, Jenson's trinitarian treatment of theology and culture is mediated by means of his Christology.

The book that follows is chiastic in structure. The first three chapters will focus upon the major presuppositions of Jenson's thought and theology. As intimated moments ago, the first of these has to do with Jenson's distinctive treatment of time. Before all else, the created order is interpreted by Jenson as evidence of the God who has time for us. The roots of this belief lie deep within his own philosophical inheritance. As in each of the first three chapters, our discussion will compare and contrast Jenson's work with one of his chief informants. In the case of time, we will turn to G. W. F. Hegel. While not pleased to be called a "Hegelian," Jenson's position within the tradition, and his subsequent treatment of time, merit the description. This said, Jenson's work presents a profound revision and significant departure from his predecessor's position.

At the heart of Jenson's notion of time is a refutation of classical theology's polarization of time and timelessness. In Jenson, the triune God is a temporal infinity, and his creation is the time that he takes for his creatures.[14] As a result, divine temporality is regarded as the presupposition of created reality. In almost every area of his work, Jenson reinforces this position by balancing the ontological and eschatological nature of reality. In Jenson, our desire to grasp the reality of creation and the creator is but an attempt to rhyme our hope and history. In this striving, Jenson declares, we can come to know the God who has time for us.

Following swiftly on the heels of time, comes space. While the categories have often fought against one another for pre-eminence, in theological terms they are inseparable. In Jenson, his elaborate theology of time initiates his exploration of space. We now identify the influence

13. Wilken, "Is Pentecost a Peer of Easter?," 176.

14. *ST* 1:218.

of Jonathan Edwards upon Jenson's thought. Drawing upon Edwards' use of Newtonian science, Jenson explores the spatial implications of his work on time. The God who has time, suggests Jenson, is his own triune space, and it is through the extension of this space in creation that we live and move and have our being. As with Hegel, Jenson revises and extends his forerunner's conclusions. Rebutting the notion of God's existence as pure unassailable spirit, Jenson draws attention towards God's eternal embodiment within the triune life. Pointing to the Son, or Word, Jenson posits Christ as the embodiment of the Father through the power of the Spirit. The development proves crucial. It is now possible, in created time and space, to identify the Son as God's temporal embodiment for and with us.

Having placed time and space within the triune life, and consequently as precedents of existence, Jenson's third theological presupposition concerns language. As we confront one another in time and space, we use language to confirm our existence and identify the realities that surround us. As one of the pioneers in the interface between theology and linguistic philosophy, Jenson is quick to make use of the work of Ludwig Wittgenstein and asks whether theology might function as a language-game through which the realities of time and space can be explicated and fulfilled. As in both prior cases, Jenson modifies and extends the Wittgensteinian scheme and proposes that God be included in our language-games. Through the history of Israel, the incarnation, and the community of the church, God has revealed himself as a Word in time and space. According to this divine self-disclosure, all of creation is dependent upon the words spoken by, and between, the triune God. For Jenson, the temporal infinity of God is constituted in the eternal conversation between the members of the Trinity. If all existence, and hence all language, is premised upon the Word that constitutes God's own triune conversation, then far from resisting the import of theological categories to language, the philosopher must agree that language is itself the export of revelation.

As the third presupposition of existence, language gives birth to culture as the totalized discourse concerning the nature of reality. In this realm there are no longer any clear internal epistemological boundaries and so all talk is to be regarded as God-talk.[15] Premised upon the God who invites creation to join the conversation that constitutes his triune life, the existence of language is to be understood as the mandate of heaven. By calling all creatures and cultures to join his discourse, God invites creation to prayer, praise, and proclamation. And while all language is premised upon the triune conversation, one defining language-act is central to any adequate account of reality. In the historic story of Jesus' life, death, and resurrection, we discover the vocabulary and grammar through which mankind can interpret reality. In the narrative of Christ's incarnation, we identify, at first hand, the God who has time, space, and language for us. And in our ecclesial re-enactments of his life-story we both remember and anticipate his coming. The telling of the gospel story, as lived in the community of the church, mediates God's real presence within creation. God is embodied in created time and space, by the power of the Spirit and through the resurrected Christ in his church. The church is here deemed the *totus Christus,* or unifying presence of Christ and his church.

Jenson's ecclesiology forms the central point of our chiastic conversation. In the preceding treatment of time, space and language, Jenson constructs a stage for, what will be, some of his most dramatic pronouncements. The concept of the *totus Christus* not only fulfils Jenson's previous theological strivings but also provides the starting point for consideration of culture. In his lofty estimation of the church, we witness Jenson's theology of culture in its most revealing and startling light. While his reliance upon the doctrine of the *totus Christus* betrays an inherent Lutheran streak, it would be wrong to address his ecclesiology as the mere premise of his tradition.[16] Tuomo Mannerma sums up Jenson's ecclesial aims and expectations most succinctly saying, "He works out his theology in the context of the *one* church and in the anticipation of the *one* church."[17]

Amidst all the earth's philosophies and religions, Jenson envisions the culture of the church as the very language by which all existence is to

15. Jenson, *Essays in Theology of Culture,* 223–24. Jenson's appropriation of Patristic thought is evident at this point. See: Williams, "Parlement of Foules," 189.

16. *ST* 1: vii.

17. Mannerma, "Doctrine of Justification and Trinitarian Ontology," 139.

be determined, expounded, and fulfilled. As a story, drama, and polity, the church's internal and external address constitutes Christ's embodiment within the world and his speech to creation. As Christ's own body-language, the church draws together past and future and, in so doing, rhymes its hopes and history. From here, the chiasm plays out in ever widening circles as we consider the implications of Jenson's theology for culture and the arts. The final chapters will both relate back to the first three chapters of the book and venture forward into unexplored ground. In each chapter we will utilize theories of culture and the arts to confirm or deny Jenson's theological presuppositions, while further applying his conclusions to the cultural life of the church.

Returning at first to language we consider Jenson's linguistic theory of culture. As "one of the most distinguished efforts in twentieth-century theology to bring the problem of Christianity and culture into focus," Christoph Schwöbel highlights the significance of Jenson's work in this domain.[18] In over thirty years of publications, Jenson has searched and scrutinized a bewildering array of subjects, issues, and art-forms. More recently his published lectures entitled, "Christ as Culture," and a subsequent essay on "Christian Civilization," have outlined a more systematic approach to the subject.[19] In the life of the church, the language of the gospel gives birth to a new culture. For Jenson, this culture is the language of the *totus Christus,* and hence, in the church, God's word is embodied in a cultural form and thus Christ becomes culture. As the *totus Christus,* Christ and his church act to transform nature and, in so doing, call forth new creation. Through dialogue with Richard H. Niebuhr and Kathryn Tanner we will test Jenson's theory further.

The life and language of the church comprises all manner of cultural forms. In the final chapters we will further investigate Jenson's position on the nature of reality and the *totus Christus,* by examining the role of certain art forms in the world and in the church. In the first instance, we will explore the place of art and architecture in our grasp of space and in Christ's embodiment of his church. Both in the artist's appropriation of space and in Christ's life in the church, we witness an

18. Schwöbel, "Once Again Christ and Culture," 115.

19. Jenson, "Christ as Polity"; Jenson, "Christ as Art"; Jenson, "Christ as Drama"; Jenson, "Christian Civilization."

experiment with a possible world. As a result, the church's artists and architects labor to interpret creation and, in so doing, build a platform upon which Christ can be present to, and with, his people. As in the previous section, our discussion will be enhanced by two notable inter-locutors, namely, Paul Tillich and Nicholas Wolterstorff.

Finally, we come to music and the completion of the chiasm. With this art form of considerable ineffability we conclude where we com-menced. Hardly concretized in space, music exists as an experiment with time. That which is the most under represented of all art-forms within Jenson's writing, makes for a curiously fitting finale. Through our dialogue with Augustine and Jeremy Begbie, the language of music is posited as the ultimate object lesson and cultural outworking of Jenson's theological conception of time. This particular cultural language deep-ens our awareness of temporality and provides new resources for the language of theology. The cultural converse of music returns us to the God who has time for us. Having appropriated the language of music for theology, Jenson can proclaim that God is a fugue, and as J. Augustine Di Noia reminds us, this word play is more than metaphorical.[20] As a community, Christ invites the church to join the capacious musical movement that constitutes the triune fellowship. In this, music charac-terizes the eternal life that is experienced and anticipated in the *totus Christus*. Like Edwards before him, the end for Jenson is music. In this musical event, theology and culture become one, and hope and history rhyme forevermore.[21]

The sights and sounds of Jenson's theology of culture are undoubt-edly impressive. They are always eye-catching and rarely fail to demand our full attention. However, at times the prevailing view may prove un-easy on the eye and the background noise disturbing to the ear. Few, if any, spectators will reach the end of this book without the occasional, and potentially perpetual, sensation of discomfort and disquiet. In my

20. Di Noia, "Jenson's Theology," 99.

21. Colin Gunton, Richard Neuhaus, and Francis Watson all refer to Jenson as "America's Theologian." The characterisation highlights Jenson's connections with Edwards in particular, and with the history and culture of America in general. While reflection upon Jenson as a distinctly American theologian would no doubt prove fascinating, it is beyond the scope and remit of this study.

research, I have seized upon every available opportunity to present and discuss Jenson's theology of culture. While much of these presentations have slipped into my subconscious, the discussions that followed remain vivid. Jenson never fails to instigate energetic dialogue, excited pontifications, vigorous debate and, occasionally, outright offence. It is this provocative, innovative, and courageous streak within his work that makes him one of contemporary theology's most compelling figures.[22] For Jenson, theology is the drama of the cosmos and thus incident, tension, crisis, and resolution are all essential tools of his trade. Jenson's lectures provide onlooking theologians with the same breathless anticipation that a cinema audience enjoys through the climax of a spine-tingling thriller. Although one is fully aware that he will leave us with Christ, the Trinity, and the church, one remains persistently uncertain as to where he might take us along the way. In Aristotle, as Jenson is fond of reminding us, a perfect drama comprises a chain of events which the audience could not have foreseen, only to discover with hindsight that it could not have been any other way. Short of the eschaton, it is impossible for any theologian's work to live up to this definition. However, as both systematician and dramatist, Jenson is certainly bold enough to try.

While hardly a kamikaze theologian, Jenson is not shy of the potential perils and pitfalls of his own program. At times in our study, helpful detraction may turn into unhelpful distraction. Along with many of his critics, it is impossible to ignore Jenson's optimistic tendency towards the grand unifying theory by which the gospel rhymes all hope and history. Likewise, Jenson's routine reification of the church may occasionally grate with our ecclesiological experience. His unyielding insistence upon God's immanence may cause frustration. His unremitting conviction of the oneness between God and his church might well prove disconcerting. However, whatever the theological irritation or discomfort, the solution lies not in a quick recourse to our doctrinal default, but rather in our ability to rest a while, to engage in dialogue and, in so doing, to endeavor to understand this profound and occasionally elusive thinker. Despite his criticisms of Jenson's systematics, Douglas Farrow eloquently characterises the man and his work: "I find

22. Gunton, "Creation and Mediation," 82.

the work (like its author!) congenial on a number of levels: its eschewal of extensive prolegomena, of apologetics, of political correctness; its critical acumen and creativity, by which traditional *loci* are dislocated and relocated in stimulating ways; its ecclesial orientation and its devotion to the narrative footing of the gospel, especially to the measure of the resurrection; its concern always to be theology, and . . . its attention to things creaturely."[23]

One surprising aspect of Jenson's work concerns the comparative lack of theological response and secondary literature that has emanated from the theological community. As Gabriel Fackre and others have pointed out, other than Wolfhart Pannenberg, there are few living theologians who can claim such a significant and sizeable contribution to the discipline.[24] While the former has been the subject of multiple monographs, essays, and articles, Jenson's contribution has yet to receive the attention that it so richly deserves. It is sadly beyond the capacity of this work, and its author, to provoke such a conversation. However, it is my honest prayer that the church, which has so much to gain from this important body of work and this seminal figure, will be enriched by the theologians of culture who cherish his legacy and follow faithfully in his footsteps.

23. Farrow, "Jenson's Theology," 89.
24. Fackre, "The Lutheran Capax Lives," 98.

1

A Brief History in Time:
Jenson and Time

THE FIRST VOLUME OF Robert Jenson's *Systematic Theology* is subtitled, *The Triune God*. Having devoted much of his life to the exploration and exposition of trinitarian theology, the subtitle must surely have written itself. As Richard Neuhaus suggests, in Jenson, "the doctrine of Trinity is the conceptual hardware that runs any software."[1] Having devoted the second volume of his systematics to *The Works of God*, Jenson's programme is classical in its conception. However, this straightforward ordering hides, beneath its shine and polish, a more illusive, chiastic design. This structure, in turn, reveals a second essential theme. For if the triune God is Jenson's primary subject, then time is his "pet" subject; with large parts of his work providing variations upon this theme. At the climax of the first volume, Jenson uses time to build his grand finale, namely the establishing of the triune identity.[2] Having cleared his throat in the introduction of the second volume, time returns. The remaining pages comprise the outworkings of Jenson's "timely" trinitarian theology.

In Jenson, time is the trinitarian presupposition of creation and as such predicates our grasp of reality. This treatment of temporality

1. Neuhaus, "Jenson in the Public Square," 243.
2. *ST* 1:165–223.

is among Jenson's most marked contributions to current theological debate.[3] For this reason, any investigation of Jenson's theology must include a discussion on time. It is "an old and central insight," Jenson declares, "that creation is above all God's taking time for us."[4] In the context of this study, time forms both the beginning and end of our story. In this commencing chapter, we will consider Jenson's work alongside those who have influenced his thinking on time. In particular, we will focus on the work of G. W. F. Hegel. While I am by no means the first to point to a Hegelian streak, the observation is never welcomed by Jenson himself. Later on, we will introduce another Hegelian to the debate, namely Karl Barth, but for now we turn to Hegel.

A Brief History in Infinity: The Concept of Time in G. W. F. Hegel

Karl Barth once asked why Hegel had not "become for the Protestant world something similar to what Thomas Aquinas was for Roman Catholicism?"[5] That said, Hegel's influence stretches far beyond Protestantism. Having himself witnessed the impact of Hegel on Barth, Hans Küng pronounces Søren Kierkegaard, Paul Tillich, Karl Rahner, and Jürgen Moltmann, all within Hegel's line of succession.[6] This is not to mention the countless philosophers, historians, artists, and political theorists who have also worked in his wake. G. W. F. Hegel, we can conclude, casts considerable light and a sizeable shadow over much of modern thought. As a leading exponent of Hegelian philosophy, Michael Inwood captures the complexity of his subject. While renowned as a most systematic thinker, his work reflects two, almost contradictory, philosophical characters. "One of them is a grim, forbidding metaphysician . . . He tried to reduce the world, the mind, nature, and anything else he could think of, to pure thought. He held perverse theological doctrines which, while more digestible than his logic, are no less unap-

---

3. Although not alone as a trinitarian pioneer within postmodernity, his illations on time distinguish him from the crowd.

4. *ST* 2:25.

5. Barth, *Protestant Theology in the 19th Century,* 384.

6. Küng, *The Incarnation of God,* 1.

petizing. He was more than just tempted to claim that history ended with himself. The other Hegel is a more amiable fellow."[7]

While ever searching for that final synthesis and ultimate resolution, the forefather of dialectical philosophy came to embody the thesis and antithesis of his thought.[8] It is this extraordinary capacity to absorb diverse, complex, and occasionally contradictory elements, that provided a system capable of containing human logic, the supernatural, physical nature, the arts, science and politics, and, for our present purposes, finitude and the infinite. The vast scope of Hegel's work can be summarized in one attendant ambition: In a time of epistemological crisis, Hegel attempted to provide a universally warrantable truth, applicable to all aspects of the corporate human project. This lifelong quest is characterized in his notion of God as *Absolute Spirit*.

In Hegel, Absolute Spirit is "the one" ground of all being and reality.[9] In this God, being passes over into essence thus vindicating him as the Absolute Being, or the absolute idea; the fact that reality matches the concept.[10] God is here to be regarded as the conceptual sum of all forms of reality.[11] An implicit bias towards pneumatology is there for all to see: "In the first place God is Spirit," Hegel reminds us, and "in his abstract character he is defined as universal spirit that particularizes itself."[12] As a result, mankind's reality is defined by his own spirit and his ensuing connection to the Absolute; human spirit flows out from, and eventually returns to, the Absolute. Ever caught between ontology and eschatology, man's existence incorporates finite and infinite realities. Although mortality is the curse of finitude, man's evolving connection with the absolute provides him with infinite possibilities.[13] For while one can dis-

---

7. Inwood, *Hegel,* xvi.

8. Whether Hegel is first and foremost a philosopher or theologian has been the cause of much recent discussion. What is apparent is that he is clearly both.

9. Hegel, *Lectures,* 1:366–68.

10. Hegel, *Lectures* 1:426–27.

11. In Hegel, God is not to be treated as a category distinct from the concept of God as, for instance, a lion is distinct from the concept of a lion. Inwood, *A Hegel Dictionary,* 113.

12. Hegel, *Lectures,* 3:191.

13. Hegel, *Lectures,* 3:208–11.

tinguish between finitude and the infinite in Hegel, the two categories are never treated as antinomies. On the contrary, summoning the finite and infinite together, Hegel proclaims their meeting as the mutual basis of faith, hope and life: "In this profound sense the Christian religion is the religion of spirit, though not in the manifold trivial sense of being a spiritual religion, venerating abstraction, regarding it as substance, essence. On the contrary, the Christian religion is the unification of the infinite antithesis, the one and only genuinely speculative enjoyment of the nature of God, or of spirit. This is its content and vision, and it is there for the ordinary, uneducated consciousness."[14]

Hegel's connection of the finite and infinite is formed in reaction to Kant. For Hegel, the Kantian confinement of rationalism to the finite realm undermines reality itself. If God is reason, then how can reason be finite? Hegel asks. Furthermore, finite rationality presupposes the infinite as, having decided upon what is finite, we have presupposed infinity and travelled to its borders. James Yerkes paraphrases the Hegelian suspicion: "A careful observation of reason 'in its actual employment' will show that all philosophical agnosticism about the nature of the infinite is *ipso facto* self-contradictory."[15]

The infinite, in Hegel's thought, cannot simply be considered as the polar opposite of the immediate finite. To do this, would be to constrain all human activity within the finite and, at the same time, to deny the presupposing reality of the infinite realm itself. To idealise the finite is simply to ignore the fact that the infinite consumes and consummates the finite. Finite reality is not without end but rather, finds its own end in the reality of infinity. For Hegel, "Kant's so-called critique of the cognitive faculties . . . amount[s] to nothing but the absolute restriction of reason to the form of finitude."[16] Furthermore, if thought has only the finite at its disposal, then "limitedness" itself has been made "into an eternal law."[17] Since Hegel considers all truth to be infinite, this move proves unbearable. If finite limitation demarcates our rational reach, then the discovery of truth has been stretched into sheer impossibil-

14. Ibid., 140–41.

15. Y erkes, *The Christology of Hegel*, 78.

16. Hegel, *Theologian of the Spirit*, 80.

17. Ibid., 80.

ity. The resulting damage to humanity is considerable, as its essence has been replaced by "an absolute sensibility" and thus, mankind is no longer "a glowing spark of eternal beauty, or a spiritual focus of the universe."[18]

It fell to Hegel to reinstate the connection between the finite and infinite, and thus reaffirm the holy mystery of humanity. The solution was to be found in a modification of Kant's own subjective idealism. In Kant's notion of idealism, inner experience is predicated upon outer experiences.[19] By connecting the self-conscious to the infinite, and thus locating man in relation to God, Hegel creates his own form of "absolute idealism." Here, God's infinity is not disconnected from man's finitude, but rather becomes the purposive and teleological ground of personal being. Our identity is thus constituted in our mutual experience of finitude and the infinite. It is now possible to elevate ourselves beyond the finite and reach the infinite consciousness of the Absolute. God holds both the finite and the infinite together and thus reconciles man with the reality that he himself is as Absolute Spirit. Spirit, in Hegel, "is an eternal process of self-cognition in self-consciousness, streaming out to the finite focus of finite consciousness, and then returning to what spirit actually is, a return in which *divine* self-consciousness breaks forth."[20]

The challenge this presents to orthodox Christian thought is apparent. If finite reality occurs within the infinite, or Absolute Spirit, then it follows that finite existence takes place within God. Furthermore, if God is defined merely as Spirit, and has no other embodiment, then all externality must be sublated into him. Hegel continues: "The unity of divine and human nature has a significance not only for the definition of human nature but just as much for that of the divine. This is because all differentiation, all finitude, though it is a transitory moment, is a moment of the process of the divine nature, which it develops, and hence it is grounded within the divine nature itself."[21]

In his attempts to reconnect the finite and the infinite, Hegel performed a great service for theology. However, having followed him to

---

18. Ibid., 81.

19. Caygill, *A Kant Dictionary*, 239–40.

20. Hegel, *Lectures*, 3:233.

21. Ibid., 3:110.

the logical conclusion of his thought, it is surely a case of pantheism or bust. With finitude's return to the infinite, Hegel relocates temporality within the God who is Absolute Spirit. Time and history now not only belong to God but have become his eternal manifestation. "God in God's eternal truth is represented as a state of affairs in time."[22]

A Brief History in Eternity: The Concept of Time in Jenson.

For Hegel, revealed religion is predicated upon two indispensable realities. The first, concerns God's existence in and for himself, and the second denotes his existence for others. Jenson utilises a similar couplet. Firstly, in Jenson, God exists for his own glory and secondly, because of that glory, he has time for creation. Creation, for Jenson, is the accommodation of others into God's own triune life. We may call this accommodation "time."[23] It is Hegel's re-evaluation of the relationship between finitude and the infinite that makes the formulation possible. Convinced that God is the ground of all reality and knowledge, Jenson, like Hegel before him, proves prone to the grand unifying theory. However, while common ground is evident, a critical delineation between Jenson and Hegel soon becomes apparent. While Hegelian philosophy pursues reason as the fount of all knowledge, Jenson remains convinced that it is the gospel narrative which provides our best access to reality. "Were the gospel fully spoken," Jenson asserts, "it would be a word about every item of reality . . . every person, every atomic particle, every galaxy, every animal."[24] For this reason, Jenson holds that all cultural and philosophical converse is the subject of Christian theology. "We may press theology's claim very bluntly by noting that theology . . . claims to know the one God of all and so to know the one decisive fact about all things, so that theology must be either a universal and founding discipline or a delusion."[25]

---

22. Hegel, *Theologian of Spirit*, 229.

23. *ST* 2:25.

24. *S&P*, 76.

25. *ST* 1:20. Jenson cites another Hegelian, Wolfhart Pannenberg, as a key contemporary exponent of this position.

While the pursuit of universal truth leads Hegel to the infinite, the grounding of all reality within the gospel transports Jenson to time. In a paper written for "The Center for Theology and the Natural Sciences," and later published in the collection, *Essays in Theology of Culture,* Jenson posed a question that has recurred from hereon throughout his thought. "Does God Have Time?" he asks: "It is the common opinion that deity is defined by not having to have time, or in the language of the tradition, by 'impassability', i.e., immunity to temporal challenges and opportunities alike. The very concept of eternity is supposed to come about by negating our experience of time."[26]

Jenson's suspicion is that much of Christian theology has got the wrong time. The problem was inherited initially from the ancient world. In a series of passages in the first volume of Jenson's *Systematics*, and a further essay entitled, "Aspects of the Doctrine of Creation," Jenson outlines his dissatisfaction with pre-modern theology's treatment of temporality.[27] Greek philosophy offered the early church two distinct, yet largely inadequate, formulations of time. In the first, or Platonic model, time exists as an ever-turning wheel with eternity as its central point. Such a repetitive notion would appear to render God unable to direct, or intervene upon events within time. The endless revolution and repetition of time provides God with a circle that cannot be squared. For Jenson, Plato's revolving wheel is not a true eternity.

In the second ancient account, or the Aristotelian model, time was regarded as the "metric of external and physical movement provided by a standard such movement."[28] This measurement was provided by the movement of the heavenly bodies. As mediators of divinity, these planets and stars enabled Aristotle to approximate the motion of time to that of eternity. Exported from Greek mythology the model soon ran aground within the church. As a Jewish sect, the church knew what Israel had known from her outset, namely that while sun, moon and

---

26. *ETC,* 190. With some irony, Jenson suggests that this doctrine is often expounded by those who do not believe in God yet somehow consider timelessness to be a defining quality of deity if such a category were possible.

27. *ST* 1:94–100; 1:138–39; 1:216. Jenson, "Aspects of the Doctrine of Creation," 17–28.

28. *ST* 2:31.

stars may have been the "lamps and clocks that" YHWH placed in the sky, gods they certainly are not.[29] That said, Aristotle's conception proves equally problematic within his own context. Jenson takes up the commentary: "The Greeks' great fear was brought to a formula by Aristotle: 'Can it be that all things pass away?' Mythologically: 'Father Time eats his children—will he get them all?' All Greek religion and its theology, that is, 'philosophy,' is a passionate insistence that the answer be no. Deity is that in which the quest is fulfilled."[30]

Since deity is a quality in Aristotle, it must, Jenson suggests, "admit participation in lesser degrees."[31] Therefore, the more divine something is, the greater its chance of avoiding the seemingly insatiable appetite of Old Father Time. If "the soul, for example, can be conceived as imperishable but mutable in other ways; then it is divine but not *so* divine as the immutable truths to which it looks."[32] Despite the inbuilt contradiction of time and eternity inherent in Greek metaphysics, the model established some security for centuries to come. However, the secularizing impact of the gospel in Europe rendered Greek temporality increasingly inadequate.[33] With God now identified in the person of Christ and the community of the Trinity, the church, and the communities in which she found herself, progressively rejected the ancient tendency to deify the celestial bodies and view the starry host as a heavenly pantheon. It would eventually fall to Augustine to reshape time for a rapidly Christianizing continent. Here, the immanent connection between God and time is formalized for the first time. Jenson acknowledges his debt in this regard: "It is an old and central insight, that creation is above all God's taking time for us; the point is primally established in Augustine's *Confessions,* where the effort to understand God's creating turns out to have as its material content in but one question: 'What is time?'"[34]

29. Gunton, *Doctrine of Creation,* 50.

30. *ST:* 1:94.

31. Ibid., 94.

32. Ibid., 94.

33. Jenson: "Very early in my theological reflection I was struck with the secularizing impact of the gospel." *ST* 1:ix.

34. *ST* 2:25.

Despite a promising a start, the age-old problems soon reappear. For Augustine, God is sheer presence and hence eternity itself. But if God, as the ground of all existence, is characterized as sheer presence, how then can Augustine account for past and future? Furthermore, if God himself admits no past or future, does this not negate all history and eschatology? The problems deepen the further we go. "If the present, in order that there be time, must pass into the past, how can it be said to be?"[35] Having established a connection between God and time in creation, Augustine's link may be about to be severed. We then are forced back to Augustine's original question, "What is time?" Given the Augustinian treatment to date, Jenson can envision but one answer, "Nihil."[36]

Like Aristotle before him, Augustine looks to the soul for resolution. In Augustine, the soul is the image of the infinite presence and forms a geometric point that is also a temporal nullity. However, if the soul is itself temporal, then it can neither defy nor transcend the movement of time. At this point Augustine introduces the concept of memory, ascribing to the soul both an enduring presence that moves with time's flux, and the capacity to both remember past events and anticipate the future.[37] In Augustine, "the presence of past things is memory, the presence of present things is direct apprehension, [and] the presence of future things is expectation."[38] But are there now not three types of time? In Augustine, Jenson concludes, the soul has become, an "ontological oddity," and time, an infinite extension, or *distentio*, of the soul itself:

> What Augustine seems at bottom to have assumed is the Platonic picture of the turning wheel of time with the geometric still point of eternity at its center. As a Christian he could not be content with this picture; he cut the circle and stretched it out as a line, to model the biblical understanding of reality as history. But he continued to think of the point of eternity as equidistant from all temporal points.

35. Jenson, "Aspects of Creation," 25–26.

36. Ibid., 26.

37. This point is made by Pannenberg in an essay in Jenson's honor. Pannenberg, "Eternity, Time and the Trinitarian God," 62.

38. Jenson, "Aspects of Creation," 26.

Many puzzles within Western discourse about time result from this oxymoronic root metaphor.[39]

While more Christian than his Greek predecessors, Augustine's theory of time is fatally flawed. "In few products of intellect," Jenson declares, "are profound insight and obvious muddle so mingled as in Augustine's doctrine of time."[40] From this day onward, Jenson points out, two models of time became proliferate within pre-modern theology. The first is inherited from the Augustinian model above, in which time acts as a measure of internal experience, and the second is a modification of the Aristotelian view, wherein time becomes the measuring device of external movements in space. For Jenson, neither proves satisfactory: The former "doctrine keeps God and the soul in the picture, but constantly threatens to dissolve the otherness of the world out there," while the second "eschews idealism by falling to atheism."[41] Gunton confirms Jenson's verdict: "[With] Augustine's interpretation of God as 'sheer Presence, that is, as sheer timeless consciousness' . . . the created order tends to be evacuated of its significance. The outcome is the apparent implication that only God and the soul have true ontological weight, so that a choice often appears inevitable between idealism and atheism."[42]

Augustine's stretched and indefinitely prolonged linear sequence of the soul is, what Hegel would term, a "bad infinite."[43] No matter how far the line is extended it can never become true infinity. For Jenson, Hegel's re-categorization of the finite and the infinite provides the "chief competition" to the Augustinian view, leaving him to propose what is "undoubtedly . . . [a] Hegelian sort of solution."[44] "Time is precisely the *horizon of experience,* with both nouns demanding full weight . . . Time is indeed, a la Augustine, the 'distention' of a personal reality, and that just *so* it provides creatures with an external metric of created events.

---

39. *ST* 2:32.

40. Ibid., 31.

41. Jenson, "Aspects of Creation," 26–27.

42. Gunton, *Doctrine of Creation*, 7.

43. McCarney, *Hegel on History*, 128.

44. *ST* 2:34. "And why not?" Jenson continues.

That is: the 'stretching out' that makes time is an extension not of finite consciousness but of an infinite enveloping consciousness."[45]

In Jenson, the distention that enables time is not an extension of a created soul, nor a finite personality, but is rather the distention of the triune God. Gunton agrees, suggesting that the Trinity provides the only solution to the Augustinian dilemma.[46] In the perichoretic interplay between the three persons of the Trinity, Jenson suggests, we witness a dramatic narrative "with its [own eternal] *extension* of complication, crisis, and resolution."[47] Here, God is not a sheer point of presence, nor is he the center of an eternally spinning wheel, but rather he is a relational space within which creation find its own place: "Therefore, whether we want to talk about God's 'time' or not, creation is not a problem for God and the posit of time imposes no strain on the character of being. God is roomy; he can make room in himself if he chooses; if he so chooses the room he makes we will call time; and that he creates means that he so chooses."[48]

While timelessness remains for Hegel a defining mark of God's being, Jenson's temporal application of the idealist's scheme enables him to move beyond his predecessor. Working with his own minor modification of Aristotelian time, Hegel is left clinging to the immortality of the soul as Christianity's "definite doctrine."[49] However, having declared timelessness as essentially unreal, Jenson is able to assert the connection between temporality and eternity as the presupposition of all created reality. In so doing, Jenson guarantees that which Augustine cannot safeguard. Creation, in Jenson, is reliant upon the relationship between eternal and temporal time in such a way as to protect both while underlining the reality and importance of the latter.

---

45. Ibid., 2:34.

46. Gunton, *Doctrine of Creation*, 7.

47. Jenson, "Aspects of Creation," 27.

48. Ibid., 27.

49. Hegel, *Lectures* 3:186–87. Martin Heidegger has argued that Hegel's model of time was a reproduction of the Aristotelian model. Inwood, *Hegel Dictionary*, 295. Gunton's critique of Augustine applies here also. In time, Hegel, the idealist, will be forced to choose between pantheism, and atheism.

Having located time within God's eternal life, Jenson is at pains to point out that this same life represents the possibility of creation, and thus of realities which are, by their definition, not God. The creation that God has time for provides evidence enough. Furthermore, in Jenson, the temporality of created reality necessitates God's own eternity for both its past and its future, its hope and its history. In this, Jenson modifies and extends the Hegelian formula. In Jenson's theology, God is free, beyond limitation, and is thus free to be with his creatures in the time and space that he opens for them. With his own Hegelian extension, Jenson declares that God's infinity is to be regarded as a temporal eternity. With this, time is no longer eternity's antinomy but rather its consequence. So once again we ask, "What is time?" The answer is found in Jenson: "Created time is accommodation in God's eternity for others than God."[50]

Now and Then: Eschatology and History according to Hegel

Hegel's exigent teleology, not unlike Jenson's theology, is eschatologically weighted. For Hegel, reason is the idea of history, and thus the passing of time provides the fulfillment of reason's ontology.[51] Through time and history the eternal truth, so embedded within the rational, is revealed as God himself. Here, reason has become the very mode of God's immanence. It is not static, but dynamic and nurtures man's spirit as it goes. Ultimately, Absolute Spirit brings human reason to the point whereby mankind can realize both its beginning and end in God's glorious oneness. "The true is the whole," declares Hegel, "but the whole is nothing other than the essence consummating itself through its development. Of the Absolute it must be said that it is essentially a *result*, that only in the *end* is it what it truly is."[52] In Hegel, creation is driven towards her perfection and completion in God.[53] Reality presupposes perfection, for "God is all reality and hence the reality of being . . . is

---

50. *ST* 2:25.

51. Hegel, *Phenomenology of Spirit*, 27.

52. Hegel, *Phenomenology*, 11.

53. This element of Hegel's thought is redolent throughout Jenson.

contained in the concept of God"[54] Man's journey towards this realization is the course of history itself. The progressive revelation of Absolute Spirit, through philosophical and historical reflection, provides the inner dynamism of Hegel's system:[55] "Spirit is never at rest but always engaged in moving forward . . . so likewise the Spirit in its formation matures slowly and quietly into its new shape, dissolving bit by bit the structure of its previous world, whose tottering state is only hinted at by isolated symptoms."[56]

Hegel remains modernity's chief protagonist of progressive revelation.[57] For Hegel, as Joseph McCarney points out, history is the unfolding of God's own nature.[58] God is subsequently, and progressively, mediated through the movement of history. As a result, creation will be perfected when it attains its final goal, namely the universal realization of Spirit. While initially unconscious of this eschatological drive, the entire business of time and history is viewed by Hegel as creation's awakening to this inherent revelation. For just as a seed contains the tree's future form, so also do the first traces of spirit contain the whole of history. With this, ontology and eschatology become sublated into one and history becomes transformed into God's plan and providence for creation.

God rules and directs this movement through the great figures of history, or the "world historical individuals," as Hegel calls them. These sainted men and women, the heroes of Hegel's faith, identify, expound, and proclaim Absolute Spirit within their own history and culture. However, at the head of this heavenly host stands Christ himself: "The infinite idea of humanity could attach itself only to Christ and see itself realized only in him, for the time had fully come, the idea

54. Hegel, *Lectures* 3:70–71.

55. McCarney notes Hegel's own rejection of circular models: "The circle is ultimately not . . . the most fitting emblem of spirit's development in time." McCarney, *Hegel on History*, 131.

56. Hegel, *Phenomenology*, 6.

57. Hodgson argues that Hegel "did not subscribe to a naively progressivist view of history; rather his vision was deeply tragic, though encompassed within a tragicomic metanarrative for which both alienation and reconciliation are ongoing realities." Hegel, *Theologian of Spirit*, 148.

58. McCarney, *Hegel on History*, 24.

was completely mature in its depths."[59] For Hegel, Christ's incarnation forms the defining drama in the revelation of Absolute Spirit. It is for this reason that Christianity constitutes his Absolute, or Consummate religion. Within the Hegelian system, human history comprises the very unveiling of God's personality and thus, as Hans Küng argues, his system forms an account of God's incarnation throughout history. In Hegel, Christ's incarnation of divine Being comprises the religious revelation and manifestation of the absolute.[60] Through Jesus, the universal is unified with the particular and thus "God is beheld immediately and sensuously as a self, as an actual human individual; only thus *is* God self-consciousness."[61]

At first, Hegel's scheme appears to be a straightforward philosophical extension of classical Christology. However, the development is secured by a somewhat circuitous route. As a self-proclaimed philosophical historian, Hegel's concerns are not motivated by a desire to affirm or enforce the factuality of particular historical events.[62] Rather, he is driven by the rational possibilities that these episodes offer to his own cultural context. This makes for an interesting, and largely self-serving, interpretation of the incarnation. For while the incarnation of Christ is of prime philosophical importance within the Hegelian schema, the establishment of the event as a historical fact is, at best, of secondary importance. While, in Hegel, understanding of the present demands a knowledge of the past, one cannot grasp the meaning of an event by simply knowing its history.[63] Hence for Hegel, theological understanding involves more than simply recording and maintaining past beliefs.

59. Hegel, *Lectures* 3:145.

60. Küng, *Incarnation of God*, 207.

61. Hegel, *Theologian of Spirit*, 121.

62. Hegel uses two words for history. The first, *historia*, refers to written accounts, historical inquiry and narratives of history. When Hegel turns on theologians for being overly historical, this is the word he uses. The second, and more commonly used term is, *geschichte*, and translates as story, affair or business. In the eighteenth century, *geschichte* came to mean "the systematic investigation of past events." Inwood, *Hegel Dictionary*, 118–20.

63. This trait is noticeable within Jenson. While reserving far greater respect for the history of Christ than Hegel, Jenson's Christology is certainly eschatologically motivated.

In Hegel, Christology is driven by three historical considerations. The first results from Hegel's own philosophical context and consists of an inbuilt skepticism towards the reliability of historical claims. The second is a reaction against an overly historical approach to theology. Anxious to bring Christian faith to life, Hegel turns upon a generation of theologians who resemble clerks in a mercantile house. These shadowy figures keep great account of the wealth of strangers, without ever experiencing these riches themselves. The third was brought about by Hegel's overblown sense of his own importance. In short, Hegel was convinced that he himself had reclaimed the full revelation and historical implications of Christ's incarnation: "Christ as reconciler and savior is still constantly made the focus of faith, nevertheless what formerly was called in orthodox dogmatics the work of salvation has taken on a significance so strongly psychological and so very prosaic that only a semblance of the ancient doctrine of the church remains."[64]

The verification of the truth of the incarnation, for Hegel, derives from the answer to two questions.[65] Firstly, is it true that God does not exist apart from the Son that he sent into the world? And secondly, was the man we know historically as Jesus of Nazareth really the Son whom God sent? If Jesus is the Son then Hegel's program is confirmed. However, if Jesus is not the Son, then we still await him. For according to Absolute Spirit, all reality presupposes the incarnation of the Absolute idea as either a past or future event. Either way, Hegel's own thought is validated by his Christology. The importance of the incarnation, for the idealist, is not that it should happen as an historic event, but rather that reason record its reality, and consequently its inevitability. In short, Hegel's philosophy is an adequate and authentic expression of the incarnation in its own right, regardless of any actual event or historic verification. For this reason, Küng confesses, "We shall search in vain . . . in the whole of the *Phenomenology* for the name of *Jesus Christ*."[66]

In his interpretation of the incarnation we discover a dialectic that even Hegel was unable to resolve. As Yerkes points out, Hegel emphasizes both the absolutely indispensable function of the historical

---

64. Hegel, *Lectures* 1:156.

65. Hegel, *Lectures* 3:330–33.

66. Küng, *Incarnation of God*, 207.

incarnation, while at other times rendering such an event as eminently dispensable.[67] What's more the contradiction between Hegel's views on the incarnation and history seem irredeemable by either Christ's first, or second, coming. Having attached such importance to the incarnation within human history, the incarnation exists as an exercise in mental gymnastics. One might even suggest that Christ could have been spared the incarnation safe in the knowledge that Hegel would have subsequently brought the event and its implications to life in his work anyway? As Inwood suggests, the inference is hard to escape: If Hegel was correct, "Christ would be no more than his lisping precursor."[68]

The ambition of Hegel's eschatology is ultimately undermined by the porosity of his own view of history. It would take a far stronger, and more realistic theory of history to bear the weight of such an overarching eschatology. In short, Hegel has limited ontological capital upon which to stake his expansive eschatological vision. Hegel believed that he stood at the dawn of a new day in Western culture. With the incarnation as little more than a self-supporting conceptual proof text, Hegel's eschatology must find hope in reason alone. "Only by philosophy can this simply present content be justified, not by history [*Geschichte*]. What spirit does is no history [*Historie*]."[69] Hegel believed that his work was to herald a new kairotic era and, beyond this, the end of history itself. After much waiting for the trumpets of the eschaton, he became frustrated by this delayed dawn and looked hopefully towards the birth of a new nation. America is "the land of the future," he declared, "a land of desire for all those who are weary of the historical lumber-room of old Europe."[70] With this, we look hopefully towards a Hegelian who has been heralded, by some, as "America's theologian."

Now and Then: History according to Jenson

Due to the influence of Greek philosophy and the attraction of mysticism, Jenson insists, Christian theology has too often translated the

67. Yerkes, *Christology of Hegel*, 130.

68. Inwood, *Hegel*, 519.

69. Hegel, *Lectures* 3:232–33.

70. Yerkes, *Christology of Hegel*, 108.

"logos" as God's idea, rather than his word.[71] This common misconception, perennial in Hegel, results in an interpretation of the incarnation through reason alone and with little, or no regard, for the historical narrative that establishes the event in the first place. Outside of the history of the biblical word, Jenson declares, dialogue concerning the incarnation is nothing but conceptual acrobatics. Jenson cites and attacks the work of Rudolph Bultmann as one recent manifestation of the Hegelian position. In Bultmann, the existential attempt to underplay historical events in a bid to amplify their revelatory character, simultaneously divorces history from eschatology. Alas once more, time is cast adrift from eternity. In Bultmann, the concurrent turn of eschatology towards the eternal, and history towards the temporal, undermines the interpretation of both, and ultimately proves theology's undoing.

Although pre-modern theology's commitment to timelessness frequently compromised the historical character of the biblical narrative, pre-modern theologians were rarely deflected from the proclamation of the gospel as an historical state of affairs. However, following Hegel, theology's attempts to connect the Christ of faith with the Jesus of history reaches a crisis point. In the full face of modernity, with its subsequent denial of all possible connections between existence and timelessness, the historical claims of the tradition appeared meaningless.[72] Through its values based-religion, and revivalist theologies, Jenson suggests, Evangelicalism rolled on in a state of denial, while Liberalism's enthusiasm for the discussion eventually bankrupted its own faith.[73] The necessary breakthrough would be provided by another Hegelian, whose influence upon Jenson is even greater than that of Hegel. The christological notion of history, which leads to Jenson's trinitarian treatment of time, would be impossible without the work of Karl Barth. Reinforcing the historical nature of the gospel, while infusing it with new possibility, Barth's Christology proves the salvation of Western theology. "I am convinced" Jenson exclaims, "that Barth's thought is a watershed in the history of theology, that discussion must now be pursued for or against

71. *ST* 2:6.

72. Jenson documents his own position on the continuing debate in, Jenson, "The Jesus of History and the Christ of Faith," 118–24.

73. *A&O*, 13–20.

Barth, and that a theological position must now be dated before or after Barth."[74]

The christological resources that Barth makes available accompany Jenson through much of his work. From his early publication, *Alpha and Omega: A Study in the Theology of Karl Barth,* Jenson commandeers Barth's biblical Christology. Here the redressing of the historical balance of the gospel is driven by three christological assumptions.[75] Firstly, the whole of history must be seen as the field of God's activity with mankind; with the primary aim of such activity resting in God's simultaneous work of salvation and revelation. Secondly, God's involvement in the field of history is preserved, not by metaphysical formulae concerning possible connections between time and timelessness, but rather by the fact that God has a history. Thirdly, God's history is the ground of all existence. In Barth, Jenson asserts, God is not an ahistorical being but the eminently historical being. As a result, reality is ontologically predicated upon the notion of eternal history, as opposed to timeless being. As a history, God abandons the present and leaps towards the future and in so doing, abandons self in order to confront others. The eternal God, in Barth, is pre-temporal, supra-temporal, and post-temporal. Hence, time flows out of his eternal history and is enveloped by the history that he is. The content of the history between God and man is salvation itself. Such divine sanctification comes to us from eternity and is revealed to us as Jesus.

Until now, we have hardly deviated from the Hegelian track. However, the next move is decisive. In Barth, Jenson points out, "God's decision is the eternal event of that which is decided. It is not a mere intention to do something but a real occurrence, the most real of all historical events."[76] In Christ's history, God implements and reveals an eternal act and decision to save creation, hence, Jesus' temporal history is to be regarded as the outworking of this eternal history. As both the eternal basis of salvation, and the temporal reflection of the God

74. Ibid., 19.

75. A detailed assessment of Jenson's interpretation of Barth does not concern us here. Our primary objective lies in Jenson's appropriation of Barth for his own theological purposes.

76. Ibid., 84.

in whom such salvation occurs, Christ's eternal history is mirrored in time. Jenson's reading of Barth is crucial for a sufficient grasp of his work hereafter. Any theology that rests content with God as the mere guide to history and salvation is too weak. In Barth, Jenson declares, God is the primary reality and thus the truth of all history: "The eternal origin of the events of human history is not a static 'Being,' nor is it the forming of a 'plan' of salvation by a puzzled or ingenious God. The eternal origin of the temporal history of salvation is nothing other than that history itself in its own deepest character as an event in the life of the eternally active God."[77]

While classical Christology viewed the history of salvation as a history between God in Christ and mankind, Barth's Christology rests upon the history between God and man as present in Christ's own nature. The implications of the shift are considerable: "Jesus Christ as God and man . . . [becomes] the one great history of the eternal covenant between God and man."[78] In Barth, we are what we are in Christ, for our very existence is only ever accomplished in him. Christ's life is, by definition, eternal life for us, and thus our history consists of a participation in his eternal history. Jenson's timely vision of God and the gospel would not be possible, but for Barth's radical departure from his own Hegelian inheritance: "To put it somewhat crudely, Barth has solved the problem of the disappearance of the timeless by retaining the general structure of classical theology but putting the historical event of Jesus' existence in the place formerly occupied by changeless 'Being' . . . Where 'Being' stood there now stands Jesus Christ. Where 'Beauty,' 'Goodness,' 'Truth' in the abstract stood there now stands the life-history of Jesus."[79]

In Barth, the incarnation is the center point of history. By revealing the humanity of God in Jesus, and asserting the place of humanity within him, Barth's Christ, far from embodying a series of uncomfortable contradictions between time and timelessness, provides a meeting point for history and eternity. The scheme retains its Hegelian flavor, but is now significantly Christianized. Hegel's lack of confidence in the history of the biblical narrative made such a development impossible

77. Ibid., 110.
78. Ibid., 139.
79. Ibid., 140.

within his own body of work. However, this is hardly a problem for Barth, nor for Jenson for that matter. In Jenson's Barthian Christology, the events of the incarnation, and in particular that of the resurrection, are to be regarded as the potent meeting place of all historical contingency and biblical revelation. In these moments Jesus heralds God's eternity as truly immanent:[80]

> [In the resurrection,] what is otherwise an antinomy at the heart of the Old Testament is resolved. Israel is to be a blessing to all nations, who are to be gathered to her God. But when it is seen that Israel's destiny can be fulfilled only by the conclusion of the world's history and the beginning of a new reality, no historical space is left in which the ingathering can occur. By Jesus' Resurrection occurring "first," a sort of hole opens in the event of the End, a space for something like what used to be history, for the church and its mission.[81]

For Jenson, the Bible tells a story about God. In this story God is identified by a complex, yet clear, set of historical contingencies, thereupon revealing that, "God is one with himself just by the dramatic coherence of his eventual actuality."[82] This is why Hegel's attempt to transcend the biblical narrative, in search of the "real" God behind the story, proves so disastrous. Having rendered the original story as, at best, incomplete, Hegel's move can do little more than testify to the ultimate falsity of the gospel which he had sought to expound. Returning to the story, Jenson extends Barth's christological reading of the gospel into a trinitarian one. While the biblical narrative is undoubtedly christological, Jenson draws our attention to the three active agents within its plot. All three of these characters perform a series of selfless and divine actions within the drama of human history, while concurrently confess-

---

80. *ST* 1:175-178.

81. Ibid., 85.

82. Ibid., 64. It is this interdependence between the triune drama and the revelation of scripture that makes Jenson reluctant to draw distinction between immanent and economic forms of the Trinity.

ing the divinity of the other two persons.[83] It is this trinitarian extension of Barthian Christology that establishes the triune God as a dramatic event within Jenson's own thought. As a history, the triune God exists as a dynamic temporal eternity and is thus intrinsically related to all other temporalities: "The proposition that God's self-identity lies in dramatic coherence is in any case mandatory for those who wish to worship the biblical God. For if we cannot construe the biblical God's self-identity in this way, then we cannot construe it at all; then we do not know any one such reality as the biblical God. Otherwise than dramatically, the Bible's theological descriptions, accounts of divine action, and worshipful invocations are too mutually conflicted to suggest referral to a same someone."[84]

If the triune God, to use Barth's terminology, is a "pure duration," then it follows that God's being is not a simple contradiction of time, but rather that this duration is the subsistence of temporal reality.[85] In theological terms, God's relationship with this reality, is termed "creation" and this reality consists of both objects within time and time itself. Therefore, Jenson asserts, created time and existence appear within the dynamic duration, or triune narrative, which is Father, Son and Holy Spirit. We inhabit the story of God. In this divine history, we live and move and have our being:

> God's eternity is temporal infinity. Can we then speak of God's own "time"? The life of God is constituted in a structure of relations, whose own referents are narrative. This narrative structure is constrained by a difference between whence and whither that one cannot finally refrain from calling "past" and "future," and this is congruent with the distinction between the Father and the Spirit. This difference is not relative and therefore not measurable; nothing in God recedes into the past or approaches from the future. But the difference is also absolute: the arrow of God's eternity, like the arrow of causal time, does not reverse itself. Whence and whither in God are not like right and

83. Jenson, "Does God Have Time?," 2.

84. *ST* 1:64.

85. Ibid., 217.

left or up and down on a map, but are like before and after in a narrative.[86]

Then and Now: Eschatology in Jenson

From his earliest theological reflections Jenson identified what he would later call, "the antinomy of hope."[87] Put simply, we either confess that hope always transcends, and is thus pie in the sky, or we live the possibility of hope's fulfillment, namely the offer of steak on our plate. Either way, hope loses its attraction. With the former, hope becomes impossibility, while with the latter, hope promises the abrogation of all hoping: "I recall as a small child sitting in a pew and trying to comprehend the pastor's talk of eternity; I decided that it would make little difference whether one were in heaven or hell, since a truly endless on and on and on . . . would merely be itself intolerable."[88]

For this reason, difficult and unfashionable though it is, talk of eschatology's content is vital to the successful exposition of the gospel of truth and time. "It must be said at the beginning," declares Jenson, "that Christianity . . . anticipates an event that is so fundamental a transformation of created being that even calling it an 'event' stretches language to the breaking point."[89] This event demands metaphysical language of its own. For this reason, eschatology has proved the downfall of many a theologian.[90]

In Hegel's case, history has become the calamity of eschatology, and on this occasion Barth is unable to provide a resolution.[91] By connecting eschatology to God's enduring presence, Jenson accuses Barth, along with Bultmann, of stripping eschatology of its temporal structure

86. *ST* 1:218.

87. *S&P* 57.

88. Jenson, "The End is Music," 169.

89. Jenson, "Eschatology," 407.

90. Jenson's critics would cast the same aspersion in his direction. See Farrow's critique later in this chapter and the summary of the dialogue between Jenson and George Hunsinger at the conclusion of this thesis.

91. As often the case in Barth, the problem may result from a lack of adequate pneumatology. Jenson's eschatology, on the other hand, is marked by its pneumatological breadth.

and consequently removing the necessary drive towards fulfillment. This contradiction exchanges the proper content of eschatology for a series of meaningless metaphors and mythic representations. Having previously reconnected the categories of time and history, Barth's eschatology now risks a relapse into the realm of timelessness. While his Christology may save history, Barth's eschatology does not avoid the Hegelian trap. In search of the eschaton behind the biblical narrative, all eschatological content disappears into timeless myth.[92] The seriousness of the situation is heightened in Bultmann. Having retained Barth's maxim that all Christianity be seen as eschatology, Bultmann fails to give the category any meaningful definition.[93] Eschatology is here, Jenson suggests, subjugated for a single moment of "authentic decision, when the world of the cross calls me."[94] The Bultmannian tendency to sublate time and eternity by mutual negation proves overwhelming.[95] While remaining an historic reality, the eschaton no longer occupies any temporal space.

"To understand the Christian hope," Jenson declares, "we must speak of the final future as a time of its own. Refusal to do so was the fault of dialectical theology—its only fault, but one that drove it to otherworldliness despite its own primary intention."[96] A high view of history, such a Jenson's, demands a more weighty eschatology than is provided by any above. For Jenson the eternal temporality of the Trinity provides the possibility for remembrance and anticipation to join together. Without this, history and eschatology all too easily become one another's undoing. For Jenson, it is the dramatic and timely event of the triune God that ensures the possibility and coherence of past and future, and thus the possibility that hope and history might rhyme. "The Lord's

92. The criticism goes also for Schleiermacher. Jenson, "End is Music," 162.

93. Ibid., 163.

94. Jenson, "Eschatology," 414.

95. This is why the resurrection causes so much trouble for Bultmann. Having died on the cross Jesus exchanges history for eternity. As Jenson points out, if we posit the resurrection as an historical event then Jesus remains as both an eternal and historical figure. *ST* 1:169–72. Furthermore, with no historical category capable of containing the miraculous, the question arises, as to what kind of eschaton Bultmann awaits?

96. *ETC*, 22.

resolve to meet and overcome death," Jenson argues, "and the constitution of his self-identity in dramatic coherence are but one truth about him. For if death and resurrection occurs, this is the infinite dramatic crisis and resolution, and so God's own."[97] Returning to the incarnation, Jenson declares, "Faith in Jesus and eschatological expectation are but two aspects of one mode of existence."[98] The eschatological crisis of Old Testament faith, according to Jenson, represents the challenge of all existence.[99] It can be glimpsed most starkly in the moments when Ezekiel is brought out of the Temple and into the valley of dry bones. Here, God himself asks the ultimate eschatological question, "Can these bones live?" With the hindsight of the incarnation we can reword the question in such a way as to posit God's own answer. "Is it possible that God's own Son could be resurrected from among the dead?" In Jenson the possibility of past and future, whence and whither, and history and eschatology hinges upon the subject of resurrection. Without resurrection, all talk of the future is simply fatuous: "Apart from the Resurrection, the future seen by the apocalyptic prophets, the future as it is determinate for God, is determinate only *as* future, as what is not yet. The risen Son, however, is an accomplished reality within the history of this age, possessing a mother, a narratable story, and a historically placeable executioner."[100]

For Jenson, the content of eschatology lies in the anticipation of resurrection. "The chief difference," Jenson points out, "between a dead man and a live one is that the live man can still surprise us."[101] Having defeated death, Christ is freed for the future and thus can continually surprise us. Such surprises are the stuff of Christ's coming kingdom. As both a meaningful word and action, Christ's kingdom represents an unconditional promise. As a result of the resurrection there is no gap

97. *ST* 1:66.

98. Jenson, "The Great Transformation," 34–35. Jenson suggests that popular acknowledgements of historical eschatology in the shape of "bumper stickers about the Rapture are closer to biblical faith than are most mainline Christians." For Jenson, modern theology's, largely non-biblical, re-workings of eschatology have become so vacuous and unthreatening, as to completely undermine the biblical reality of history as eschatology.

99. Jenson's reading of the Old Testament is typological at this point.

100. *ST* 1:201.

101. *ETC*, 22.

between the making of this promise and its fulfillment.[102] Through the resurrected Christ, remembrance and anticipation become essential aspects of the same temporal event, and thus, hope and history begin to rhyme. This exposition of the resurrection was the cause of a lively exchange between Jenson and H. Paul Santmire.[103] Having been accused of "Jesusology," an incandescent Jenson responds: "The 'Jesusology' he wants to attack . . . [states that] 'God's reality is the history of Jesus.' . . . If God raised Jesus, then God is separate from Jesus. Yet apart from what happens with Jesus there is no God; God's reality is the history of Jesus. 'God is triune' is merely the attempt to say both of these in one slogan."[104]

It is this trinitarian extension of Barth's Christology that enables Jenson's distinct formulation of time.[105] Here, past and future are fulfilled without mutual sublation. In Jenson, history really is in the past and can realistically be remembered, while eschatology is most definitely the future and can thus be anticipated. The occurrence of past and future within the perichoretic life of the Trinity ensures their distinction within one aspect of the triune life. As Douglas Knight has pointed out, in Jenson, there are two types of time at work.[106] There is the fullness of time when "God will reign . . . [and] fit created time to triune time."[107] And there is the coming to be of that fullness of time, or in this case 'our time.' In Jenson, God "*is* the end and he works *from* the end. God has a time that is now perfect and complete, and he has a time that is now *working* perfection and completeness. He has the finished object, and finishing the object is what he is now doing."[108]

The momentous ingathering of past, present, and future within the death and resurrection of Christ represents the outworking of the triune

---

102. *S&P*, 41.

103. Santmire, "A review of A Religion Against it Itself," 227–28.

104. Jenson, "Response," 229–30.

105. Without this move, Jenson would be guilty of both Jesusology, and, more worryingly, a failure to move beyond the immediate existentialist eschatology for which he attacks Barth and Bultmann.

106. Knight, "Jenson on time," 71–79.

107. *ST* 2:369.

108. Knight, "Jenson on Time," 78.

drama. The Father who sends forth the Son, appears as the "whence" of divine events, the given from where such incidents originate and must one day return. Correspondingly, the Spirit, who anoints and reconciles the Son to the Father, appears as the "whither." The Holy Spirit is the power of the future, from where he comes to break open the present unto himself. Finally, the Son becomes God's own "specious present." As the Father finds himself in the Son, so too, the Spirit's liberation is accomplished in the Son's resurrected body. As a result, the goal of history is God himself in the person of the Holy Spirit. Like Hegel before him, Jenson stakes much of his eschatology on the power of the Spirit; although the Spirit in Jenson is recognizable as the Holy Spirit of Scripture. For Jenson, the final promise of God is that creation be identified with, and in, his life and the Spirit is both the content and the medium of this promise. Hence, where the Spirit works he makes history enter the end times.[109] There is no need for progressive revelation here. Such capitulation is merely the prerogative of those unable to assert the historical contingency and closure found within the biblical narrative.[110]

In Jenson, there is future in God: "God anticipates his future and so possesses it, and so there is a present tense of creation's future with God, and therefore there is also its place with God."[111] In this moment, faith and hope will pass over into the love that constitutes the triune life, and all human hopes will become both fulfilled and transcended in a process of infinite reinterpretation. Hope is not ended, nor abolished, in these moments for this would be akin to death itself, but rather it is continually realized and extended as love; the perfect openness to possibility.[112] "Eternal life is rather, the infinite *appropriation* and interpretation of accomplished lives within the discourse of the triune life."[113] For all his attempts to balance past and future, ontology and eschatology, Jenson remains a most enthusiastic eschatologist. No matter how difficult the task or elusive the subject, Jenson proves persistent in

109. *ST* 1:157.

110. Ibid., 65.

111. *ST* 2:121.

112. Jenson, "End is Music," 169.

113. Jenson, "Eschatology," 415.

his attempts to describe eschatology's fulfillment. "Perhaps one may in almost unintelligible summary speak of an infinite implosion of love," he ventures, "of a created community pressed and agitated into perfect mutuality by the surrounding of the triune God."[114]

Concerns of Pantheism and Questions of Panentheism: Hegel, Jenson, and Farrow

As the conclusion of this chapter draws near, one question demands our attention. In both, Jenson and Hegel, time exists within God's own life. The question now arises as to whether these immanent models can avoid slipping into pantheism. In Jenson's case, the charge will recur with some regularity. His refutation of the allegation is deliberate. The notion that humanity lives, moves, and has its being in God, Jenson declares, is nothing but a fundamental tenet of classical Christian teaching. On the other hand, he concedes that his treatment of time may be considered panentheist and insists that such a differentiation can and should be made. Underlying his refutation, there appears a slightly mischievous response. "There are worse things to be called than a 'pantheist,'" Jenson seems to suggest. However, the issue at stake is not whether Jenson's work strays into panentheism or pantheism for that matter, but whether or not Jenson's formulation can be defended as *Christian*. This is of greater concern to the outcome of this project, not to mention Jenson himself, and as such will create the framework for these discussions as and when they arrive. In this first instance we must address whether it is possible for Christian theology to view time and creation as aspects of God's own life.

The initial danger appears twofold. In the first place, creation is so identified with God's existence that divine personality becomes abrogated. Here, God exists as the conceptual category bracketing all reality, and thereafter pantheism gives way to atheism. In the second place, God's intrinsic identification with the world causes creation to overrun divine personality. While his own thought strays into both domains, Hegel fashions an escape by means of his own appeal to the Trinity. This results in a somewhat unorthodox configuration of the doctrine.

114. Ibid., 405.

"Whether this amounts to atheism or not," Inwood asks, "is another of those ambiguities."[115] While Hegel also refuted allegations of pantheism, at times he is forced to choose between that worldview and atheism. Given the choice, the former would appear to offer the lesser of two evils.[116] The lasting impact of these contradictions means that scholarly consensus is yet to be gained as to whether Hegel was a Christian, an atheist, or a pantheist.[117]

Jenson is quick to deny the proposition that Hegel be considered as Protestant's Aquinas. For Jenson, Hegel is a heretic![118] However, Jenson would appear to leave his own work open to a similar attack. One such critique is offered in Douglas Farrow's response to Jenson's *Systematic Theology*.[119] Here, Farrow claims that Jenson's treatment of time is essentially panentheistic. "Only an inverted Eutychianism such as Hegel's can finally account for the temporalizing of God as God," he suggests.[120] It is Farrow's conviction that Jenson's model of time places both the distinctiveness of God and creation in jeopardy.[121] He continues, "It is an imposition on the biblical narrative . . . to suggest that the God who has decided not to be God without us is therefore only God by being God with us."[122] That Jenson comes close to this assertion can be argued; however, to go so far as to suggest that God's economic existence is dependent upon the immanent creation is to infer a Hegelian sublation that Jenson does not permit. Jenson's point is *not* that God could not do without us, but rather that we have no way of knowing what kind

115. Inwood, "Hegel," 747.

116. For Hegel, while atheism has too little of God, pantheism holds too much. Hegel, *Theologian of Spirit*, 148–49. Hegel's program might best be classified, "were it not for its air of paradox, . . . [as] Christian pantheism." McCarney, *Hegel on History*, 50.

117. Inwood, *Hegel Dictionary*, 115.

118. Interview with author, (Princeton, 16 July 2005).

119. Farrow, "Jenson's Systematic Theology," 89–95.

120. Ibid., 90.

121. David Bentley Hart mounts a similar critique alleging that, despite his trinitarian intentions and credentials, Jenson has ultimately been led astray by Hegel. Hart, *The Beauty of the Infinite*. Similarly, in his response, Jenson suggests that Hart "seriously misrepresents" him. Jenson, "Review Essay," 235.

122. Farrow, "Jenson's Systematic Theology," 91.

of God he would be outside of his history with us. To outline detailed hypotheses in this regard is, to Jenson's mind, an exercise in presumption and hubris beyond that of Hegel, and the outworking of an almost entirely vacuous and meaningless philosophy. While Jenson's program, at times, flirts with these possibilities, his insistence upon the biblical narrative does not force the Trinity and creation into a relationship of co-dependence, but rather confirms that the only reliable knowledge of God is contained within God's revelation as mediated through creation. Douglas Knight provides a précis of the point: "Definitions of . . . time that contrast humanity and divinity are not adequately theological. These concepts must receive their reference from the work of the Creator who puts his creatures before him and is with them. They are a function of the doctrine of creation, which is about the course and destination of the world as the work of God. The creature is not in a position to tell God that God may not be with his creatures."[123]

Farrow further claims, that Jenson's treatment of time eternalizes creation itself and thus undermines the form of temporality that he is anxious to protect.[124] While occasionally close, at no point does Jenson formally adopt such a stance. Furthermore, it is, in part, the delineation of created time in Jenson that makes the creature/creator distinction possible in the first place.[125] We have time *because God has made time for us*, and this created time is the very possibility of existence that is other than God. While, as the presupposition of our own reality, time is intrinsically related to the history that God lives, our respective temporalities are not one and the same. In Jenson, the distinction is made possible by a classical configuration of the doctrine of the Trinity. "The triune God is not a sheer point of presence; he is a life among persons. And therefore creation's temporality is not awkwardly related to God's eternity, and its sequentiality imposes no strain on its participation in being."[126] Although illuminating, Farrow's critique puts words into Jenson's mouth. However, what is clear is that in his notion of time we

123. Knight, "Jenson on Time," 76.

124. Farrow, "Jenson's Systematic Theology," 91.

125. We will return to the creature/creator distinction in our discussion on "space" in chapter 2.

126. *ST* 2:35.

witness Jenson at his most imaginative and controversial. His modification of the Hegelian treatment of time both critiques the tradition and encroaches upon the limits of orthodoxy. At times, the complexity of the subject, along with Jenson's exposition, make this depiction of temporality difficult to decipher. However, Jenson's treatment of time is largely consistent with the central tenets of Christian doctrine and, as such reinforces our understanding of the triune God.

Conclusion

Although his critique pushes Jenson too far, Farrow rightly pin points the origins of Jenson's views on time. In the first place, Jenson expresses a preference for the Cappadocian formulation of the Trinity, as opposed to that of Augustine. Secondly, he modifies Barth, and, thirdly, he is drawn to Rahner's axiomatic formulation concerning the immanent and economic Trinity. While Jenson acknowledges these influences, the labeling of his work as "Hegelian" proves more controversial. Having declared the idealist a "heretic," Jenson's defensiveness is unsurprising. However, when pushed, he states, "If you are asking me if I am a premodern theologian, the answer is 'no.'"[127] To this end, Jenson can no sooner deny Hegel's influence than he can any other formative figure within Western theology.

As we have seen, it is in Jenson's treatment of time that Hegel's influence comes to the fore. His subsequent, and enthusiastic attempts to export these considerations into almost every other aspect of his theology, increases the weight of the charge. Finally, whether by his appropriation of Hegelian categories, the influence of Karl Barth, or his place within the tradition, Jenson is a Hegelian theologian. However, we would be in error to end our assessment here. While undoubtedly influenced by Hegel, Jenson's work represents a *radical departure* from the well-worn paths of Hegelianism. Unlike Hegel, Jenson's account of time presupposes and promotes an orthodox conception of the Trinity. Having extended a modern conception of time into a postmodern context, Jenson's formulation retains a classical scope and content. In his reclamation of the biblical narrative and subsequent trinitarian treat-

127. Interview with author (Princeton, 16 June 2005).

ment of time, Jenson could even be said to have Christianized Hegel's thought on the subject.

"The substance of every human act," Jenson suggests, "is the particular way it joins the poles of time."[128] In Jenson, time is the premise of all reality, both temporal and eternal, past and future, fallen and perfect, created and divine. In time, we can grasp both the reality of creation and the one who creates. For God's temporal infinity is universal enough to contain his own life and yet particular enough to make our own moments meaningful. While ancient enough to contain history and prehistory, God's time is also futuristic enough to embrace eschatology. In his time, we will share in the perichoretic drama and dance of the triune life.[129] In this movement, God's reality will be opened to us and all our hopes and histories will begin to rhyme. Where this discussion is concerned, we have run out of time. For as Jenson points out, while God has both time for himself and creation, we rarely have enough time for anything, and that is the great difference between us.

128. *ETC*, 191.

129. Paul Fiddes has used this as the basis of his recent work. Fiddes, *Participating in God.*

2

Explorations in Outer Space:
Jenson and Space

In the previous chapter, we discussed the fundamental role of time in Jenson's theology. Here, temporality provided the key for our understanding of creation and the creator. God has time, declares Jenson. Furthermore creation comprises the specific time which God takes for us, his creatures. With this, Jenson's concept of time becomes stretched into space. For in the eternal triune God, we discover a temporal infinity in which we ourselves live, move, and experience being. By having time for us, God also has space for us. As a result, our grasp of reality requires both an understanding of time and space. It is the spatial implications of Jenson's notion of time which will form the focus of this next chapter.

"The metaphysical tradition has tended to interpret time in terms of space, pointing to the need to use spatial language when speaking of time. But of course we also need to use temporal language to speak of space: a distant point is where we now are not but could be in the future, and so on."[1] Jenson's ordering of these principles is indicative of his situation within the tradition. While pre-modern theology usually placed space before to time, this trend has become reversed in modern and postmodern thought.[2] In Jenson, time precedes space, for space is

1. *ST* 2:46.
2. Inge, *A Christian Theology of Place*, 5–13.

but the horizon of the present tense, the confirmation that the now is God's present, or gift to us. In Jenson, God is not primarily the maker of matter nor the sustainer of spatiality, but rather the creator of history. And henceforth, we exist as temporal-spatial histories. As time is a distention in God's life, so too space is a feature of the same distention. By importing his temporal conclusions into the realm of space, Jenson sets a precedent for the rest of his work.[3] However this soon to become familiar formulation creates its own quandary. "A dilemma appears here similar to that which characterized our intuition of time." Jenson continues, "We want space to be *both* an a priori of consciousness and a sort of container within which we and all our consciousnesses are to be found," but is such a dual model possible?[4] In an essay entitled, "A Space for God," Jenson surveys the challenge of space as handed down through the tradition: "John of Damascus formulated a maxim for all subsequent theology: God is his own space, in himself he is 'in' nothing but himself. If he creates a world, God occupies the space that he himself is, and the world is another space. And these do not overlap; there is no space to accommodate mixtures of God and creature or almost-gods or a little-more-than-creatures."[5]

If John of Damascus is correct, our own spatiality and physical nature cannot be defined in connection, collision, or collusion with the creator. In this case, creation becomes disconnected from the creator, and created reality is torn from its own ontology. Despite this, classical theology maintained a perennial insistence upon God's real presence for and with his creation. For as the central event of Christian revelation, the incarnation enforces this view upon us. In these moments we witness the human Jesus as both fully man and fully God, and neither his human physiology, nor his earthly geography appear to disturb this reality. The gospel story is thus reliant upon a formulation of space in which created reality can house divine presence and personality. Jenson

3. Colin Gunton has spoken of this directly. The complexities of Jenson's theology in this regard, "are to be found in the fact that we are here in the realm not simply of the relation of eternity and time, but also of infinity and space." Gunton, "Creation and Mediation," 87.

4. *ST* 2:47.

5. Jenson, "A Space for God," 51.

emphasises the point in his description of the Icon of The Virgin of the Sign.[6] The picture here discussed, portrays a pregnant virgin Mary with Jesus also depicted within her womb. The accompanying inscription reads, "The Container of the Uncontainable."[7] According to Jenson, it is of critical importance that Christian faith and theology authenticate this dictum. For in the person of Mary, the nation of Israel, and the community of the church, the uncontainable God has made himself present in the container of created space.

Having previously registered the influence of Hegel, this chapter will feature another theological informant from the eighteenth century. Jonathan Edwards is a faithful companion throughout Jenson's theological journey. In particular, Edwards helps Jenson to negotiate space.[8] This discussion will also make use of the work of Thomas F. Torrance, one of theology's leading authorities on the subject of space.

Time in Space: Edwards and the Place of Space

To counter those who would class him a straightforward pietist, and to underline his substantive contribution to Western thought, Jenson calls directly upon Edwards' theology of space. Here "we find a different Edwards," pronounces Jenson. "A born rationalist. His 'view' of God is . . . revealed as a thoroughly intellectual vision."[9] While for Jenson, time is of prime importance, in Edwards, it is space that forms reality's chief precedent. In Jenson, we are nothing without time. In Edwards, our existence is inconceivable outside of space: "Space is this necessary, eternal, infinite and omnipresent being. We find that we can with ease conceive how all other things should not be. We can remove them out of our minds, and place some other in the room of them; but space is the very thing that we can never remove."[10]

6. Ibid., 49–51, 55–57.

7. Ibid., 51.

8. As with Barth before, the discussion will emphasise Jenson's interpretation and use of Edwards, as opposed to evaluating his work as a piece of Edwards scholarship.

9. Jenson, *America's Theologian*, 20.

10. Edwards, *The Works of Jonathan Edwards*, Vol. 6, 203.

In his book, *Incarnation, Space and Time,* Torrance provides a useful survey of the place of space in theology before and after Edwards. Prior to the Reformation, Torrance argues, theology utilised two distinct models of space.[11] The first, inherited from Plato and Aristotle, and fundamental to Latin theology, viewed space as the container or receptacle of all created matter. Torrance calls this the container, or receptacle model of space.[12] The container is envisioned as either a finite entity, as in Aristotle, or as infinite, as with the Atomists and the Pythagoreans. In the finite receptacle, container and contents are seen as interdependent entities, whereas within the infinite version, both container and its contents are independent of one another. The second vision, drawn from the Fathers and inherent within Medieval theology, saw space as the rational means by which God has made himself known to us. Here, the rational grasp of spatial reality is objectively grounded in God's own transcendent rationality. Typified as the "relational notion" of space, this model is typified within "natural theology" and is of structural importance to modern science.[13] While the Latin vision emphasises the metric structure of spatial reality, the Medieval alternative pays heed to the possibilities of spatial deduction and interaction.

Where Latin theology came to grief, according to Torrance, was in its attempts to develop an Aristotelian notion of space aside from God's interaction with nature. The problem is most noticeable in Western accounts of God's presence within the incarnation and the sacraments. Using the Aristotelian premise, one questions how Christ, as the creator of the container, can be simultaneously both inside and outside of it. Furthermore, how can Christ subsequently coexist within the multiple containers that constitute the church's many members? In the most part, Torrance reports, the church proposed an Aristotelian solution to her Aristotelian problem. However, the ensuing notion of transubstantiation remained inadequate for the task: "The doctrine of transubstantiation had attempted to get round the rigidity of the Aristotelian concept of the container while taking seriously the real presence of the body of Christ. But this was achieved only at the cost of a highly artificial

11. Torrance, *Space, Time and Incarnation,* 1–21.

12. Ibid., 4–5.

13. Ibid., 11–17.

separation between substance and accidents and was questioned . . . on the grounds that the container is not independent of what it contains— space [after all,] is not different from a spatially perceived object."[14]

The need to affirm Christ's presence in the church gave theologians little option but to bypass all philosophical contrariety by the direct invocation of God's absolute and inexplicable power. In this conceptualization, God's presence is experienced not by any rationally verifiable schema but through his own omnipotent will to be present to us.

The implications of such muddled metaphysics, as Torrance points out, were felt far beyond the church, as "Renaissance physicists rejected the Aristotelian concept of space only to return to that of the Atomists."[15] The resultant promotion of space over matter created scientific difficulties for centuries to come. In another corner of the tradition, reformed sacramentalism rejected the receptacle notion altogether. Suspicious that this may cut all spatial and temporal ties, the reformers insisted that Christ's presence in loaf and cup was an active self-presentation of Christ within time and space. However, if Christ has ascended to the time and space that is heaven, how is he also present to us in created time and space? The unanswered question reinforced suspicions of a Calvinist "extra" and subsequently forced Lutherans to attribute degrees of timelessness to Christ's real presence within the sacraments.[16] In short, both models forced their protractors into an unenviable choice, for while reformed thinking entailed contradictions damaging to space, the Lutherans equivalent resulted in an abrogation of time.

The breakthrough, Torrance declares, belongs to Isaac Newton. Adapting Aristotle's model, Newton rejected the tendency to separate time and eternity and thus promote one facet above the other. Instead, Newton proposed that space and time together form an infinite receptacle for all creaturely being. "He thus developed a dualism of space and matter, or volume and mass, in which space and time were given an absolute status independent of material existence but causally conditioning its character and qualities."[17] Hence, the God in whom we live

14. Ibid., 27.
15. Ibid., 28.
16. Ibid., 32.
17. Ibid., 38.

and move and have our being becomes the eternal, and infinite, creator and container of existence. In this way, space and time are recognized as divine attributes.

It was this new scientific vision of space that Jonathan Edwards appropriated for theology. For Edwards, Newton's work made possible a receptacle model of space without the Aristotelian flaws. "Whatever 'mass' or 'matter,' or 'space' or 'motion,' mean *within* Newton's laws," Jenson notes, "they mean for Edwards. It is Aristotle Edwards wants to be rid of."[18] Despite being cautioned against the new philosophy by his peers, Newton's thought forms the basis of Edwards' account of space.[19] In Edwards' descriptions of Newton, "the adjectives 'divine' and 'immortal' became practically compulsory."[20] However, far from being lured into heresy, as Stephen Holmes points out, Edwards "grasped with considerable insight what . . . [Newton's] discoveries might mean for Christian theology."[21]

Edwards' account of space as the underlying premise of all reality begins with a Christian reclamation of "substance."[22] Never relying upon a closed universe impervious to divine interruption, Edwards' appropriation of "substance," as Jenson points out, was directly opposed to any notion of God as the necessary unmoved mover. Substance in Edwards, "is a God-concept."[23] In Edwards, substance finds its irreducible state, in the form of the Newtonian atom. His theory, as Jenson suggests, relies upon "his entirely unoriginal definition of the atom."[24] As the existence of finite atomic life presupposes the existence of an infinite power, or creator, Edwards is left to conclude, atomic structure must be constructed and maintained by God himself.[25] Solidity then,

18. *AT,* 27.

19. The "new philosophy it was said would soon bring in a new divinity and corrupt the pure religion of the country." Holmes, *God of Grace and God of Glory,* 14.

20. Gay, *The Enlightenment,* 131.

21. Holmes, *God of Grace* 79.

22. The use of "substance," may first appear to be an Aristotelian throwback. However, Edwards' use of the concept owes far more to Locke's development of Aristotelian thought, than it does to Aristotle.

23. *AT,* 26.

24. Ibid., 28.

25. Edwards, *Works* 6:214–15.

by its very nature, is the result of God's active presence, and since body and solidity are the same, all bodily forms are the result of the exercise of divine power, purpose and placement: "The substance of bodies at last becomes either nothing, or nothing but the Deity acting in that particular manner in those parts of space where he thinks fit."[26] It follows then, that each body in space, and the very forces of gravity that hold these elements in place, are the direct result of God's immediate action.

Next, Edwards concentrates on the role of movement. Motion is "the communication of . . . resistance, from one part of space to another successively," and is therefore also God's own immediate act."[27] Newton's laws thus enabled Edwards to depict the existence of matter and the movement of bodies as a perpetual miracle, and thus established the possibility of a natural science that is not inimical to moral meaning and the teleological drive of creation. Given our discussion of time, it is not hard to see the attraction that the scheme holds for Jenson. In fact, through Edwards' interpretation of Newton, Jenson suggests that we can discover "the harmony of God's 'immediate,' that is, personally present agency."[28]

Edwards' challenge lay not in adopting the Newtonian model but rather in avoiding its potential problems. Having escaped one dualism, Newton rushed head long into another, with the assertion that space and time constitute the infinite container with deity himself. While this removes the unhelpful dualism of space and matter, it reinforces an older, and potentially more damaging Hellenic alternative. Torrance describes the dilemma: "If God Himself is the infinite Container of all things He can no more become incarnate than a box can become one of the several objects that it contains."[29] Newtonian science, at this point, leads us straight to Deism. While his ontology of time and space appear more convincing, Newton's container projects a rigid, objectivist, and ultimately static spatiality that is closed to divine intervention. The Newtonian depiction of the world as an independent and fully functioning system, or machine, has mitigated calamity far beyond the realm

26. Ibid., 215.

27. *AT,* 28.

28. Ibid., 28.

29. Torrance, *Space, Time,* 39.

of science. "Too often," as Torrance illustrates, "the God of Newtonian Protestantism has been shaped according to the static, isotropic receptacle of space and time."[30]

While impressed and informed by Newton's scheme, Edwards both identifies and avoids the slide into a mechanistic view of reality. Following his first encounters with the new science, Edwards penned a series of writings on the subjects of metaphysics and the natural sciences. While asserting a natural order in mathematical terms, Edwards is determined to avoid any inference of an underlying "world machine." It was, as Jenson remarks, Edwards' faith that saved him from this capitulation:[31]

> Edwards's interpretation of the newly burgeoning scientific knowledge was austerely phenomenalist and operationalist . . . He regarded the mechanist world view as an obscurantist anachronism, produced by a hangover of antique notions. But unlike many others who have held such positions, he had an answer to the question . . . God has neither constructed a machine nor instituted a game of craps. The play of phenomena is the play of God's imagination.[32]

In Edwards, the immediate power that creates and supports space, with all its rules and conventions, is not that of static, timeless, and unreachable deity but rather one of active and eternal thought. Despite its utility, Edwards' appropriation of Newtonian terminology defies the demise of spatiality into inert object and static atom, and turns instead towards the possibilities of a theological notion of substance. Contrary to Newton, Edwards locates the origin of substance in the interactivity and inter-subjectivity of the triune God. Thus, if space is to serve as the field of God's own personal activity, then it must derive from the active

---

30. Ibid., 48.

31. "Edwards was a phenomenalist and an operationalist, rescued by faith in God . . . from these position's usual deficiencies." *AT,* 27.

32. Jenson, *End is Music,* 165–66. Jenson regularly provides insight into the negative historical outcomes of America's adoption of the Newtonian mechanism. In *ST* 2:38–41, he rehearses his conclusions on Edwards' program and once more elects music as a more fitting metaphor than that of the machine.

person that God is. In short, space both results from and is an extension of God's own dynamic consciousness.

By predicating his notion in this way, Edwards argues that created space and physical reality ultimately presuppose the spatiality of the triune God. This fusion of Christian theology and Newtonian science insures Edwards against a mechanistic view of reality and prevents God's suspension from creation. In Edwards, God's real presence grounds all spatial realities. Where space, in Newton, presupposes *static* deity, in Edwards it is premised upon the notion of divine *dynamism and harmony*. In this way, God thinks and communicates space into being by consciously willing all that space consists of and contains. In Edwards, space is the presupposition of all reality. What's more he is prepared to push his notion further. In Edwards, "Space is God."[33] And this divine space forms the substratum wherein all things "move and have their being. In each and every space, according to Edwards, God's presence dwells: 'To be precise, it is the mind of God, apart from whose knowledge nothing can exist.'"[34]

Room for Three and More: Edwards and Triune Space

Jenson's notion of time holds much in common with Edwards' treatment of space. The positing of spatiality within God's life and the predicating of substance upon the work of the creator, provides Jenson with the perfect platform on which to build a theory of space consistent with his conclusions on time. By joining these schemes it becomes possible to pronounce time and space as both mutual presuppositions of reality and as eternal characteristics of the creator. However, if these suppositions are to provide this denouement, they must do towards a *trinitarian* end. For Jenson is ever insistent that the study of created phenomena be verified by the trinitarian nature of the creator, and vice versa. The question now arises as to the trinitarian credentials of Edwards' scheme. For if God has space for us, then this space must be marked by his triune nature. "In Edwards' interpretation of being," Jenson reports, "the triune God, as harmony in himself, thinks other true partners of

33. Edwards, *Works* 6:203.
34. Holmes, *God of Grace*, 88.

this community, and so there is the world posited by physics, as the inter-subjectivity of the expanded community."[35] Or, as Holmes puts it: "Material things are objective, are other than each other, . . . because that is how God thinks of them, and His faithfulness is the only guarantor (and the only one needed) of that. In the more developed form of this metaphysics I have postulated, the creation exists through being known by God, and so the Father holds the creation in being through His Son and His Spirit."[36]

At first, the resting of physical space upon an entity as seemingly immaterial as consciousness appears strange. However, far from turning Edwards' world into a dream, this move ensures that God's "consciousness envelopes what it apprehends, and that [this] enveloping is the 'being of beings.'"[37] As we grasp reality through our consciousness of the physical and material world, so too, God creates and maintains reality through the engagement of his consciousness with spatial possibilities.

At this point, a further question arises as to the independence of created conscience. Is Edwards suggesting that all our thoughts are only God's thoughts? Edwards goes on to explain: "God directly 'communicates' to each of us the ideas that are the content of our consciousnesses, and it is this communication that is his thinking and so his creating of the universe of bodies."[38] A counter question then occurs as to whether God is hereby stripped of his own independence. Edwards defends his claim once again, suggesting that God's independence is guaranteed by the fact that he is, in himself, triune and thus, communal, whereas we are only communal in that we are found in him. "The secret lies here: that which truly is the substance of all bodies is the infinitely exact and precise and perfectly stable ideas in God's mind, together with his stable will that the same shall gradually be communicated to us, and to other minds, according to certain fixed and established methods and laws."[39]

35. *AT,* 34.

36. Holmes, *God of Grace,* 88.

37. Jenson, *America's Theologian,* 30–31. From here Jenson is able to confirm his suspicions that God's faithfulness characterises the eternal time and space of the triune life.

38. *AT,* 31.

39. Edwards, *Works* 6:344.

As with Jenson's concept of time, Edwards' formulation of space may carry an implication of pantheism. The charge is surprising against one so famed for his bombastic preachments at sinners caught "in the hand of an angry God." However, Edwards' belief that space is God, incurs its own vulnerability to the pantheist critique. While far less drastic than Hegel's doctrine of absolute immanence, Edwards' insistence upon divine immediacy has invoked much response at this point.[40] The question that we must once again address concerns whether Edwards' program fuses the space of God and creation to such an extent that either party is in danger of being overcome by the other. Jenson himself observes the inherent danger of such an immediate notion: "Indeed, that God himself was creation's immediate support and coherence would only imprison us in *pantheos*."[41] However, this need not be our conclusion if we are able to resist a monadic interpretation of God's life. Edwards' refutation, according to Jenson, is constructed similarly to his own defense against pantheism. Firstly, the space that God himself takes up is that of a creator and so is also the very possibility of another space, or an outer space, which is not God. Secondly, this other, or outer space is premised upon the communal nature of the triune God.

If, as Edwards suggests, all space is supported by God as the only proper substance then the claim that all spatial reality is ontologically presupposed upon him seems unremarkable. At no point, is Edwards forced to imply that creation is identical to its own spatial presupposition, but rather, as Holmes points out, the excellency of existence, which so personifies God's creative being in Edwards, is a relational excellency, which further ensures the distinction between creator and creature, for without such distinction no relationship would be possible. Furthermore, Edwards' relational ontology is primarily premised, not upon God's relationship with the world, for this would certainly incur God's absorption into the life of his creation, but rather upon the relationship which God himself enjoys as triune. Jenson picks up on this trinitarian hypothesis in an article entitled, "Mr. Edwards' Affections."[42] "It is by the trinitarian distinctions in God that the distinction between

40. One notable attack can be found in Gunton, "The End of Causality," 78–79.

41. Jenson, "End is Music," 166.

42. Jenson, "Mr. Edwards' Affections," 169.

God and our consciousness is maintained even in our illumination. The difference between natural religion and spiritual new life is that God the Spirit chooses to play a role in the saints' consciousness the same role that he plays in God's triune inner life. Plainly, only the *triune* God can be in this way interlocked with the factors of his creatures' consciousness."[43]

While Edwards' trinitarian defense of the creature/creator distinction is largely effective, one problem remains. The necessary pneumatological extension outlined by Jenson above, while theologically nonexpendable, appears lacking in Edwards' exposition. As Holmes points out, although Edwards is at pains to develop a christological mediation of God's relationality, the pneumatology necessary to support his scheme is both idealistic and inadequate.[44] Despite this deficiency, Holmes declares, Edwards was able to rewrite Reformed theology through his appropriation of the best secular science and philosophy of his day.[45] Edwards' utilization of Newtonian science enabled him to resolve inherent spatial conflicts and to mould space and time into a unified vision of created reality. For the Reformed tradition, Edwards provides a vision of space whereby God's presence is not dissected between heaven and earth, nor doubled up as in the Calvinist extra. Here, God's presence or location (i.e., his own consciousness) is the self same place in which he is present for us in the incarnation, Eucharist, and parousia. Furthermore, Edwards' assertion that creation finds its very existence in the conscious will and communication of a triune God provides the ground for God's continued, promised, and indeed, necessary involvement within spatial reality. In Edwards' work, God is the real presence of the world and, as such, all harmony and created order point to him. God's presence here seeks not to escape or deny time, but rather embraces it. While celebrating his achievement, Jenson himself bemoans the fact that Edwards' treatment of space has failed to come to fruition in the life of the American church:

43. Ibid., 172.
44. Holmes, *God of Grace*, 97.
45. Ibid., x.

It is surely worth considering whether . . . [Edwards'] interpretation of Newton's world is not that demanded by faith . . . Behind all the nihilisms of modernity is the vision of our world as a deaf and dumb apparatus, within which we live but to which our converse is irrelevant . . . In its participation in this self-alienation, one-half of the American church has become simply unbelieving, disguising its abandonment of prayer by doing other things— meditation, self- or group-therapy, etc.—and calling them prayer; the other half thinks it can maintain belief only by relativizing the Newtonian harmony and making God an extra entity who sometimes "intervenes." The American civil community is flattened and perverted by the same religious triviality and ideological demonism.[46]

Room for God: Jenson and Triune Embodiment

Space, Jenson suggests, must provide both "an a priori account of our consciousness and a structure within which we locate ourselves."[47] The resolution has already been anticipated in Edwards' notion of "God's enveloping consciousness."[48] Echoing Edwards, Jenson places space, ontologically, alongside time. Much of what we have learned from Edwards is imported directly into Jenson, and from hereon our discussion will focus largely upon the distinctions between the two accounts.[49] We begin, where we left off, with the problem of pantheism. In Jenson, the pantheistic threat is largely overcome by the God who knows and creates "others." While we may find our spatial existence within his own life, "our accommodation in him has the present dimension of separateness."[50] Jenson arrives at the point, not by abandoning Edwards' triune notion of consciousness but, rather, by developing it further.

46. Jenson, *America's Theologian*, 34.

47. *ST* 2:47.

48. Ibid., 47.

49. To list the commonalities between Edwards and Jenson, while beyond the space available here, would make for an interesting study in its own right.

50. *ST* 2:48.

Like Edwards before him, Jenson does not hide from the difficulties entailed in conversations about consciousness. Jenson is quick to draw our attention to the role that consciousness plays in mediating our experience of physical reality. Through my consciousness, I become aware of the space in which I live and come to understand myself as one place within that space. Likewise, my consciousness enables me to acknowledge other objects and subjects, as other places within a shared space. I can identify these places as others because my consciousness assures me that they are not the same as me. Space is now both the communal container in which we exist as human beings and the process by which we locate and measure our spatial movements and interactions. Furthermore, as we are recognizable through our own physical distinctives, our very identity is predicated upon certain spatial calculations.[51] "To address myself to one addressing me," Jenson writes, "I must be able to pick him out from the maelstrom of actuality. I may do this by merely pointing—to his body, not his spirit," nor his consciousness, we might add.[52] In the same way that consciousness enables the spatial calculations between ourselves and others, it also enables us to identify our otherness, as creatures, to God. Hence consciousness, in Jenson, equips human beings both to locate themselves within the divine life and to differentiate themselves from it:

> If the transcendental focus of my consciousness is indeed a participation in divinity . . . then I am not myself the space within which this focus is located but must belong rather to that in which I am located . . . And if the transcendental focus of consciousness is thus indeed "behind" the field of my consciousness, and indeed in some sense a geometric point, it is not therefore *timeless*, since that within which we live and move and have our being is the triune God, who is an eternal *life* and so neither a single point nor merely timeless.[53]

---

51. Ibid., 355–56.

52. Jenson, "The Body of God's Presence: A Trinitarian Theory," 84.

53. Jenson, *On Thinking the Human*, 26. These echoes of Kant will return before long.

Developing Edwards' Newtonianism, Jenson combines time and space to provide both the horizon of human consciousness and the measurement of spatial reality. In Jenson, the two receptacle models of space are merged. Creation, as the finite container of created space, is now contained within the infinite receptacle that constitutes God's own life. Finite space is no longer to be considered in diametrical opposition to infinite space, and thereby, Jenson's interpretation of space merges, once more, with his treatment of time. In the same way that our temporal reality is related to God's eternal reality, so too, our finite spatial existence is dependent upon God's own existence as an infinite space. Using Edwards' concept of God's consciousness, Jenson is successful in fusing the two receptacles together, thus making the created space, that we call creation, into the meeting place for God and his creatures. Knight emphatically describes the results: "We are placed by and contained within the Ptolemaic container of God's working, and it is by this same working that this container is broken open."[54]

Having borrowed much, Jenson resists Edwards' suggestion that "space is God."[55] In distinguishing his own position Jenson reminds us of the maxim of John of Damascus: "God is his own space." For Jenson, God is not all space neither is he our space, but he is his own space, and while we ourselves find our space in his consciousness, this space is set apart from him as other. As we utilize use our consciousness to differentiate ourselves from others, so too, God uses his own consciousness in the mutual willing and distinguishing of finite and infinite realities. Without this ongoing act of divine distinction, creation itself would be impossible: "Since there are in fact creatures, their otherness from God establishes that God is one place, and creation is spatially located by not being *at that* place. God is one place and creatures another, and just and only so there is created space."[56]

The diversity and otherness of creation occurs firstly within God's mind, in that he wills it into being. It is this conscious act that initiates and delineates all creator/creature distinctions.[57] Having engaged

54. Knight, "Jenson on Time," 76.

55. Edwards, Works 6:203.

56. *ST* 2:47.

57. Jenson, "Creator and Creature," 219.

with Jenson on the issue, Gunton suggests an important terminological clarification. For while it is one thing to state that reality exists "*in* the mind of God and the minds of finite beings," it is something else altogether to claim "that the 'in' should be taken literally."[58] Applying David Berman's work on George Berkeley, Gunton suggests that the phrase "in the mind," be used metaphorically. For when we promise someone that, "we will keep them in mind," we are not making a literalist assertion. To promise to keep someone "*in* mind," is not to use the word "in" in the same way as when we say that that, "the apples are *in* the basket."[59] It is this careful use of spatial language that maintains the essential balance between internality and otherness. As Jenson points out, "The Father's love of the Son as other than himself is the possibility of creation's otherness from God."[60]

With this clarification made, Jenson continues: "the absolute difference between Creator and creature is an automatic classification . . . 'Creator' is simply equivalent to 'God' . . . and 'creature' is simply equivalent to 'everything.'"[61] In this differentiation we grasp hold of reality and anticipate its teleology. "In the purest abstraction," states Jenson, "what is other than God necessarily has God as its final and formal cause. Its being must be participation in God who is Being—or in God's ever-renewed transcendence of being."[62] God is both the ontological and eschatological presupposition of all spatial realities; we find in him both our origin and our goal. Along these lines, Jenson equivocates the doctrine of justification with the Orthodox concept of *theosis*. However, even now the creature/creator distinctions are maintained: "So there is a life that is God. And this life is communal in and of itself; there are three personal individuals who enact it among themselves. Therefore, they can rope us in. Thus as Cappadocian trinitarianism understands God, we can become God without acquiring the divine nature, and so without becoming additional instances of that nature. We indeed could

---

58. Gunton, "Creation and Mediation," 89.

59. Berman, *George Berkeley: Idealism and the Man*, 39.

60. *ST* 2:48.

61. Jenson, "Aspects of Creation," 17.

62. Jenson, "Creator and Creature," 219.

not share divine nature without ceasing to be human and without God ceasing to be unique."[63]

In the end, all spatial reality will be found in the God who is his own space. However, to achieve this oneness with God and to be identified by him, with him, and in him, according to Jenson, is not to *become* him. Although undoubtedly subtle, this point is of crucial importance for what is to come.[64] While it is possible, nay inevitable, for us to become *unified with* God and to be *located in* him, this is *not* to say that we will, or can, attain his personality and attributes. If the tale of temporality talks of the God who is timely and the time he has for us, then the story of space declares that God is roomy and points to the room he has for us. Like Edwards before him, Jenson envisions this roominess as an extension of trinitarian relationality. Through the act of creation, the triune God has created a space for us from within his own life. However, this space is marked by being both *in* God and being *other than* God, as without this distinction all interaction would become impossible.[65] Here lies the all-important distinction: To be "one with" something, in Jenson's thought, is not to become "the same as" that something.[66]

The point is illustrated by Christian teaching on marriage. In theological terms, it is possible to claim, in fact to insist, that I am one with my wife; however, it is unlikely that anyone would mistake us for the same person. It is also conceivable to suggest that having become one in our wedding ceremony, this oneness has increased over the years of our marriage; however our growing oneness neither endangers nor undermines our individual personalities. To lose this would be to relinquish the very nature and possibility of our relationship in the first place.[67] When Jenson talks of creation existing within the space opened up

63. Jenson, "Theosis," 110.

64. The mutual affirmation of our complete unification with God, and perennial identification as other than him, will be of particular importance in our consideration of the *totus Christus* in chapter 4.

65. *ST* 2:120.

66. It is important to hold on to this distinction in future discussions concerning the *totus Christus*. See chapters 4–7.

67. Jenson suggests that marriage is mimetic, in its reliance upon the communion that God is. "A great mystery of communion with Christ in the church, marriage is assuredly is." *ST* 2:65.

within the triune life, he is not proposing a Christianized Brahmanism. This mystical notion of oneness, whereby personality evaporates into the thin air of divine cosmos, is the opposite of Jenson's vision. However, the Brahmanist model is not ruled out due to its embrace of pantheism, but rather because it denies the triune subject of the Christian faith. A properly *Christian* theory of space must elide all personal declivities towards nothingness, and present the physical fulfillment of human-ity, as opposed to its demise. "To be deathless disembodied spirit," as Jenson points out, is one thing, "to bring off death and resurrection is another."[68] The Christian hope is thus, "irremediably antithetical to hope for dissolution into abstract divinity or for rescue from the wheel of karma or for reincarnation or soul transmigration, or any other state that represses personhood."[69] Resurrected saints experience God as though they are one, but not the same: "Those accommodated as par-ticipants in the divine life do not thereby become persons of that life. Space, we may say, is the form of God's own experience of this other-ness, which experience, of course, enables it. It is therefore not merely because of the limitations of our finitude that we inevitably imagine God as 'beyond' or 'above' us, . . . it is simply the reverse of the fact that we are beyond for God."[70] Gunton characterizes these immanentist instincts by citing Jenson's emphasis upon "withinness." According to Gunton, unlike Hegel, Jenson's less realized eschatology prevents these instincts from driving his program towards pantheism.[71] For all his talk of oneness and subsequent unifying tendencies, Jenson's notion of space is separated into two categories. The first consists of the place which God *is*, as Father, Son, and Holy Spirit. The second is the outer space that he makes for himself and his creatures.[72] This second, created space, although other than God, is both "immediately and inwardly ad-

---

68. Jenson, "Body of God's Presence," 89.

69. *ST* 2:354.

70. Ibid., 47.

71. Gunton, "Creation and Mediation," 90–91.

72. At this point, Gunton recalls Coleridge's argument that creation demands one of two possible explanations; either pantheism or trinitarian theism. Only the latter can establish an outer space to the creator and yet maintain the connection between creator and creation. Ibid., 90.

jacent to him."[73] Pointing to the significant influence of Johannes Brenz and the Swabian School of Lutheran theology in this regard, Christoph Schwöbel, illustrates Jenson's position further:[74]

> For God the whole created universe is one single place so that God can be present to the whole of creation simultaneously in a manner that is not distinguished by the locations of creation but by the modes of divine activity. God's presence to creation is different in the word of the gospel and the sacraments and in the hearts of believers, different again in the creative presence that maintains the being of the whole of creation. However, all these modes of presence are not to be spatially differentiated; they follow the differentiation and relation of God's Trinitarian self-giving.[75]

Once again, Jenson extends Edwards' own model of space. While his own estimation of Edwards's scheme is generous, it is safe to say that Jenson's investigations enable a fuller account of God's triune nature and its impact upon space.[76] In "The Body of God's Presence," Jenson introduces the concept of converse to further develop his own trinitarian theory of space.[77] As the eternal Word, Jenson's first premise denotes, God exists as an unending address, or conversation, between the three members of the Trinity. The ensuing dialogue constitutes God's self-revelation. Following on from this, the fact "that God reveals himself, means that an object which we intend as we seek to reply to God's promise, is the same object that God intends in the immanent Conversation that he is."[78] For Jenson, consciousness is not simply awareness of one's self but rather an admission of another. Consciousness has here become a *communal* experience made possible by the communal nature of the

73. *ST* 2:254.

74. The influence of the Swabian School is evident throughout Jenson's Christology.

75. Schwöbel, "Once Again, Christ and Culture," 118.

76. Is Jenson eager to amplify Edwards' program in this regard, or does his interpretation project his own conclusions from Edwards' work? The answer is, most likely, both.

77. Jenson, "Body of God's Presence," 82–91.

78. Ibid., 88.

creator. While Edwards echoes still, Jenson's point is more Kantian than his predecessor's: "Immanuel Kant undoubtedly got it formally right when—in his pompous language—he spoke of a 'transcendental unity of apperception,' of the structured unity that items in consciousness have with each other simply in that they *are* items in one—someone's—consciousness, a focusing whose point of focus is 'transcendental' in that it is never itself such an item."[79]

By identifying divine consciousness in the converse of the triune God, and in the dramatic location of each of its members, Jenson hereby gives Kant a trinitarian twist.[80] The idea of a transcendental unity of apperception, according to Jenson, while flawed in its anthropological inception, provides a perfect fit with the Christian interpretation of the triune life. Hence, the ultimate application of Kant's concept lies not in the inner workings of the human consciousness but rather in the mutual love of the godhead. If other conscious reality exists, Jenson concludes, then it does so by its participation in this life. Once again, the triune God is not here to be interpreted as sheer being but as a story: "The Father sends the Son and the Son obeys the Father and the Spirit frees this sending and obeying to be love. Since focused consciousness is either God's or by participation in him, we may conclude that *all* focused consciousness is focused by and as narrative; its location is its location within a story and it is a unity if and because the story is coherent."[81]

Our own consciousness confirms Jenson's notion that spatial reality forms the context for community. Consequently, consciousness becomes the key by which we discover the divine community in whom we exist and through which all consciousness is made possible. However, if Jenson is to follow through on his intention to root all spatiality in the life of the Trinity, he must go further than linking divine and human consciousness. If physical space is to receive a trinitarian ontology, Jenson must move beyond an affirmation of God's consciousness and establish a place for physical space within the Trinity itself:

79. Jenson, *Thinking the Human*, 23.

80. The Trinitarian twist may also be considered a Hegelian extension. Hegel's complaint against Kant at this point concerns Kant's finite limitation of consciousness. Jenson's move puts an end to such limitation. See chapter 1.

81. Jenson, *Thinking the Human*, 27.

If this is so, then I can be one consciousness—that is again, I can be conscious at all—only if location within the triune life and location within created human history and community are somehow congruent. In contingent fact, they coincide at one place, that at which is focused the consciousness of the specific man who is the Son. The *Son's* "transcendental unity of apperception" is identically a specific location within the human narrative and community and a specific location within the human narrative and community. He is a Jew, the child of a woman named Mary with a particular lineage, one of Rome's victims, and so on. And he is the Son and Word of the Father, the recipient and giver of the Spirit, and so on. *And* these are not two locations but only one; by classic doctrine, Jesus the Son is but one "person," one identity.[82]

For Jenson, the transcendent power of God to create or to will otherness is presupposed by his own internal experience of otherness. In short, otherness is possible for God because the Son is other than the Father and the Spirit is other than the Son. For this personal otherness to be substantive, Jenson suggests, it must bring with it the possibility of embodiment. For if God were only to exist as Spirit, how could he be identified as three persons? As the word of the Father, Jenson claims, the Son exists as God's own embodiment. Pushing further, he suggests that our own created bodies are also intrinsically connected to God's own embodiment in the life of the Son. For if Jesus is to be considered as "truly God," so the argument goes, trinitarian theology must provide an account of such embodiment.

Here we arrive at the second premise of Jenson's trinitarian theory of space. For Jenson, it is necessary to state *both* that "God has a body" *and*, as such, that God transcends himself.[83] If the triune God is eternally embodied, then revelation becomes a grant of divine objectivity, a dem-

82. Ibid., 28–29.

83. Jenson, "Body of God's Presence" 89. For Jenson, the thought of God as sheer, eternal, disembodied spirit is unthinkable, as such a deity would have no capacity for relationality and seek only to enslave his creation. This is also part of Jenson's critique of Hegel. See, chapter 1.

onstration of God's own embodiment. Jenson supposes that Christian theology has not taken space seriously enough at this juncture. The "bowdlerized version of standard theology understands God's embodiment as achieved by addition of Jesus' body to God. That God is triune is what makes such an anomaly possible."[84] In Jenson, the Spirit frees the Father from the temptation to retain all existence within himself. It is then the Son's role to mediate between the Father's originating and the Spirit's liberating and thus to hold open the space for creation.[85] Once again, this spatial configuration is replete with temporal significance: "To say that God has a body, is to say that God transcends also himself. There is in God beginning and goal, what is left behind and what is set ahead, past and future . . . All the analysis and rhetoric of idealist and existentialist doctrines of human existence, fit God before they fit us."[86]

We will return to the christological implications of triune embodiment with Jenson's third premise, but for now, Jenson asserts, God's embodiment represents his transcendence and, thus, the possibility that other bodies might encounter him. However, where could such a meeting take place? In Jenson's words, God needs a "pad"; "a created space to be his own, besides the uncreated space that he himself is."[87] First and foremost the tradition has denoted God's pad as "heaven." When it comes to space, Jenson posits, "the biblical notion of heaven is . . . not dispensable: For God to have a history with us, he must have a place not only in himself but in our world, in our space. And the Bible first calls this place heaven."[88]

For Jenson, heaven is spatially differentiated from earth, not by geometry but, rather, by *history*; God's ability to transcend space being also his ability to transcend time, Jenson's heaven is not spatially related to the earth in the same way as two earthly spaces but is rather differentiated on the basis of time. Heaven is "created future's presence—*as*

84. Ibid., 91.

85. *ST* 2:26–27. As Gunton points out, this position retains an inbuilt resistance to allegations of emanationism within Jenson's account of creation. Gunton, "Creation and Mediation," 88.

86. Jenson, "Body of God's Presence" 89.

87. Jenson, "Space for God," 51.

88. Ibid., 52.

future!—with God."[89] There is future in God, but not so as to transcend God: God *anticipates* his future and so possesses it, and so there is a present tense of creation's future with God, and therefore there is also its place with God.[90] For Jenson, heaven is the fulfillment of history, a place of completion where time and place are perfected and God's transcendence is immediate to his creation. In this reality, time and space are fused and fulfilled beyond anything that we can at presently imagine. Here, resurrected human beings transcend sin and death through the God who himself embodies this eternal transcendence. In short, the outer space of heaven exists as this world's perfect future tense. Knight illustrates Jenson's point:

> [In heaven God is] in place—his own place—in a more solid sense than we are. He is "here," though this "here" is not a here available to us—we cannot say where it is. We are entirely present to him, the function of his making and holding us to him; but we are neither properly to each other, nor, other than by Eucharistic epiclesis, using one particular name, is he accessible to us. In this world, which we so insouciantly take for our own, we are not yet what he determines we will be.[91]

Knight's reading does much to resolve the complex and potentially contradictory tension within Jenson's treatment of space. While ever immanent within the temporal and spatial reality of creation, God's unremitting presence with us is only ever directed from one side of the creature/creator divide. God is present within the outer space of his creation because he wills to be present for others. Hence, while his continuing converse with creation maintains our very reality, it is impossible for us to identify the space in which he is, save from his own revelatory embodiment among us. In the act of communion or the utterance of his name we do not call upon him as much as confirm the promise

89. *ST* 2:121. Jenson here develops Barth's theory that heaven was created as mysterious boundary. Jenson later suggests that his development of the Barthian scheme is the solution to the problems posed by Copernicus concerning heaven's physical location. Jenson, "A Space for God," 52.

90. *ST* 2:121.

91. Knight, "Jenson on Time," 75.

he has already made to be present with us. It is as though God opens the door between heaven and earth, and thus enables his creatures to experience the future that he already has for them. Each glimpse of this ultimate spatio-temporal reality is but a promise, and in each promise a new space/time continuum is opened. All this is performed by the work of the Spirit, who characterizes God's possession of the future and opens it to us. Hence, all knowledge of God, in Jenson, is a Spirit-enabled anticipation of and movement towards God's own future.

Here, we discover the pneumatology so lacking in Edwards: "The creation is liberated to its End and Fulfillment by God the Spirit," Jenson declares, "heaven is the *telos* of this dynamism insofar as it is a teleology within creation itself."[92] From here, it becomes possible for God to be simultaneously present in heaven and the Temple. Likewise, Christ can be both on the throne and in the Eucharist, without the need for a Calvinist extra. There is neither spatial stretch nor contradiction implied in these claims. If any dimension is being transcended it is a temporal one. This journey is not across space but across time, and, as such, makes what is already present in God, namely our future, present to us now. In Jenson, to anticipate God's future, namely heaven, is to be positioned alongside it.

Having spoken of God's embodiment within the Trinity's eternal converse and transcendence, Jenson establishes and validates his theory with a third and final premise. We return, once more, to Jenson's Christology and, in particular, his emphasis upon the resurrection.[93] In Christ, triune embodiment becomes more metaphysically manageable and difficult to deny: "God identifies himself by Jesus," declares Jenson. "This is the deepest and most quickly made statement of God's embodiment."[94]

We began this chapter with the challenge that space presents to the tradition and one question in particular. So what does it mean for creation to contain the uncontainable? In the search for a christological

---

92. *ST* 2:121.

93. David Demson's suggestion that Jenson ascribes an eternal fleshly existence to Christ, is a misreading of this point. Demson, "Robert Jenson's Systematic Theology: Three Responses," 96.

94. Jenson, "Body of God's Presence," 90.

conception of space, we return now to Mary. In her response to Gabriel's promise, Jenson asserts that Mary offered her womb to be "God's space in the world."[95] Mary's *fiat mihi* provided the platform for history's encounter with the God of space and the embodiment of the triune life, namely, Jesus. However, Jenson is anxious to point out that the incarnation is neither the beginning nor the end of God's embodiment for us. The christological reality, present in Mary's womb and in the incarnation, had long before been manifest in the nation of Israel. It was the very nature of God's embodiment within Israel that made the nation's religion peculiar to her neighbors. To this end, Jenson reminds us of the shock experienced by the Philistines when, upon opening the Ark of the Covenant, they found it completely empty.[96] Israel's prohibition of divine objects, images, and idols defied the religious norm. In the Holy of Holies, where YHWH dwelt, there was no spatial object to which this divine subject was tied.

While in material form the texts of the Torah offer a more concretized artifact of God's self presentation, these writings are but the story of God's people, and their commands are fulfilled only in their being read out and lived out. In the Old Testament, YHWH manifested his spatial power and presence primarily through the bodies, or body, of his people Israel. YHWH was similarly embodied in the lives of the prophets and these "mobile Temples" became known as the sons of God. Jenson concludes, "God takes for himself the space enclosed by the Tabernacle or the most Holy Place in order to dwell among the *people*, not vice versa. It is the people as a whole who are thereby the 'Container of the Uncontainable.'"[97] In this, Jenson suggests, God's Son was physically embodied in created time and space, long before Mary's encounter with Gabriel: "It is of course the heart of Christian faith that God's presence in Israel is gathered up and concentrated in Immanuel, God with us, in this one Israelite's presence in Israel: he is in person the Temple's *shekinah,* and the Word spoken by all prophets, and the Torah. And if that is so, then the space delineated by Israel to accommodate the

95. Jenson, "Space for God," 55.

96. Ibid., 54.

97. Ibid., 54.

presence of God is finally reduced and expanded to Mary's womb, the container of Immanuel."[98]

As the container of the uncontainable, Mary can be called, "Israel in one person," for her obedience has made her Temple, and arch-prophet alike.[99] By providing a physical space and home for God's Son, Mary constitutes Israel herself. While the embodiment of God's Son within the life and people of Israel is not fully answered by the Old Testament, the New Testament provides us with christological clarity. In these chapters and stories, divine and human spatiality collide in God's outer space.[100] Here, in the person of Christ, God's embodiment for his creation is no longer a case of "containment in one set of places instead of another but one of availability to experience in one set of places instead of another."[101] As Schwöbel points out: "To replace the notion of containment as the guiding idea for understanding what a 'body' is with availability has for Jenson a twofold corollary. Availability is our becoming present for others and so intending others, but at the same time allowing others to intend us. Both are held together in the understanding of body as availability."[102]

Having rested his case for God's spatial embodiment within the availability of the incarnate, risen Christ, Jenson is able to pose one of his favorite questions. "Where has the body gone?" he asks. His point is both simple and profound. The body of Jesus is risen and lives as the body of believers who have witnessed his availability and become available to him. Following his resurrection and ascension, the Son is embodied *in the church* and thus, in the church we witness the *totus Christus*.[103] With Christ, as her head in heaven, and the Christian com-

98. Ibid., 55.

99. Ibid., 56.

100. As Schwöbel points out, Jenson's Cyrillian, Lutheran Christology not only asserts the unity of the person of Christ, but also forbids an interpretation of deity whereby Christ's deity can be conceived or experienced aside from his humanity, for this would represent a relapse into Nestorianism. Schwöbel, "Christ and Culture," 117–18.

101. *ETC*, 219.

102. Schwöbel, "Christ and Culture," 119.

103. We will return to this temporal and spatial embodiment of God's Son at some length in chapter 4 and regularly from thereon.

munity, for her body on earth, the church is the continued christological embodiment, transcendence, and availability of the triune God in the outer time and space of creation. It is for this reason, Jenson suggests, that the church finds herself at the gate of heaven.[104] These very issues will form the central chapter of this work and will recur regularly from then on.

Conclusion

Considerable ground has been covered in this chapter. Having witnessed the pioneering work of Jonathan Edwards, we can testify to the significant impact of the revivalist's thought upon Jenson's notion of space. Acknowledging the loyalty and deep respect that Jenson has for Edwards, it is right also that we acclaim the sizeable scope, individuality, and imagination displayed in his own approach to the subject. In Jenson, we have witnessed a more deliberate and developed trinitarian model of space. With both theologians, the discussions concerning pantheism will, no doubt, continue. However, Jenson's intentions not only to refute the allegations but also to provide a distinctly trinitarian account of space are clear.

Where Jenson differs most from Edwards is in his prioritizing of time over space. In his work on the place of space in Christian theology, John Inge argues that Newton's influence inevitably led to the reordering of these principles.[105] Despite his Newtonian tendencies, Edwards resists this temptation. However, while Jenson's work represents an almost extreme outworking of Inge's theory the question now arises as to which order is correct. However, the common ground and direction within Edwards and Jenson would seem to suggest that the order in which we tackle time and space is of secondary importance. What Newton, Edwards, and Jenson have all taught us is that the categories must be treated together.

Whether one model or theorem can fully elucidate the complexities of space is doubtful. However, in Jenson we have discovered an account that utilizes the contribution of the tradition, proposes new ways

104. *ST* 2:172.

105. Inge, *Theology of Place*, 5–13.

of thinking and, in so doing, tackles a number of significant historical and philosophical problems. Finally, we can assert, along with Jenson, that our existence is premised by two ontological realities rested upon the triune God. *We exist because God has time and space for us.* Through our experiences and reflections upon these entities, we come to terms with the reality of creation. In the future, it may even become possible to view and experience God's own perfected time and space, or that which we call "heaven."

3

Heaven's Mandate:
Jenson and Language

GOD HAS TIME AND space for us. Here we have witnessed the two primary presuppositions of created reality within Jenson's theology. In the same way that Jenson's treatment of time stretched into space, so too his account of space leads us directly to language as the third and final presupposition of reality. As we witnessed in the previous chapter, Jenson's trinitarian account of space is reliant upon the christological conception of God's embodiment in the Word. In Jenson, the triune space is delineated by the divine discourse between the three members. It follows then that our own grasp of reality, or the created time and space in which we find ourselves, is made possible by the dialogues that we share with one another and, more specifically, through the language which constitutes this conversation.

The following chapter is dedicated to the place of language within Jenson's theology. In particular, we will ask whether Jenson is warranted in placing language, alongside time and space, as a presupposition of reality. To succeed, language must prove itself doubly theological. Firstly, it must enable mankind to come to terms with the temporal and spatial realities of creation and, secondly, it must articulate the identity and nature of the creator, in whom created time and space finds its being. Jenson's most specific dealings with language emanate from the early part of his career. His most notable publication in this regard, *The Knowledge of Things Hoped For: The Sense of Theological Discourse,* was written in the 1960s, while Jenson was teaching at Oxford. The book combines a critical conversation with the great thinkers of the tradition along with a survey of leading trends in contemporary theology and philosophy.[1] "In particular," Carl Braaten remarks, he brings "the insights of the then regnant Oxbridge linguistic philosophers (e.g. Ludwig Wittgenstein, John Wisdom, J. L. Austin) to explore the meaning of statements of Christian eschatology."[2] In this chapter, the first, and most influential of these figures assumes the role of our chief interlocutor. Having listened in upon Wittgenstein's and Jenson's discussions concerning language, our discussion will be enhanced by the inclusion of a further dialogue partner. As a fellow Lutheran, George Lindbeck's work represents one of the most sophisticated appropriations of Wittgensteinian thought for theology.

Philosophy and the Game: The Convergence of Language in Wittgenstein and Jenson

Although famed for his philosophy, Wittgenstein is often considered as "the opposition" for the orthodox theologian. The same goes for much of Wittgensteinianism, to categorize those who have followed in his philosophical wake. Alan Keightley goes as far as to suggest that "in *some* theological circles, Wittgenstein is thought of as philosophy's 'bogey man.'"[3] Upon reflection, the roots of this fear may be mistaken. The predominant tendency to posthumously label Wittgenstein as a "fideist," does not wholly reflect the philosopher's position. Having no means of making him into an atheist, atheistic philosophers have often chosen the title, "fideist" as the next best category by which to describe

---

1. Jenson, *The Knowledge of Things Hoped For.* These early preoccupations with language and theology remain present through the entire body of Jenson's work. Latterly, this treatment of language enables much of Jenson's Prolegomena in the first volume of his *Systematics. ST* 1:3–62.

2. Braaten, "Robert William Jenson—A Personal Memoir," 6.

3. Keightley, *Wittgenstein, Grammar and God,* 11.

him. However, as Fergus Kerr points out, Wittgenstein's experience of faith was more defined, decisive, and dramatic than the term implies.[4]

A thorough going evaluation of Wittgenstein's philosophy and its implications for theology are beyond the scope and frame of this work. However, a more focused investigation concerning the impact of Wittgensteinian philosophy upon Jenson's notion of language proves promising.[5] In appraising their work, a number of kindred qualities are evident. In his characterization of Wittgenstein, David Pears highlights a refusal to submit to skepticism, a philosophical pull towards the description of reality, a willingness to unravel the Western philosophical tradition, along with its claim to ultimate authority, and a rare ability to see the particular within the general.[6] Although much of this resonates with the tenets of his own thought, it is the theological *utility* of Wittgenstein's analysis of language use that proves irresistible to Jenson.

While philosophers have wrestled with his theology, theologians have often struggled with Wittgenstein's concept of the "language-game."[7] This central notion instantiates Wittgenstein's refutation of the claims of empirical philosophy to know the inner workings of the human understanding. Such an end, Wittgenstein declares, is an impossibility. In the renowned *Tractatus Logico-Philosophicus*, Wittgenstein asserts that essence, far from assuming some form of pre-linguistic determination, exists within language itself.[8] As George Lindbeck explains: "It seems clear that the pre-sensory or preperceptual selection

4. Kerr, *Theology after Wittgenstein*, 28–36. Reflecting upon Wittgenstein's encounter with Tolstoy's account of the Gospels, Bertrand Russell disapprovingly noted that the Russian had converted his colleague from being "dogmatically anti-Christian" into a kind of philosophical mystic. Cell, *Language, Existence and God*, 132.

5. Jenson's employment of Wittgensteinian thought is independent of any admiration that he may, or may not have, for the philosopher's own theological standing. As with Hegel, Jenson's theology regularly employs those on the fringe of, and even far removed from, the tradition's inner circle. His theology is, in part, distinguished by the utility it makes of thinkers with whom he holds the most significant disagreements.

6. Pears, "Wittgenstein," 812–13. Both Jenson and Wittgenstein are suspicious of formulations of the God *behind* the God that we can grasp in language. As we will soon see, this aversion will lead them in two quite different directions.

7. Kerr suggests that this is, in part, due to the misinterpretation or misappropriation of the concepts by theologians themselves. Kerr, *After Wittgenstein*, 28–29.

8. Wittgenstein, *Tractatus Logico-Philosophicus*.

and organization of stimuli is not entirely prelinguistic. The classification and categorial patterns embedded in language, once it has been acquired, help organize the inexperienceably chaotic confusion that bombard our senses."[9]

The language we use and the rules that determine its usage are, according to Wittgenstein, ineradicable expressions of our own existence. The game brings to prominence the fact that language is a form of life, or "life-form," and, as such, is an essential aspect of every human activity. Hence our attitudes and beliefs are not the stuff of pure noetic energy awaiting verbal interpretation and expression, but rather consist of and are embodied within words and speech. In Wittgenstein, language contains and reflects the organization of our whole experience. "In fact, all propositions of our everyday language, just as they stand, are in perfect logical order.—That utterly simple thing, which we have to formulate here, is not a likeness of the truth, but the truth itself in its entirety."[10]

The rules of a language-game do not exist for their own independent study, but are rather the means by which we take part in the game in the first place. For it is in our playing of the game that we grasp hold of reality. "The main mistake made by philosophers of the present generation," Wittgenstein remarked, "is that when language is looked at, what is looked at is a form of words and not the use made of the form of words."[11] Each and every facet of life depends upon this linguistic interplay. In pursuit of reality, theologians, philosophers, historians, mathematicians, scientists, and artists, to name but a few, all engage in language-games. In the case of the former, the theologian's use of language to explicate the cause and nature of creation comprises a theological language-game. As with all games, the rules of theology dictate what players can and cannot do within the life of the game. Speech that is considered true, faithful, and honoring is encouraged, while words that may be deemed inappropriate, heretical, or obsolete are ruled out. Importantly, in Wittgenstein, the theological language-game is not constrained within the academic domain nor among believers, but is played universally by all humanity.

9. Lindbeck, *The Nature of Doctrine Religion*, 37.

10. Wittgenstein, *Tractatus*, 67.

11. Wittgenstein, *Lectures*, 2.

Theology and the Game: The Divergence of Language
in Jenson and Wittgenstein

Wittgenstein's notion of language is redolent within Jenson's own reflections upon the subject. In Jenson's most basic constructions, language comprises a series of sounds produced via semantic function, or as a series of physical gestures that generate a communicative, or expressive effect.[12] In its broadest evaluation, this grand unifying category encompasses linguistics, semiotics, sociology, the sacraments, body language, violence, art, culture, and more besides. In all cases, linguistic action enables mankind to evaluate and construct the reality with which it is presented. Through language, Jenson asserts, man organizes his experience of time and space, and thus grasps hold of his existence. For reality is that which "you and I create with sentences and other signs."[13] An important point of departure between Jenson and Wittgenstein, concerns their respective use of time. For Wittgenstein, time, or timelessness to be more precise, pushes language to its uttermost limits. While philosophers and theologians pretend to talk of timelessness, Wittgenstein asserts, their efforts are doomed to failure for all language is bound by time itself, hence philosophers who say, "'After death a timeless state will begin,' or: 'at death a timeless state begins,' do not notice that they have used the words 'after' and 'at' and 'begins' in a temporal sense, and that temporality is embedded in their grammar."[14]

Attempting to resolve the dilemma, Wittgenstein makes use of Augustine. Faced with the challenge of time and timelessness, Augustine turns to music and verse. In verse, language can measure time's passing without the need for a clock or a sundial. In this way, language enables our grasp of created time. However, the retention of verse is made possible by memory, or the timeless soul. Verse by its nature, Augustine concludes, transcends time and timelessness.[15] This view proves irre-

12. Jenson, *Visible Words*, 57.

13. *VW*, 20. Language constructs reality. Jenson's point is that we use language to experiment with, and build, our own reality. Later on we will have cause to consider his ontological notion that speech creates all reality and existence. *ST* 2:259.

14. Wittgenstein, *Culture and Value*, 22.

15. Augustine's observations on time, memory, and music will feature prominently in chapter 7.

sistible for Wittgenstein.[16] In Wittgenstein, while our understanding of language is time-bound, there remains an unspeakable element stretching far into timelessness. "The solution of the riddle of life in space and time lies outside space and time," concludes Wittgenstein.[17] The philosopher is unapologetic about the scheme's philosophical roots: "I read: '. . . philosophers are no nearer to the meaning of 'Reality' than Plato got . . . What a strange situation. How extraordinary that Plato could have got even as far as he did! Or that we could not get any further!"[18] With this, Wittgenstein settles for a Platonic division of time and timelessness, and assigns language as the connection between the realms. However, what appears an appropriate resolution soon unravels in time.

In assigning language to both the temporal and the timeless, Wittgenstein risks contradiction. For if language is reliant upon time, then what can be said about timelessness? And likewise, if language contains that which is timeless, how do our words avoid becoming de-temporalized? It becomes hard to see how Wittgenstein's troublesome connection between the temporality of language and the timelessness of eternity can avoid undermining his program. We will return to these challenges later, but for now we turn to Jenson. Having outlined Jenson's multiple rejections of timeless reality in the first chapter of this work, it will come as little surprise that his treatment of language diverges from that of Wittgenstein. In Jenson, language is framed by perpetual temporality: "Time is qualified succession. It is the continuing occurrence of meaning . . . Time and word belong together. The word *narrates* . . . what has occurred in time and thus lets it live on in time. Its function is re-presentation . . . In the word what has been is present and real: in the word what is coming announces itself."[19]

Jenson's linguistic theory lives up to Heidegger's famous declaration of language as the "house of being."[20] The power of language to contain and communicate reality is derived from the God who has time, space, and a word for us. For Jenson, the temporal-spatial event that we

16. Hudson, *Wittgenstein and Religious Belief,* 62.

17. Wittgenstein, *Tractatus,* 87.

18. Wittgenstein, *Culture and Value,* 15.

19. *KOTHF,* 206–207.

20. Ebeling, *Introduction to a Theological Theory of Language,* 95.

call creation is made possible in language. Therefore, language retains no independent existence over and against what it says, for the givenness of the world and our experience of humanity rely utterly upon it. Through language, Jenson implores, "we take up the task of coming together in our lives . . . [as such,] your life and mine become intertwined only by a shared environment, posited by language, *in* which we meet."[21] Similarly to Wittgenstein, language, in Jenson's theology, enables our negotiation of, and location within, temporality. In every speech act we orientate ourselves between the poles of past and future, between "memory and promise."[22] Take, for example, this standard greeting: "Good Morning." These two words represent, first, an ancient routine; second, a current convention; and, third, the possibility that someone new is about to break into our lives. In Jenson, language is a gift of the past that challenges us to the future and thus it is the very temporal nature of language that makes hope and history possible. In our use of sentences and symbols, we construct and interpret reality so that "we can live humanly together."[23] Therefore, by detemporalizing the act or content of language we abort the meaningful nature of history and render all hope as impossibility: "The word is the opening to us of the future. The word is the reality now between us of what neither of us is yet. Every address of one man to the other poses to the hearer the possibility of becoming something other than he is."[24]

Jenson extends this thesis in an essay entitled, "God, the Liberal Arts, and the Integrity of Texts."[25] Analyzing the role of language within the life of the community, Jenson cites the part played by shared texts. "A community subsists, in that as a group created by a certain past it jointly chooses a future."[26] In this way, a community's hope and history are realized through the temporal construction and conservation of corporate texts. Whether in the form of written accounts, artistic depic-

21. *ETC*, 1–2.
22. *S&P*, 74.
23. Ibid., 6.
24. *ETC*, 41.
25. Ibid., 209–15.
26. Ibid., 209.

tions, or oral histories these language-acts contain and comprise the community's story and identity.[27]

It is Wittgenstein that we have to thank for one of the most important revelations of contemporary thought, namely that all human experience and understanding of reality is *mediated by language*. Although the potential relapse of the Wittgensteinian scheme into the realm of timelessness provides ground for concern, Jenson's own extension and temporal reinforcement of the program has amplified the key claim that language provides our access to reality. In answer to our first question, we can confirm the theological nature of language. For Jenson, the theme of language is human existence as a whole.

God and the Game: Revelation in Wittgenstein, Lindbeck, and Jenson

We come to the second question with which we commenced this chapter. Can language be the means by which we understand the instigator of reality, namely the creator? Jenson himself frames the question in Wittgensteinian terms: "May not a language activity be played with a key piece 'God'? May not a language-activity be concerned with positing and manipulating the relation to this key piece of such words as 'me,' 'future,' 'salvation'? May we not have a game with its own rules, by which its sentences are meaningful in their own way, so long as we follow these rules?"[28]

The request initially appears modest, with Wittgenstein himself crediting the notion to one of Jenson's heroes. "Luther said that theology is the grammar of the word 'God,'" recalls Wittgenstein, and "I interpret this to mean that an investigation of the word would be a grammatical one."[29] In Wittgenstein, grammar provides the patient and painstaking

27. Along these lines, Jenson claims that Western civilization has lost faith in the historical power of texts. "Is there a *story* to tell about the Western political community? A story that is *true* and the chief thing needed for us to understand our communal life?" Jenson asks. "We are currently inclined to doubt it." Ibid., 213–14.

28. *KOTHF,* 4–5.

29. Wittgenstein, *Wittgenstein's Lectures.* 32. Susan Wood has argued that the scriptural foundations and ecclesial connotations of Jenson's own theory of theological language are built upon the Lutheran doctrine of *sola scriptura.* We will ex-

route to all theological converse, for just as we access our thoughts and experiences linguistically, so too our knowledge of the divine is dependent upon our life in language.[30] In Wittgenstein, everyday language becomes evidence of God's closeness to us, as opposed to his distance from us: "It is very *remarkable* that we should be inclined to think of civilization—houses, streets, cars, etc.—as distancing man from his origins, from what is lofty and eternal, etc. Our civilized environment, along with its trees and plants, strikes us then as though it were cheaply wrapped in cellophane and isolated from everything great, from God, as it were. That is a remarkable picture that intrudes on us."[31]

Running against the grain of accepted metaphysics, Wittgenstein insists that in our search for the meaning of existence, we have nowhere else to turn other than the complex system of signs, which is language. However, while supporting the theological nature of the language-game, on the one hand, Wittgenstein is ultimately unable to affirm Jenson's request. Admitting God as a particular, discernable piece within the game, according to Wittgenstein, would be to introduce a "paranormal" factor to the interplay and thus to break the rules. In this moment, we thrust against the limits of language. In Wittgenstein, all attempts to give voice to the divine through language are doomed to fall short. For "the sense of the world must lie outside of the world," and thus beyond the grasp of language.[32] "What we cannot speak about," he declares, "we must pass over in silence."[33] However, Wittgenstein's silence is not the denial of God's existence but rather a denial of language's ability to expound the universal truths contained within it.

The failure to include God in the language-game is, in part, brought about by Wittgenstein's capitulation towards the timeless. For while language provides our purchase upon temporal reality, it cannot stretch to explain the timeless reality upon which our existence is premised. As our only connection between time and timelessness, the best

---

amine the link between these further in our next chapter. Wood, "Robert Jenson's Ecclesiology," 78–187.

30. Kerr, *After Wittgenstein*, 145–48.

31. Wittgenstein, *Culture and Value*, 50.

32. Wittgenstein, *Tractatus*, 86.

33. Ibid., 89.

that language can offer us is a mysterious transcendence all of its own. Henceforth, the divine remains present in everyday language as long as it goes unmentioned, for in every temporal attempt to explain that which is timeless, divinity itself is immediately banished. If we do not attempt to utter what is unutterable, Wittgenstein suggests, then nothing will get lost. Furthermore, that which is unutterable will remain in all that we do utter. Trapped in its own temporal and circular ontology, language appears to have no hope of articulating that which, by its own nature, is simply beyond. Where religion is concerned Wittgenstein is forced to "retreat into silence." However, pushed to its own logical conclusion, this move threatens Wittgenstein's entire program.[34] For if the linguistic nature of reality is subject to a religious dimension—which, upon reflection, remains closed to linguistic description—the power of language to grasp and expound existence is brought into question.

George Lindbeck's theological engagement with Wittgenstein has provided fresh impetus to the theological dialogue concerning the concept of language-games. In *The Nature of Doctrine*, Lindbeck proposes that theological language comprises both discursive and non-discursive elements along with a distinctive logic or grammar by which this language can be meaningfully communicated.[35] It is Lindbeck's intention to present theology as the language-game for the language-form that we know as Christianity: "Just as a . . . 'language-game,' . . . is correlated with a form of life, and just as a culture has both cognitive and behavioral dimensions, so it is also in the case of a religious tradition. Its doctrines, cosmic stories or myths, and ethical directives are integrally related to the rituals it practices, the sentiments or experiences it evokes, the action it recommends, and the institutional forms it develops."[36]

The language-game of Christian theology is, for Lindbeck, the result of a particular story. From here, Lindbeck's theory appeals to the language of biblical narrative and the tradition. This language precedes our own experience and provides a set of grammatical rules for our use. Theology is here largely regarded as a descriptive exercise used by

34. Cell, *Language, Existence and Go,* 136.

35. Among others, Lindbeck draws into his Wittgensteinian schema, the work of Karl Marx, Max Weber, Emile Durkheim, and Clifford Geertz.

36. Lindbeck, *Nature of Doctrine,* 33.

believers in their faithful attempts to participate in the game. The comprehensive story which the Christian community utilizes to structure the dimensions of her own experience "is not primarily a set of propositions to be believed," according to Lindbeck, but is rather a "vocabulary of symbols . . . used for many purposes, only one of which is the formulation of statements about reality."[37]

While promising much, Lindbeck's limitation of theological language to an internal dialogue concerning religious practice strips theology of much of its propositional possibilities. With this vocabulary lacking, theology's purchase upon reality is severely restricted. Ontology is here sacrificed for what Lindbeck terms, "intrasystematic coherence," and eschatology is exchanged for a theological description of the here and now. In Lindbeck, the claims of history appear almost as unimportant as they are uncorroborated. At this point, Lindbeck serves only to theologize the same contradiction that we identified in Wittgenstein. The flawed assumption—that the description of creation can be isolated from propositional statements about the creator—recurs in Lindbeck's schema. As Jenson himself points out, implicit to the proclamation of Jesus' story are its implications for our own reality.[38] Unable to maintain a non-propositional stance, Lindbeck capitulates, confessing that, "as actually lived, a religion may be pictured as a single gigantic proposition."[39]

Jenson's rejection of Wittgenstein's rules of engagement can be seen most clearly in his critique of Lindbeck. Jenson's twofold rebuttal strikes at the heart of Lindbeck's appropriation of Wittgensteinian grammar.[40] Firstly, Lindbeck's refusal of essential ontological and eschatological ingredients undermines his defining notion of theological language. Jenson remains insistent at this point, for "if Christian theology is grammar, then it is prescriptive grammar," and must make

37. Ibid., 35.

38. Jenson, "Proclamation without Metaphysics," 22–29.

39. Lindbeck, *Nature of Doctrine,* 51. If this is the case, then Christianity is surely the gigantic sum of an inestimable number of other propositions. Lindbeck fails to address this. Subsequently we have not journeyed far beyond Wittgenstein. God remains the conceptual sum of all our language-games and life-forms.

40. Novak, "Theology and Philosophy," 56–57.

meaningful mention of God's past and future.[41] Secondly, his semiotic treatment, and subsequent denial of theology's capacity for external reference prompts Jenson to remind Lindbeck that theology cannot avoid the extralinguistic entity that constitutes its subject.[42] In a most stinging harangue, Jenson concludes that Lindbeck's Wittgensteinian extension "may not have shaken off [its] positivist prejudgments."[43]

The Revelation-Game: Theological Language in Jenson

Can theology be played as a language-game with "God" as a key piece? We return to the question with which we commenced the last section. Having witnessed Lindbeck's failure to resolve the Wittgensteinian dilemma, Jenson must now look elsewhere. "What Wittgenstein seems not to believe," Michael Foster suggests, "is that God has spoken. But what is it to believe this?"[44] In his own tribute to Jenson, David Novak testifies against philosophy's perennial tendency to undermine theology with the misplaced insistence that, while the universal must include the particular, the particular cannot direct us to the universal.[45] It is this tendency that has, too easily and too often, rendered talk of revelation as philosophically crude or invalid. However, as Paul Helm has suggested, far from extricating itself from philosophy, "the idea of revelation bristles with philosophical issues."[46]

In *The Knowledge of Things Hoped For,* Jenson proposes that God be included in our theological language-game via the linguistic tradition of the church. While this position may appear closer to Lindbeck, Jenson's starting point, method, and conclusion are markedly different. Furthermore, the barrier between language and divinity in Wittgenstein provides a bridgehead for Jenson's linguistic account of creation and the creator. While Wittgenstein considers ultimate reality as beyond the boundaries of time, Jenson posits time as itself evidence of the temporal

41. *ST* 1:20.

42. Ibid., 18.

43. Ibid., 19.

44. Foster, *Mystery and Philosophy,* 28.

45. Novak, "Theology and Philosophy," 44–45.

46. Helm, *The Divine Revelation,* xi.

infinity of the creator. In Jenson, the timeliness of God's eternity means that the ultimate reality for which we search, far from being permanently ensconced within the extrinsic limits of timelessness, exists as the very ground of our own temporal existence. As a result, each aspect of time-bound creation is a revelation of God's own temporal eternity and thus remains connected to his own life.

With language and time's coalescence re-established, Jenson is able to assert that the God who has time for us, also has language for us. In theological terms, such temporal description of God's personality and activity is denoted as revelation. The theological language of revelation, Jenson proposes, is already at our disposal as the enlivening of our theological language-game. In his temporal self-revelation, God has unveiled a language by which all reality can be described. The notion "that grammar cannot prescribe usage but can only describe it," can only be maintained in the absence of one who is able "to give the prescriptions."[47] As Novak points out, it is Jenson's revelatory presumption that enables his breakthrough in this regard. For while descriptive grammar can never convey an extra-linguistic entity, prescriptive grammar can provide such a possibility. Such prescription becomes possible when we locate "a person behind the commanding voice, *someone* whose will is being enunciated, and someone who cannot be reduced to an internal function of the prescription itself."[48] Speaking *about* God and, as we will soon see, speaking *to* God is possible, thinks Jenson, *because God has first spoken to us.* Jenson draws on the work of Gerhard Ebeling in this regard: "Something has been revealed to faith, it has learned something, and so is able to speak, and in particular to give an account of its own basis and consequences. Faith is given and experienced in words. Because it lives by the words it receives."[49]

This move towards God's identification is enabled by a threefold proposition. Firstly, according to Jenson, an adequate formulation of time enables us to talk of God through his own revelation to us. Secondly, the word that God speaks in revelation demonstrates the christological nature of creation. And thirdly, christology comprises a conversation

47. *ST* 1:20.

48. Novak, "Theology and Philosophy," 58.

49. Ebeling, *Theory of Language*, 25.

within the wider dialogue which is the life of the triune God. It is this movement that characterizes the development of Jenson's theological language from hereon. Jenson begins by making a direct appeal to revelation as the immediate evidence for the reality of God's speech in time. Once again, Jenson declares, God cannot be divorced from his word as his own linguistic act of revelation. As a result, the language of revelation constitutes God's actual presence within the theological language-game and the life-form that we know as the church.

In his survey of revelation, Jenson turns initially to Origen and Thomas Aquinas. The critical contributions made by these pioneers of theological language prove decisive to this day. In his reading of Origen, Jenson alights upon the underlying insistence that Scripture be regarded as the re-creation of the images received by the disciples at the incarnation. Origen thus asserts that God-talk is only made possible by God's direct interaction and self-revelation within time and history.[50] While wedded to Platonism, Origen's historical-biblical approach reinforces the fact that God is not only the author of divine revelation but is temporally present within it. Jenson paraphrases him further suggesting that, "when God deals in history with men, he makes himself the subject of anthropomorphic predicates. These predicates are not mere metaphors: God really has—*somehow*—become what these words say He is."[51] Having lauded Origen, Jenson applauds Aquinas' use of analogy as a breakthrough in the language of theology. "The perfect mutual necessity of the parts of Thomas' analysis is amazing," remarks Jenson. "It directs us to use the ordinary language that we use to make statements about objects and to make certain special stipulations."[52] Through Aquinas, it becomes possible to use everyday language-acts to describe God's nature equivocally, without these utterances being interpreted univocally. Analogies used to explicate God's attributes and activities can be understood realistically and truthfully, while not being interpreted literally.

As with Wittgenstein, Origen and Aquinas both fall for the trap of timelessness. Origen's Platonism undermines his notion of history

---

50. *KOTHF,* 45–47.

51. Ibid., 55.

52. Ibid., 88.

and Aquinas continually struggles to establish a stable position between equivocity and univocity. In spite of the problems, Jenson insists, "Thomas' insistence on the informative character of theological utterances and Origen's insistence that only the history of Jesus Christ makes such utterance meaningful" provide the basis for our theological propositions concerning the creator.[53] "While Jenson criticizes both his predecessors," as A. N. Williams indicates, "his choice of figures is augural, indicating how large a role both patristic and medieval theology will play in his later work."[54] The ancient confirmation of God's involvement within history, combined with the assurance that humanity is not deaf or dumb in the presence of the creator, provide the essential assumptions for Jenson's theory of theological language: "The telling of the church's story requires two kinds of words. It requires ordinary words with which we narrate matters of fact: 'born,' 'preached,' 'died.' And it requires, as a story which determines the lives of its hearers, the special words which man seeks to grasp, indeed to create, the meaning of his life: the words of myth, ritual, metaphysics, existential analysis. It requires words like 'sin,' 'history,' 'eternal' or 'god.'"[55]

As with Lindbeck before him, Jenson's conception of theological language centers upon the biblical narrative. However, unlike his colleague, Jenson's notion rests upon the propositional nature of these particular revelatory events and their universal implications in time and space. For Jenson, the church is part of God's address to creation and thus exists as both an embodiment of, and a response to, a divine word. The nature of this address is, first and foremost, to be found in the gospel narrative concerning the life, death, and resurrection of Jesus. Either side of this event, God's story is relayed both by and in the history of Israel and the life of the church. These are not to be seen as three independent, or even interdependent narratives, but as the self-same story.[56] What's more, in its narration, the main character of the story is not only

---

53. Ibid., 97.

54. Williams, "Parlement of Foules," 189–94. Williams identifies three stages in the development of Jenson's theological language. Commencing with the biblical narrative, Jenson goes on to explore the liturgical nature of language and finally, dogma.

55. Jenson, "Proclamation Without Metaphysics," 22.

56. It must be noted that this move does not turn Jenson into a supersessonist.

described or promised, but is actually present. Jenson asserts, "the biblical God's unique self-identity as God is established by his history on a narrative line parallel to the temporal line of our own history."[57] In the language of this narrative, God reveals himself to be the central piece, and player, in our theological language-games.

The revelation of the gospel narrative makes the particularity of God's identity historically and eschatologically explicit. For "God is whoever raised Jesus from the dead, having before raised Israel from Egypt."[58] Once again, far from removing himself from time, God is identified by the temporal language of history, and his very being and self-identity are constituted in the dramatic coherence and closure of this narrative. In Israel, God is understood as the narrator of her national history and as the enemy of death. In the incarnation, Christ fulfills this historical revelation through his identification with Israel and his triumph over death in the cross and resurrection. Therefore, to proclaim Christ as risen is to declare that God has happened. Thus, the infinite and dramatic crisis and resolution of all time belongs to God and his own history, or story, with us. From here on, the church community represents the historic presentation and eschatological expectation of God's Son, or Word. "Within Christian theological language the fundamental utterances, evocative or expressive as they are, are all historical *narratives*," Jenson declares.[59] "Christian utterances about God," Jenson insists, "posit an attitude to life exactly as narrative language."[60] Jenson makes his stand upon the very spot where Wittgenstein fell. In his own attempt to reinforce the gospel story Wittgenstein once declared: "Christianity is not based on a historical truth, but rather, it offers us a (historical) narrative and says: now believe! But not, believe this narrative with the belief appropriate to a historical narrative, rather: believe, through thick and thin, which you can do only as a result of a life."[61]

With no means of verifying its own ultimate claims, in Wittgenstein, theological language becomes one life-form among others. However, if

57. Jenson, "The Father, He . . . ," 101.

58. *ST* 1:63.

59. *KOTHE*, 107.

60. Ibid., 108.

61. Wittgenstein, *Culture and Value,* 32.

theological language is to be considered as meaningful utterance, then its claim upon history and its expression of universal truth are but one in the same. As Jenson rightly declares, central to the language-game of the Christian faith is the narration of a story concerning a figure in history, "and we may and must demand of it that it be *correct*. If it is a purely illustrative or mythical or parabolic story, it is also false."[62] In this case, Jenson must answer as to how the claims inherent within theological language gain adequate authentication? In its precise balancing of history and eschatology, Jenson maintains, the narrative of revelation can be checked for truthfulness against the balance of past, present, and future. This is not to suggest that the gospel stands or falls with every detail of related historical research, but rather that it is finally confirmed or denied within the scope of history as a whole. "It is when Time is complete, when all events are presented as one great drama, that the issue of God will be [finally] settled."[63]

At this point, Jenson criticizes thinkers who construe their own theological language through an amalgam of religious experience and utterance. While the analyzes of Schleiermacher and Schmidt, to name but two, provide valuable insights into the nature of theological language, taken in isolation they prove wholly inadequate. In this guise, meaningful theological utterance is translated into a series of highly subjective and heavily personalized hypotheses, and thus reduces the Christian faith to absurdity. While "my private experiment may very well confirm me in my religiosity," Jenson argues, "it cannot confirm my religious utterances . . . Private religious experience cannot be the evidence relevant to the truth or falsity of theological" language.[64] Here, Jenson joins forces with Wittgenstein once more. A retreat into personal religious experience breaks the first rule of all language-games; there can be no such thing as a *private* language. While Schleiermacher and others, have tried to get around this by positing the existence of a universal religious experience, it is difficult to prove that such an interpretation of reality is possible.[65]

62. *KOTHF*, 142–43.

63. Ibid., 113.

64. Ibid., 145.

65. Lindbeck's theory of "cultural-linguistics" aims to resolve the difficulties

Wittgenstein declares that, "If a God creates a world in which certain propositions are true, then by that very act he also creates a world in which all propositions that follow from them come true."[66] From its earliest origins, the tradition has claimed this truth as her own. The gospel story is the only story capable of explaining reality. Jenson mounts a threefold defense of this conclusion. Firstly, in the gospel we have met Jesus Christ, the one in whom all hope and history finds meaning, and, as a result, we know what, and who, to expect of reality. Secondly, Christ's enactment of the gospel drama enables us to interpret the past and the present while making meaningful predictions about the future. Thirdly, the overwhelming crisis of our own reality converges with the climax of the Christ event. In Jesus' resurrection we face the possibility of our own future, namely that we might live beyond death and be raised to oneness with God. In the story of the resurrection, we discover the realized goal of our own existence and acquire the language by which we can proclaim God's eternity in created time and space. Through the narration of the gospel, Jenson reports, the church calls up as future the story of a particular man of the past, rhyming hope and history as she goes.[67] In this address to us, God has provided a unique and revelatory insight into his own reality. Therefore, every telling and inference of this gospel address is both the linguistic embodiment of an historical event and the conferring of an eschatological promise upon reality. It is these claims that distinguish Christianity from human religion: "Therefore the address of a God must be spirited *and* embodied, language *and* sacrament. It must open an infinite future, but it must rhyme that future with all the past . . . In normal religion, no visible word can more than momentarily speak the coherence of past and future."[68]

---

within one theological language-game by synthesising the polarities of propositional utterance and experiential expression. Far from reconciling the two approaches, Lindbeck pulls most of theology towards the latter and opens itself to the argument above. Lindbeck, *Nature of Doctrine,* 16–34.

66. Wittgenstein, *Tractatus,* 45.

67. *ETC,* 4.

68. *VW,* 29–30.

Words and the Word: Christology as the Language of Revelation

Jenson explores the theological implication of these ideas further in his *Systematic Theology*. Having outlined a language through which God can be identified within time and history, Jenson extends his notion of revelation further. The ensuing exploration sheds new light on the question concerning God's place within the theological language-game. What if God's own existence was constituted linguistically? If God were to apprehend himself linguistically, then surely language itself would become a logical presupposition of both the creator and his creation. In this case, language would figure, alongside time and space, as a presupposition of created existence. For Jenson, God's creative word, by its very nature, forms the centerpiece in the theological language-game that we call *reality*. If all language presupposes speech, Jenson asks, "How does our discourse ever get started? . . . Seemingly there must be a first Speaker."[69] The answer is already with us, for "the world is no less dependent on God's creating word now . . . than it was at the beginning."[70] The time and space of history are thus dependent upon the eternal word of the Father in the Son and through the Spirit. Furthermore, because God's word is an eternal word, his words in creation and the gospel story are to be considered part of the same address. "Let there be . . . ," "Christ is risen," and "He is Lord," Jenson insists, are identical "utterances of God within one dramatically coherent discourse. A creature who exists by hearing the first is indeed open to the second."[71]

The implications of Jenson's linguistic Christology are not merely temporal but also pervade the realm of space. In our last chapter we reflected upon Jenson's conclusions concerning God's triune embodiment through the Son, or the Word. Having established God's eternity as the premise of all created time in chapter 1, we were able to suggest, in chapter 2, that it is the embodiment of the triune God which provides us with the possibility of created space. Furthermore, it is this physical manifestation that enables him to be present and available to his. That this embodiment is constituted and experienced in a linguistic form,

69. *ST* 2:63.
70. Ibid., 9.
71. Ibid., 68.

namely as a Word, is of ontological importance. For it is God's embodiment in the Son, as the Word of the Father, which instigates the creation of bodies within created space. In creation, it is God's speech that makes time and space for others.

From creation forward, the premise of God's linguistic embodiment is perpetually reinforced. Through the torah, God's word forms the people of Israel whom he in turn chooses, adopts, and embodies as his own. In the incarnation, God's Word becomes flesh and lives among us. Through the Spirit at Pentecost, this resurrected Son commandeers a community to be his own body on earth. For Jenson, the ontological language, which we coin Christology, constitutes God's temporal address and spatial availability to us.[72] The christological *terra firma*, from which Jenson forms this linguistic account, provides a further parallel between the linguistic nature of God and his creation: "If we exist because we are addressed by God and if we have our specific identity as those who respond to God, then we do not possess ourselves. If I exist as I participate in a conversation, then to be myself I must hearken and respond to an other than myself. If to be in the image of God is to be embodied before God, then to be specifically human is to be available to an other."[73]

For Jenson, being made in the image of God is not a reflection upon humanity's claim to be the only featherless biped, nor is it marked by the size of human intellect. Rather, our resemblance to the creator comes from our use of *language*. Jenson's reflections upon the identity of Adam and Eve prove fascinating in this regard. These inaugural human beings were the first community to address one another with words.[74] Humanity's advent is not to be found in the first creatures to conform to the biological form that we call *homo sapiens*, but rather is instigated in the moment when men and women first realized the linguistic implications of their own embodiment. Jeremy Ive paraphrases Jenson most eloquently at this point:

72. *KOTHF*, 123.
73. *ST* 2:63–64.
74. Ibid. 63.

> Adam and Eve are those human participants in this his-
> tory, called into being by God's address, who respond
> appropriately in the vocative. They are the first historical
> human beings to whom a mandate, . . . "the mandate of
> heaven," is given . . . This gives them both embodiment,
> which is more than physical but also orientation. This
> mandate brings into being the first true human commu-
> nity . . . [This community] is made possible in anticipation
> of the incarnation and is made identifiable as one human
> community by Jesus' life and death for all.[75]

Humanity is thus defined as *a community of temporal-spatial creatures who are capable of using words*. As if this move to unite human
and divine language were not enough, Jenson presses on proposing the
following ontological finale for all language-acts:

> Were an argument for the existence of God attempted
> within the framework of thought here represented, it
> would be on such lines. We have argued that the speech
> of God by which he creates us human and our morally
> obligating mutual speech are the same event. There must
> indeed have been a first address of God by which he initi-
> ated our discourse, but we need not necessarily think of a
> voice from heaven intruding at some point in the hominid
> descent. We may think rather of an unpredictable event of
> initial linguistic community.[76]

According to Jenson, God is not only the temporal-spatial embodiment of his own words to us, but is also an event in the language that
occurs between us in time and space. In particular, God is what happens when we share and speak the eschatological promise of the gospel
in Jesus' name. For it is only this eternally living and succeeding word
that can reconcile our hope and our histories.[77] As God creates spatial
and temporal realities through the address of the Son, as the embodied
Word of the Father, so too our own experience of reality is dictated by

---

75. Ive, "Robert W. Jenson's Theology of History," 147.

76. *ST* 2:63.

77. *S&P*, 122–25.

the words that we hear and speak in our encounters with others in time and space. Inasmuch as these language-acts are made possible by God's Word, they serve as extensions of God's own creative address. It is for this reason that language-acts form both our access point to created reality and to the God in whom such reality finds its existence.

From here, Jenson is able to conclude that all human converse is, in some way or another, derivative of and directed to the creator. The implications of the discovery are widespread. The holistic converse which communities use to come to terms with reality and which Jenson assigns to the realm of "culture," are to be considered as humanity's further and inevitable embodiment in the mode of language. All of our discussions concerning theology, philosophy, history, and art, to name but a few, find their place within the particular cultural language-game of our own time and place. As a result, language is not primarily, for Jenson, that which can be achieved by the use of a dictionary, but rather, "language is all those things we do to come to understanding with each other in a world."[78] If language is the crowning moment of our human attempt to grasp the nature of our own distinctive temporal-spatial existence, then culture is the embodiment of our human desire to come to terms with the reality in which we find ourselves. The discourse that we call culture is, in Jenson, to be considered as one holistic christological language-game.

Creating Conversations: Creation and the Triune Discourse

The world in Jenson, as we have discovered, is a revelatory utterance. Hence, in creation we discover the God who has time, space, and a word for us. At this point, Jenson's question as to the possibility of a prospective theological language-game assumes dogmatic significance. With this christological view of revelation in place, we can conclude that reality comprises a language-game centered upon God's own Word. However, Jenson is unlikely, and unwilling, to assign Christology as the final goal of his linguistics. The theological language of Christology reveals God in his fullness, only in as much as it points directly to the Trinity. As discussed in our last chapter, the embodiment of God in his Word rep-

78. *ETC*, 1.

resents the very antinomy of all monistic constructions of deity. Our talk of the Son implies the existence of both a Father and the Spirit, and henceforth all talk of God is considered fanciful, if not impossible, outside of the Trinity. This important conclusion has implications for language, for a lone deity has no use for words, as all such phenomena are the proclivity of a community. To provide a fully Christian account of language, Jenson declares, we must understand the Trinity as its own eternal language-act or conversation.

The Word by which God creates the world and initiates history is part of the triune discourse. It is the opening up of this divine conversation to other beings and other worlds. The realities of time and space, in Jenson's thinking, are determined by a series of linguistic coordinates located within the triune discourse. "To be," Jenson maintains, "is to be spoken of by God. Therefore, to be located is to be referred to by him in a specific network of relations of otherness."[79] Man's identity, for Jenson, is defined by his position as God's conversational counterpart. We are, as he likes to say, "the praying animals."[80] In his own pursuit of an adequate theological language, Wittgenstein himself resorted to prayer, however the limitations forced upon him by his own rules diminished the very nature of the exercise.[81] In Jenson's work, prayer is transformed from the dead end domain of private reflection into the arena of divine discourse. He who finds his genesis in the spoken word, according to Jenson, will find his fulfillment there also, for prayer is the actuality of faith: "Humans, we may say, are those animals whose creation is not merely that God speaks *about* them but that he also speaks *to* them. Humans are those creatures who exist in that they are mentioned in the triune discourse *and* are called to join it. Humans are those creatures who not only exist by words that state God's moral will, but are given to hear and reply to those words."[82]

---

79. *ST* 2:59.

80. *ETC*, 117–31.

81. "The meaning of life, i.e., the meaning of the world," Wittgenstein declares, "we can call God. And connect with this the comparison of God to a father. To pray is to think about the meaning of life." Wittgenstein, *Notebooks*, 73.

82. *ST* 2:16.

Jenson's christological conclusions are, once again, extended in a truly trinitarian direction. In the same way that our mutually obligating speech to one another embodies God's address to us, so too our address to God becomes part of his own trinitarian discourse. We address God as, "Our Father" because, firstly, our intercession is made with and through Jesus as God's eternal Word. Likewise, Jenson adds, "once the conversation of God with humanity is under way, his speech to us in not another event than our speech for him to one another."[83] Secondly, we pray, "Our Father," because it is through the church, in which Christ is embodied, that we make our address. Our use of language is so christologically constituted that in all of our intercession, the Son, by whose words our existence is sustained, joins with us in our petition. The communal nature of the life of prayer is fulfilled in Jenson's own exposition of the *Totus Christus*. We will address this as the central theme in our next chapter: "God's word in and by the church is not an event other than the continuing antiphony of the church's own narrative in proclamation and prayer . . . And therefore it is not a paranormal phenomenon, though it may of course sometimes include such phenomena."[84]

Prayer illustrates and constitutes the language-act that is the church's very existence. As the now embodiment of God's Son, or Word, the church exists as a "gathering to perform a certain language act," namely the exposition of reality and the subsequent identification of the triune God.[85] In the church, the liturgies and rituals we perform, the theological dialogue we undertake, the communal fellowship we share and our narration of the biblical narrative, all serve as aspects of the triune conversation and thus maintain God's real presence in time and space. Mannermaa rightly identifies this as a foundational trait throughout Jenson's theology. As the internal discourse concerning the nature and mission of the church, Jenson's definition of theology combines the ancient catholic rule of, *lex orandi lex credendi,* with the Reformers equivalent, *lex proclamandi lex credendi.*[86] The story of the God who speaks the world into being and who sustains creation by his

83. Ibid., 61.

84. Ibid., 2:61.

85. *ETC*, 4.

86. Mannerma, "Doctrine of Justification," 141.

Word cannot be interpreted independently of the community that that Word instigates and fulfils, and through whose history and drama it was brought to life. As Christ's body, Jenson declares, God's Word is temporally and spatially present in the church.

In his review of Jenson's *Systematic Theology*, Francis Watson has applauded the grounding of theological language within the biblical narrative and the subsequent move to rest the Bible's authentication within the life of the church. However, Watson proposes that the program that Jenson outlines requires further development if it is to fully achieve its author's main aims. In particular, he suggests that "a theology of divine communicative agency such as Jenson's requires a more explicit understanding of the Bible as 'word of God,' and as such the book of the Christian community."[87] In his response, Jenson agrees that a more stated doctrine of God's word could have been made. However, Jenson also claims that much of this is implicit within the said volumes. In fact, Jenson declares, much of this theology, "could be read as one long insistence that the word in the church *is* God's word—including the *viva vox* of the Bible's reading in the church."[88] While ever anxious to defend his work, Jenson concedes, "I wish I had read Watson on canon before" writing the systematics.[89]

There remain wider cultural ramifications for Jenson's theology at this point. The communal discourse upon which all existence and dialogue rely is not the sole domain of the Christian believer and the church. Culture itself mirrors the communal converse of the triune creator.[90] In Jenson, culture is to be seen as the conversation that all communities share with one another. Just as words create communities to begin with, communities cannot escape the use of words in their own discourse concerning reality. The name given to these discussions is "religion," and hence every culture, in Jenson, becomes the visible embodiment of its own religious vision. As the conversational travail of a community, every culture is the enactment of a particular theologi-

---

87. Watson, "America's Theologian," 216.

88. Jenson, "Response to Watson and Hunsinger," 226.

89. Ibid., 226.

90. *ST* 2:17–28.

cal language-game.[91] We will return to this theme, and its implications, throughout the ensuing chapters of this thesis. For now, it is enough to state that no matter where we live, or to which community we belong, our culture comprises a linguistic attempt to take hold of our own existence: "Our living together depends upon the presence among us of, . . . 'the mandate of heaven.'"[92] Jenson concludes:

> Scripture and the theology of the church sustain the great maxim of the theology of culture, that the soul of every culture is a religion and the body of every religion a culture; the gods are precisely "the gods of the nations." They also maintain the prophetic critique that emerges from this apprehension: just *because* the gods are each the god of a nation or race or class or gender they are "idols," products of our own religious subjectivity, powers we envision by projection of our own values and needs.[93]

There is one community, or culture, whose language-act can truly explain the nature and purpose of creation. It is in the time, space, and language of the church that God makes himself present within history, and it therefore falls to the church to enact the triune language-game in which all creation finds its hope and history. The church presupposes the fulfillment of all language and culture by the very Word who initiated creation and, in so doing, her own communal life. This Word, namely the resurrected Christ, is God's availability in time and space.

Conclusion

In his courageous commandeering of Wittgensteinian thought, Jenson displays his own inimitable brand of postmodern orthodoxy. In his search for a plausible philosophical language, Wittgenstein acknowledged three great challenges namely, "Space, Time, and Deity." In

91. The language-games of other cultures, Jenson asserts, "are not deity but only point to it." *ST* 1:59.

92. *ST* 2:63. Jenson deliberately borrows this term from Chinese political ideology. Its fit within the present schema casts a wry glance towards its origin.

93. *ST* 1:51–52.

Jenson, our attempts to come to terms with creation and the creator entail a similar triumvirate, namely, time, space, and language. Rather than barring us from divine reality, these entities mediate God to us. God's linguistic revelation in time and space further confirms the presupposition that our reality is suspended in the language of the triune discourse. While the culture in which we find ourselves, and the theological language with which we speak, make an indelible impact upon our experience of reality, there is but one culture that can truly reveal to us the nature of creation as a whole, and this is the culture of Christ and his church. For in this community we hear and speak God's words and thus become part of the triune conversation. In the life of the church, we discover God is not simply a piece in our language-games, but rather that he is the "be all" and "end all" of language itself: "All the various ways in which the gospel has traditionally made itself effective as the final decision about its hearers are united in the word 'God.' 'Jesus is God'—here is the all-encompassing confession of classical theology. 'Lord,' 'Savior,' 'Judge,' 'being,' 'good' and a hundred other words are all united in the word 'God.' In the ancient church theology was identical with the attempt to elucidate the precise meaning of this sentence."[94]

94. Jenson, "Proclamation without Metaphysics," 27.

4

Body Language:
Jenson and the *Totus Christus*

CREATURELY AND "CREATORLY" REALITY are dependent upon the God who has time, space, and language. In Jenson's theology, we summarize, God has time for us. And because he has time for us, he also has space for us. Likewise, God's space presupposes his word, or discourse. Jenson's exposition of these themes proves doubly resonant, striking chords with our own experience of reality and the triune drama, as witnessed in the gospel narrative. This careful use of theological materials constructs the necessary platform for his exposition of ecclesiology and culture. As we discovered in our last chapter, the defining Word that God has for us is none other than his only Son. In the time and space of creation, we encounter this Word in the resurrected Jesus and in the community that constitutes his body. In the interplay between Christ and his church, Jenson argues, creation is interpreted, fulfilled, and transformed. This vision is most prominent within Jenson's exposition of the *totus Christus*.

While time, space, and language frame Jenson's theology, it is his subsequent unification of Christology and ecclesiology that forms the front and center of his work.[1] To push the analogy further, one should

1. Douglas Knight has declared Jenson, as "a pioneer of the strong ecclesiology." Knight, "Jenson on time," 71.

imagine a depiction of the risen Christ. In this theological portrait Jenson's Christology portrays Jesus' head, while his ecclesiology forms the body. As eye witnesses to Jesus' resurrection and ascension, and receivers of his Spirit, the church has become the body of Christ. In this body, within our own time and space, we join the perichoretic converse of the Trinity. Jenson's Lutheran roots, unifying tendencies, and immanentist approach provide an almost irresistible momentum towards this end. In this chapter, we will set out the main themes of Jenson's ecclesiology and one significant critique.

The Church as Story

Reverting to type, Jenson's ecclesiology soon returns us to time. His characterization of the church as the *totus Christus* is, as Gabriel Fackre points out, almost entirely derivative of his notion of temporality. "The inseparability of the Christian community from the incarnate Word and thus a 'high' doctrine of church, sacraments, and ministry; an antisupersessionist view of Israel consonant with an unfolding story; and a thoughtful interpretation of petitionary prayer," are the direct result of the God who has time for us.[2] In Jenson, the church is both the narrative consequence of the creator's temporal infinity and the subsequent fulfillment of creation's temporality: "I suggest that it is in dealing with the inescapable temporality of the whole human conversation that men need to say 'God' . . . We live in the present, because of the past, before the future. It is as we try to deal with this temporal structure of life that we come to cry 'God.'"[3]

For Jenson, each and every human act is an attempt to come to terms with time, and hereby to rhyme past and present. All our deeds and activities are to be determined as contributions to this one overarching dialogue of existence. In every moment of this conversation, mankind expresses his confidence in some form of eternity—be it temporal or timeless, Christian or nihilistic—and in so doing finds himself sneaking up on "God."[4]

2. Fackre, "Lutheran Capax," 96.

3. *S&P*, 103.

4. Ibid., 105.

> Whenever we take part in the human conversation, we act
> on faith that reality will support our deed: that the succes-
> sion of events through time is not condemned to be a mere
> succession . . . but is a succession somehow held together,
> somehow embraced, somehow fit for coherence. It is the
> reality of this bracket that men of all religions have evoked
> with some word like "eternity." Eternity is the embrace in
> which past and future come together in the present rather
> than tearing it apart; eternity is the real possibility—if in-
> deed there is one—of the rhyme of the old language and
> the new word.[5]

For Jenson, as we have seen, language provides the link between
temporality and divinity. Surveying the human conversation through
the categories of "law" and "gospel," Jenson argues that the former classification defines the divine as timeless, static, and persistent, while the
latter proclaims the possibility of temporality, openness, and promise.
The language of law promulgates God's character as fundamentally re-
actionary, whereas the language of promise proposes that he be seen
as a revolutionary. The very words we use provide us with two possible
candidates for what Jenson calls, "the God-job."[6] Either the universal
Conserver, on the one hand, or the universal Innovator, on the other. It
is God's own story, according to Jenson, that serves as the final arbiter:

> The gospel denies the eternity of timelessness . . . The
> gospel attacks the God of timeless eternity; that God is
> unmasked as Satan, who at once destroys us with the guilt
> of what we have been, and deludes us with false security in
> what we are. The Father of Jesus replaces all that men have
> called "God"; . . . The word "God" enters our language to
> evoke the transcendence of the past. The one whose word
> is the contradiction of this evocation disputes every claim
> of the old God. The gospel evokes the Transcendence of the
> future as liberty from and for the past . . . The Guarantor

5. Ibid., 105.
6. Ibid., 107.

of persistence is not God; there is rather the possibility of
novelty. Eternity is unassailable futurity.[7]

The revelation of the gospel authenticates our experience of time
and revolutionizes our understanding of the eternal God. In the life,
death, and resurrection of Jesus we discover the true nature of eternity
through the earthly manifestation of God's own transcendence. If having
died, Jesus now lives, then he exists both in our remembrance of a
historic figure and in our expectation as the promised future. Put simply,
the resurrected Christ is the conclusion of the human enterprise. His
transcendence is not primarily categorized in spatial terms, but is rather
experienced temporarily. His distance from us is not the instigation of
a human quest, for such a venture would be the mimicry of human religion, but rather the God of the gospel is remembered and anticipated
in his own coming. As disciples, we recognize this God in the historical
figure of Jesus. This man, framed in our own time and space, calls us not
to seek him but to follow him. In taking his lead we come to acknowledge the two other characters in the divine drama of his life. At first,
we confess that God is both the man Jesus and the one whom he calls
"Father." Following from this, we recognize God as the futurity of the
relationship between the Father and the Son, namely the Spirit. In this
threefold narrative we witness the triune God: "He is Goal and Origin
enacted together in the history of Jesus; he is God-Future, God-Past,
and God-Present; to use the biblical names, he is Spirit, Father, and Son.
In time, God-Future and God-Past confront each other in Jesus' resurrection; and just this Confrontation is God. If we resist the religious pull
and leave it at that, we confess the triune God."[8]

For Jenson, God is the conversation to whom all language is mere
response and the eternal miracle by which history and communication
are made possible. "If the gospel is true," Jenson claims, "the individual
human person Jesus *is*, by the initiative of the Father and in the freedom
of the Spirit, the material determinant of what generally can be and cannot be."[9] Although Jenson's narrative notion of triune time requires no

7. Ibid., 111.

8. Ibid., 117–18.

9. *ST* 2:215.

further rehearsal, the chosen bearer of this story should not escape our attention. This christological triune formula, with all of his conclusions on the theological nature of time, space, and language, is the exclusive property of the church. In short, it is the church's role to interpret God and creation for the world:

> The Christian Church . . . is the community of a particular narrative communication, of a story. It is that gathering which occurs when one man tells others the gospel-story. This is the story of what happened with Jesus the Israelite, told as a story which concerns the teller and his hearers ultimately. It is a story of the *past,* told as the last *future,* as the story of what is finally to come of our lives . . . The Church's worship is simply the total of what happens on such occasions of gospel-communication.[10]

As a body of disciples the church has embraced the gospel story as an explicit and historic act of God's eternal self-disclosure, and therefore as the explication of all reality. The gospel finale, Jenson declares, is that the final outcome of human history will dramatically coincide with Jesus' own history. From this moment on, the story of the incarnation becomes the one determining narrative of both creation and her creator. Hence, the histories of Jesus, Israel, and the church are considered part and parcel of this one plot: "'The church' is the gathering which occurs as the gospel communication occurs. Like any story (and unlike, for example, mathematical formulas or ethical proposition) the news about Jesus lives only as it is actually told and heard . . . It is a visible and very ordinary assembly of persons where what has assembled them is the communicating of the gospel."[11]

The church is defined by Jenson as the gathering of believers with the express purpose of speaking and hearing the gospel. Therefore, in that the church occurs in time, the gospel occurs also. The church is both the human teller of a divine story and a divine story told through humanity. The tradition provides first-hand evidence of this phenomenon. Through the life of the church, the gospel interprets our present

10. Jenson, "Worship as Drama," 160.

11. *S&P,* 2.

realities, ancient histories, future hopes, and greatest expectations. In fact, Jenson declares, "the story about Jesus is accurately told only if it is so told as in fact to incorporate our stories, to be about our fears and commitments."[12] In her proclamation of the gospel the church bears the temporal tension between, history and eschatology, prophecy and fulfillment. Consequently, her narration is not governed by the accepted wisdom of a certain era nor by her ability to accommodate the selfish hopes of the present age. In every gospel telling, Jenson declares, the church makes history and "evokes unpredictably new hopes and dreams. For it has the function of unconditional promise, and so on every occasion opens possibilities beyond any already entertained."[13] Through the God-given language of the gospel, we find the new words and language by which to rhyme hope and history.

The power of the gospel story to maintain its own character and yet dynamically respond to the flux and flow of successive æons, Jenson suggests, is akin to the process by which a person remains himself through the many changes of life. If the individual attempts to resist these changes he will only lose himself. Whereas, should he respond positively to the challenge of time, he will find that his identity is enhanced by the dynamics that previously threatened him. The temporal nature of existence, it would appear, demands a narrative conception of personal identity. "What differentiates a person from a mere individual," Jenson argues, "is that an individual something need not have a story. While a person not only has but, in my view, *is* a story . . . What am I? I am a story that the moving finger will one day stop writing."[14]

The symbiosis of Christology and ecclesiology that is so prevalent within Jenson's ecclesiology now begins to take hold. In the story of the church we encounter a plot through which time itself can be explained and understood. If such a narrative were possible, it could not exist merely as a story about God, but must actually be God. For Jenson, God is personally synonymous with his own story. Having merged the concepts of narrative and identity the suggestion holds little fear. God's personhood is simply to be understood as his story or plot. Therefore, in

12. Ibid., 10.

13. *S&P*, 10.

14. Jenson, "Christ as Culture 3," 194–95.

the same way that I cannot be separated from my own story, God is also one with his story, namely the gospel. While already present in the plot of creation, humanity is further drawn into the creator's story, in the church. As God's narrator, the church community takes part in Christ's story and thus embodies him. It is this notion of Christ's presence in the church that enables Jenson's conception of the *totus Christus*. From hereon, the gospel is simultaneously the story of God *and* his church. For in Jenson, the *totus Christus* is the manifestation of Christ with his church. Hence the church is not an *opus ad extra*, or simply another aspect of creation. "The church *is* the body of Christ for the world and for her members," Jenson proclaims, "in that she is constituted a community by the verbal and 'visible' presence *to* her of that same body of Christ."[15]

The Church as Drama

Having considered the church as a story in time, we return now to the realm of space. The God who is present in the church as the *totus Christus* draws together the realities of time and space. In other words, he is the one who "wholly transcend[s] spatial differences."[16] As in chapter 2, Jenson's ecclesial reworking of space is the outworking of his trinitarian notion of reality. As space itself presupposes the triune consciousness and God's embodiment in the Son, so too our own bodies presuppose this trinitarian roominess and the reality of Christ. The implications for the church, as a body of believers, are significant. In *Visible Words: The Interpretation and Practice of Christian Sacraments*, Jenson outlines three necessary steps towards the notion of God's embodiment within the church.[17]

Firstly, if we consider God to be an eternal Word, his own existence must be constituted in a process of mutual address. Put simply, God addresses God. Secondly, to say that God is embodied is to declare faith in a God who transcends himself. As such, God recognizes himself in the Son, in Christ's incarnation, and also in the church's presentation of the

15. *ST* 2:168.

16. Ibid., 253.

17. *VW,* 34–38.

gospel. Hence the triune God does not de-objectify himself, choosing to hide from our prayers and praises, but makes himself spatially available in the very words, objects, and people who re-enact his story. In bread, wine, water, and liturgy, this God intrudes upon our lives and restricts our ability to avoid him. Thirdly, God identifies himself in Jesus, which, as discussed in our second chapter, forms the deepest yet most quickly made statement of God's embodiment. It is in the person of Jesus that God is made present within the church as the *totus Christus*. This truth is authenticated, once more, by the resurrection. For if Jesus were not resurrected he would remain a merely heroic historical figure, "e.g., Caesar or great Granddad . . . he would not be the [embodied] revelation of God."[18]

Jenson's account of embodiment raises questions about God's precise location. For Jenson, the question as to Christ's physical whereabouts, and the church's challenge to speak of his temporal presence, are but two sides of the same problem.[19] For space relates to time in the same way that the present relates to the future and the past. Here, the words that we use are of the utmost significance, for a person's presence is also their temporal availability. Hence, to speak of somebody's spatial location is to identify their temporal whereabouts: "If I am present as subject to you, this occurs in that I somehow address myself to you; a word is uttered by which I enter into a common world with you, as a shaping participant in that world. I am present to you in that in the world you inhabit a word occurs that is *my* word. The classic example is always: 'I love you.' It is the same with the risen Jesus."[20]

Jenson can now equate God's Word in the church with his presence to the world. The church's identification of God occurs as a narrative of events within a certain physical space. However, this narration takes on a different form from other historical reconstructions. The risen Jesus, according to Jenson, represents the spatial embodiment of this God. Without this identifiable embodiment, he argues, God could neither

18. Ibid., 34.

19. See the discussion on the problem of space within the Christian tradition in chapter 2.

20. *S&P,* 160.

create nor transcend space.[21] With this, Jesus becomes constitutive of God's spatial transcendence, leaving Jenson to simultaneously locate the Son at the right hand of the Father and within the community of the church.[22] With Christ ascended into heaven, the church now provides the essential embodiment of the Son within created space. The church's story is both a temporal and spatial phenomenon. For if the gospel were to secure a mere temporal presence, our faith would be akin to Gnosticism. However, in the same way that Christ is temporally present in the gospel's proclamation, he is also spatially present in the church as a physical community. Through the preaching of the gospel, Jenson supposes, Christ unifies the many bodies contained within the church into one story, one body, and "one human personality."[23]

It is this act of divine embodiment that makes the gospel more than words. This particular story conscripts multifarious co-communicants for its telling. Physical actions, bodily gestures, visible symbols, and concrete objects are all redeployed in the language of the church. In the first instance, this use of body-language is utterly unexceptional. For "the body is involved in any dialogue, for it is our availability to each other. The gospel-event will therefore necessarily include touching, or at least looking at and listening to, each other."[24] In our church gatherings, the gospel is not simply spoken but is physically enacted as liturgy. This theatrical production is antiphonal, comprising both earthly cry and heavenly response. The drama here staged, moves beyond the mere "telling" of the gospel and becomes its own "dialogical narration."[25] The liturgical nature of her worship is constitutive of the church's broader life and mission. In the life of the church, the gospel combines improvised converse and fixed narrative within one theatrical production. Hence, the act of worship engages the church in a dramatic converse with the triune God and his creation: "As *praise*, liturgy is play . . . Play is meaningful action that does not need to seek its meaning in some achievement exterior to itself. It is what we do because we do not have

21. See the discussion of triune embodiment in chapter 2.

22. *ST* 2:254.

23. Ibid., 254.

24. *S&P*, 167.

25. Jenson, "Worship as Drama," 160–61.

to. It is action to which the future opens as gift rather than as burden. The life of the Trinity is sheer play. As play with the Trinity, liturgy is anticipation of life in the Fulfillment—the closest we get to freedom."[26]

In the form of liturgy, or play, Christ himself embodies the church's gospel enactment. For this reason, our proclamation entails an endless series of physical events. We eat and drink; wash and anoint; touch and embrace; stand, sit, and kneel; we parade up and down; make signs and gestures, and articulate God's story through an almost endless variety of physical actions and gestures. All manner of objects and props are utilized, without which the production would appear unrealistic. With the theater, stage, and scenery set, the ecclesial production is brought to life in choreography, rhetoric, music, and art.[27] In her embodiment of the gospel, the church is elevated from story into drama. For Jenson, the church comprises the sum of these words, liturgies, symbols, and signs coupled with the church members themselves. It is this "body-language," in the fullest sense of the word, which constitutes the presence of Christ *in* and *as* the *totus Christus*:

> The gospel is a story. For some reason, we do not merely tell it to each other, we act it out with and upon each other. So at the climax of our gatherings, one of us plays Jesus and the rest play disciples, and we act out the New Testament accounts of a last meal of Jesus and his disciples before his execution. We do not merely talk about the meal, we perform it. And the acting-out, once begun expands symbolically to become a representation of the whole event of Jesus' death and self-giving.[28]

This one liturgical gospel event constitutes the church's single greatest act of self-determination. Here we witness her dramatic acting-out of the verbal and extra-verbal elements of the gospel. Spirited and embodied in the drama of the sacrament, God makes his Son spatially available within the dramatic narrative of the church. Through this

26. *S&P*, 183–84.

27. We will detail the importance of architecture and staging for the liturgy in chapter 6.

28. *S&P*, 166.

physical manifestation, we come to know and experience the God who is his own space, within the space that he has for us.[29] This notion of spatiality is entirely premised upon Jenson's christological exposition of the triune God. For Jenson, Christ's physical embodiment of the church is guaranteed by the unconditional promise of the gospel. In short, we find Jesus in the place he has promised to be. Hence, the church finds her fulfillment in the meal that she shares in remembrance and anticipation of her Lord's coming. In this act, the Christ who holds together all time and space is physically present in our midst. As a result, all "anti-sacramentalism," to Jenson's mind at least, is to be considered as either forgetfulness or idolatry:[30] For "Christianity makes religiously odd claims about its sacraments—e.g., that God is 'really' present in them."[31]

For Jenson, it is the spatial drama of the Eucharist that enables the church's unification with Christ.[32] In this event, we partake in fellowship with one another and, consequentially, the risen Jesus. The Eucharist is both the celebration of a past triumph and the physical inauguration, and anticipation, of new creation. In the drama of the Eucharist, the church is joined with Christ in an intractable enactment of prayer, praise, and proclamation. In these moments, the gift of God's unconditional promise of salvation is embodied within the bread and the wine that Christ alone can give. While Catholic discussions of the rite often emphasize the objects, or props, Protestant dialogue is more concerned with the words, or script. Jenson reminds us that the story of the embodied Word of God requires both, for the linguistic nature of the supper demands words, objects, and actions. In this meal we remember the historic Christ through narration and action. In our re-enactment of the past we anticipate and rehearse our part in God's future: "The future is not yet; and if what we do anticipates it, this is strictly God's gift. That clearly stipulated, we may say that as embodied past-tense narrative is representation, so embodied future-tense narrative, embodied gospel-

---

29. *ST* 2:254.

30. *VW*, 32.

31. Ibid., 31.

32. "Tell me what your theology of the sacraments is, and I shall tell you what your Christology is." The dictum rings true in Jenson. Schwöbel, "Christ and Culture," 116.

promise, is anticipation. The Supper is both; but in that it is anticipation it is a sacrament, a visible word of the gospel."[33]

As an enactment of the gospel, the sacrament of the shared bread and cup is its visibility. It speaks of Christ's life in the church and confirms his bodily presence among us. This is not to say that Christ is present because bread and wine are present, but rather that he is present in the sacramental drama as a whole. In the Eucharist, the space that God is, and the space that he has for us, become one and the same:

> The human heart is not his natural abode, however much it may be Brahman's or a Boddhisatva's; the Christ comes always *to* us. And in this sacrament, his way to the heart— not, of course, to the stomach—is by a uniquely primal and total opening to the external word: the unitary sensory, organic, and mental act of eating and drinking in fellowship. The act of faith and the act of the mouth are, in the Supper, one act . . . The object of faith and of eating are one in the event. So are Christ and the elements one in the supper.[34]

By locating Christ's real presence within the supper, Jenson rejects the notion of transubstantiation. The assumption that, in Christ, the human soul is no longer subject to space nor any spatial limitation is as intolerable to Jenson as the equivalent proposal concerning the timeless soul. According to Jenson, the notion that the soul exists as pure spirit, with its implied connection between the spirited soul and the absolute spirit of the imago Dei, is a fundamental error.[35] As we have already witnessed, the Eucharist is evidence enough of God's embodied reality. Jenson's solution is characteristically Lutheran in tone. If Christ is risen to be with God and if God is, in turn, omnipresent, then Christ's body can be experienced everywhere.[36] However, as Jenson points out, for

---

33. *VW*, 78–79.

34. Ibid., 107–8.

35. Ibid., 110. Once again Jenson rejects and attacks Hegel's chief premise. See chapter 2. Here, Jenson argues that a God of pure disembodied spirit could not share relationship with his creation.

36. *S&P*, 159–63. Here Jenson's own tradition comes to the fore. The theory he outlines is a variation of the Lutheran doctrine of Christ's ubiquity.

this scheme to hold we must broaden the category of the body beyond the substantive and material notion so prevalent in Newton's laws:

> I do not define *bodily* by "material substantiality" . . . God is omnipresent in his promises . . . In that the bread and cup are the center of that rite which embodies the entire gospel, and themselves embody this gospel insofar as it is the promise of God's presence, God is present bodily when and where the bread and cup are. And in that the bread and cup *are for God* the presence also of the man Jesus, . . . Jesus has and needs no other body to be risen in full bodily splendor and solidity.[37]

For Jenson, Jesus has no supernatural hiding place high above the clouds. He is dramatically present in his own body through the church's enactment of his own story and promise. In these moments it becomes impossible to separate the story and drama of our own lives from God's own narrative with us. That the supper's thanksgiving is "accepted by God and our fellowship in it established for all eternity, and that the bread and cup are the body-presence of Christ" are not to be regarded as separate theological realities but are, instead, indivisible parts of the same revelation. Unsurprisingly, Jenson proves highly protective of the church's "sacramental language." For in these moments, we are no longer manufacturing words to suit our occasion, but are listening in on the divine discourse of the Trinity. We can only hope that our repetitions will not dishonor him nor turn us into blasphemers.[38] Hence, to rearrange the language of the sacrament, either through the spoken words or the acts performed, is to resist a divine mandate and mar God's promised

---

37. *VW*, 111. This chapter, along with the second in this work, attributes much consideration to the place of embodiment within Jenson's investigation and application of the theology of space. However, with this last quote we uncover a quandary which occurs with some regularity. While, on the one hand, Jenson's thought places heavy emphasis on God's embodiment and the place of Christ's body; on the other hand, the body itself, at least as we understand the term biologically, can appear surplus to requirement. The dilemma occurs in both Jenson's reading of the resurrection and his ecclesiology. We will return to this issue directly at the conclusion of the thesis.

38. Jenson, "Father, He," 109.

presence. Jenson illustrates his point with reference to the tendency of certain traditions to share the wine through multiple cups. This, he argues, strips the rite of its communal essence. The supper is not given to a disparate band of privatized individuals. It is not a "supply station of individual and immediate blessings," but rather is received by the one community who share Christ's hope; the corporate body who are gathered and sustained as God's own embodiment in time and space. Ive summarizes the position most effectively: "Jesus is identified through the scriptural narrative and embodied in the church and sacraments. The church provides the hermeneutical context within which the triune reality is known, and as which the participation in the triune reality takes place. Jenson calls this 'the body of God's presence,' and the church is in turn the body of Jesus."[39]

A question arises as to how the church is to make such crucial judgments, where the organization and distribution of the sacraments is concerned? Jenson's preference for a clearly ordained and unified approach is there for all to see. However, a cursory glance at the contemporary church reveals an unending array of disagreements concerning the interpretation of, so-called, sacramental language. In truth, an otherwise powerful exposition of the *totus Christus* is potentially undermined by its own application. We will return to this challenge later.

In the drama of the Eucharist, Jenson argues, we witness the dramatic fulfillment of created time, space, and language as one subject shares himself unconditionally, or eternally, with another. In this defining language-act, the church describes the origin and goal of all reality, and further anticipates the total translation of creation into the triune conversation. Just as the oneness of the Trinity relies upon a fatherhood which rejects domination in favor of an eternal movement of love, so too church hierarchies should avoid the exercising of dominion and focus on the primacy of love which constitutes communion.[40]

For Jenson, the perichoretic interpenetration of the Trinity provides the model for the church's *koinonia*.[41] As the connecting point

39. Ive, *The God of Faith*, 15.

40. *ST* 2:249.

41. A. N. Williams makes precisely this point. Williams, "Parlement of Foules," 193.

between these communities, the Eucharist comprises man's supreme, God given, and Spirit inspired attempt to make language work. In this one dramatic event all reality is opened to us and, hence, all consideration of the relation between theology and culture must begin with the drama of Christian worship.[42] The supper is God's embodiment of past events, present reality, and future anticipation. "When the bread is given," Jenson declares, "God promises all his love, bodily."[43] It is here, in the fellowship of the church, that we finally discover what it is to be made in the image of the triune God. As we take Jesus' body, we take hold of our own humanity and become co-embodiments of Christ.[44] The fulfillment of the gospel, as staged in the drama of the Eucharist, represents our most eloquent attempt to describe reality and is thus the climax of language in created time and space. This simple enactment encapsulates the antiphony between man and God in perfect proportion. For the supper's actions are both man's address to God, and God's declaration to man. In this, the supper anticipates the church's final end and her most audacious spatial claim, namely her full and perfect inclusion in the life of the triune God.[45] "We may say: the communion that is now the church is itself constituted by an event of communion, or participation, with the communion that is in the Trinity." Jenson continues, "It is this last twist that locates the church at the gate of heaven."[46]

The Church as Polity

For Jenson, the liturgical enactment of communion is not only the essential ingredient in the church's gathering, but also forms her single greatest act of self-determination. The communion that we celebrate in the supper is only realized in that it shapes the other aspects of our ecclesial life. It is in the full communion of the church, or the dramatic life of Christ together with his people, that the Son is eternally embodied in time and space as the *totus Christus*. The conversation that has gone

42. Jenson, "Worship as Drama," 159.

43. *VW*, 82.

44. *ST* 2:212.

45. Ibid., 240.

46. Ibid., 222.

before is not the private dialogue of a closed corporation but rather forms the manifesto of a community whose very nature is her mission to the world. "Every Eucharist," insists Jenson, "is a subversive gathering—in *any* nation—and a potential school of dissidents."[47] Our confession of Lordship and Christ's subsequent embodiment of the church transforms the congregation into a political community. As Stanley Hauerwas has pointed out, for Jenson, "a Christian is someone whose nation and polity is the church."[48] Debates concerning the politicizing or depoliticizing of the church are subsequently nonsensical. As one community among mankind, the church is a political force whatever her opinion about politics. "Sometimes a big force and other times a little force. The only question," Jenson asks, "is where that weight falls."[49] Jenson's proposal, as David Yeago has argued, "is not that the church *has* a polity but rather that the church *is* a polity."[50] This body politic comes with a voice by which to narrate the gospel and enact God's drama. This voice will be heard, in one way or another: "The church is to stand in the street or the temple or the palace, like Amos, Isaiah, or Jeremiah, and state the truth of the present situation by speaking the Word that evokes the future. The one who inhabits and sends the future is this Jesus whom you crucified."[51]

When the church speaks it is not only her founding gospel that is heard, nor is it merely her defining drama and ceremonies which are witnessed. Likewise, her embodied address is not limited to those who are already members of her family. The language with which the body of Christ communicates, incorporates the vast gamut of linguistic materials—be they words, signs, stories or sacraments—that make up the life of the church. For Jenson, this language comprises the church's culture, and it is this culture that determines the type of polity she becomes. In 2003 Jenson presented a series of lectures at King's College, London, entitled, "Christ as Culture." While we will return to this output frequently in the final chapters of this work, the inaugural presentation

47. *S&P*, 178.

48. Hauerwas, "Only Theology Overcomes Ethics," 62.

49. *S&P*, 179.

50. Yeago, "The Church as Polity?," 201.

51. *ST* 2:199.

is of particular interest here. Subtitled, "Christ as Polity," Jenson's first presentation provides an unparalleled insight into his application of the *totus Christus* within the cultural language of the church.[52] It is Jenson's thesis that Christ is linguistically, or culturally, embodied in time and space through the polity of the church, as the *totus Christus*.

In any given time and space, Jenson asserts, the church polity forms the meeting place of, at least, two distinct cultures. The first concerns the culture of the incarnate Christ, while the second comprises the context in which the church finds herself. In each and every manifestation, the polity of the church exists as both a contemporaneous culture and as an historic Jewish sect. While immovable from her present location within history, the story and drama that the polity of the church enacts is meaningless outside of the historic and cultural context of the gospel.[53] In Jenson, the church is to be seen as a dramatic dialogue about God's story and creation. The polity of the church is an ongoing conversation between a fixed narrative, namely the gospel, and an ever-changing world. As a result, Christ is able to rhyme hope and history through the cultural language of the church.

The meeting of different cultures within the polity of the church raises all kinds of questions concerning enculturation. As all positive acts of assimilation require a process by which cultural imports can be accepted and rejected, so too the cultural conversation, which is the life of the church, continually leads to decisions as to what is and isn't permissible within her own polity. Jenson's criticism of the use of multiple cups within the Eucharist, already cited above, provides one such example. In this case, Jenson asserts, the ceremony has been diminished by the church's extensive assimilation to the culture of the Enlightenment and in particular to the misplaced ideal of individuated autonomy.[54] Cultural capitulation, at this point, impairs the congregational polity and threatens the oneness of Christ's body: "Thus the moral history of

52. Jenson, "Christ as Culture 1," 323–29.

53. The implications of the claim are not without significance. Without ever answering the question fully, Jenson asks where the cultural connection between Israel and the church might take us. Among other issues raised, Jenson supposes, it demands a re-evaluation of the church's relationship to the Temple and the implications of Old Testament law upon Christian notions of purity. Jenson, "Christ as Polity," 324.

54. Jenson, "Christ as Polity," 324.

the church is not, as it were, pure; it is not simply other than the moral history of the communities around it. The gospel takes its ethical form just as it *interprets* an antecedent morality of those who at a time and place are there to hear and speak it."[55]

It is the church's enactment of the gospel at a given time and place which characterizes the cultural language of the church and gives voice to the Christian polity. As in any polity, Jenson holds, the church amplifies her speech through a multitude of language-acts. Music, art, architecture, dance, literature, rhetoric, and a thousand other forms are all co-opted in the church's move towards self-determination and proclamation. Through all of these cultural activities, the church community creates new language by which the gospel can be presented to the world. In the church, Jenson argues, the gospel is not a timeless tale from a land far away, but rather comprises a dynamic cultural dialogue within time and space. Through this living converse, the church interprets every element of reality and makes Christ present as its fulfillment. In support of this, Jenson cites the frequent coincidence of Christian polity and social reform within American political history. The cessation of slavery, the civil rights movement, and the end of the Vietnam War were all brought about, in part, by a dialogue between the church and other political forces. In each of these contexts, Jenson suggests, the church's proclamation of the gospel was, at the same time, an act of protest against the political status quo. Having identified a dissonance between the prevailing political prose and God's dramatic story, the church polity had no option but to speak out. Not to do so would have been to render her own gospel as, at best, spurious and, at worst, false.[56] In effecting change in this arena the church confirmed herself as a community of eschatological force and anticipation.

While, for Jenson, all politics is the stuff of eschatology, the eschatological nature of politics itself can only be fully and finally understood in the cultural life and language of the church. The language of the Christian polity, Jenson suggests, interprets all reality in the light of the

55. *ST* 2:210.

56. David Yeago has pointed out that political discourse is part of the cultural converse that humans share concerning their futures, and as such, is constitutive of human personhood in Jenson. Yeago, "Church as Polity?" 205.

resurrection of Jesus, and hence, as occasions for hope. "The church is thus a standing conspiracy in society on behalf of society's own future."[57] The conversation that constitutes the church as a polity is her preaching and sacramental enactment of the gospel writ large. The church polity, for Jenson, comprises a totalized dialogical narration of the gospel. As a result, Christ's presence within the church is not limited to her official gatherings and ceremonies, but rather permeates the entire culture of her community: "If the church is the body of Christ, that is, if the church is the availability of Christ in and for the world, and if this body of Christ, the church, is a culture, it follows then that Christ is a culture. And the sense of the 'is' in 'Christ is a culture' will be the sense in which each of us must say that he or she 'is' his or her body."[58]

It is here, in Jenson's engagement with the language of culture, and in his assessment of the church as a polity that his exposition of the *totus Christus* becomes most explicit. In the life, culture, and polity of the church, Christ is linguistically embodied in time and space as the *totus Christus*. In this guise, "he is himself simply *as* himself *and* he is himself as one with the disciples, with the members of his body; and only as he is both is he indeed himself."[59] While the resurrected Christ, as the second person of the Trinity remains one person, he is now able to draw others into the community that constitutes his own body. In so doing, we ourselves become drawn into the dramatic story of the triune God. As a result, Christ is differentiated from his church in the same way that we are differentiated from our bodies. In the same way that I stand over and against my body—and can so chose to discipline it, punish it, or enjoy it—so too Christ, as the head of the body, retains control over the church community. The theory is not merely analogical. The body language of the New Testament, and the resulting Christology, comes with a sacramental weight that cannot be undone without doing significant ecclesial damage. Furthermore, for Jenson, the relationship between Christ as the head of the body, and the church as the body of Christ, serves as the prototype for all talk of a human's relationship with his, or her, body.

57. *S&P,* 178.

58. Jenson, "Christ as Polity," 325.

59. Ibid., 325.

For Jenson, body language is also talk of the Spirit. While the church is the only community to share a body in this way, all polities share a spirit.[60] What differentiates the ecclesial community from other polities is that her body is born and raised by the same Spirit that brought about Christ's own birth and resurrection. For this reason, the conversation of the church comprises more than the mutual dialogue of a human community. The body language of the Christian polity is ever directed both horizontally and vertically. Thus, the culture of the church, as embodied by the Christian polity, is always the language of petition, praise, and proclamation. As such, it finds its highest end and defining characteristic in the antiphonal drama of prayer, whereby the church becomes one with the Son's address to the Father and, in so doing, joins the triune discourse. However, the entire scope of church culture is viewed, in Jenson, as a contribution to this divine discussion, whether it is addressed to cultures and communities outside the church, to members within, or to God himself. "So who are the people of God?" he asks. "They are the historically actual and just for that reason not always unambiguously delineable people whom God's predestining will is gathering to fulfillment in him."[61]

In an essay entitled, "Christian Civilization," Jenson sketches the history of the church as a polity. Firstly, he claims, the church has taught, demonstrated, and maintained a culture by investing in her own "high culture." This phenomenon, within the life of the polity, constitutes a cultural language that has been *"carried further,* to be that culture intensified."[62] Jenson illustrates: "Higher linguistic culture will be able to say 'On the other hand, I would have thought . . . ,' rather than just 'Wrong!'—which is not to deny that 'Wrong!' would often be preferable. Those who lament 'elite discourses' should try some time to explain what *is* an 'elite discourse' to freshmen lacking such a thing."[63]

---

60. Readers will note how long we have waited for the first mention of the Spirit. For some, the argument that follows may prove adequate. However, others might well suggest that a more developed pneumatology is necessary to support his program.

61. *ST* 2:194.

62. Jenson, "Christian Civilization," 124.

63. Ibid., 7–8.

Secondly, Jenson argues, the church has taught its own "freshmen" the moral, practical, and intellectual intricacies of what it means to be a member of the churchly polity. One cannot be born into this community and must rather learn the cultural language necessary for membership and communion. Converts "face a new culture . . . like a mountain . . . they will be climbing till they die. Where the convert does not face such challenge, one must ask if it is the church he is entering."[64] Thirdly, the culture of the church is cultivated by the work that she performs upon nature. In the case of the body of Christ, this involves nothing less than new creation. This is not to suggest that we, the church's members, can achieve such ends, but that the polity of the church exists as a demonstration and anticipation of the world that is yet to come. The Christ who is God's ultimate plan for creation is already present in the community of the church. Ive takes up the commentary at this point: "The church . . . as the body of Christ, constitutes within itself, by virtue of that identity as *totus Christus,* the new reality by which the whole universe is to be transformed."[65] As a result, the church is not merely a saved community, but is rather the saving community through which God redeems creation. This aspect of his ecclesiology mirrors the inner workings of the triune God, once more: "A culture is action to transform nature. The triune God has no nature antecedent to the mutual action of the Father, Son, and Spirit. What it is to be God is given in the Father's eternal begetting of the Son and enlivening through the Spirit, in the Spirit's eternal liberating of the Father and the Son for one another, in the Son's eternal self-giving to the Father in the Spirit."[66]

As we come to the end of this section and consider the comments of others, we would do well to remember one thing. The unique nature of the church as story, drama, and polity is also her mission. The church belongs to Christ and, as such, comprises his gift, or act of self-giving, to the world. "Whether as common grace, natural law, general revelation, or Barth's 'little lights,' Christianity has recognized the Word spoken also outside the divine polity."[67] For Jenson, the church is nothing but

64. Ibid., 8–9.

65. Ive, "Jenson's Theology of History," 151.

66. Jenson, "Christian Civilization," 10.

67. Ibid., 12–13.

the *totus Christus*. It is the telling of God's story in and through time, the enactment of God's drama in space and the presence of God's polity within culture. "In this way," David Yeago declares, Jenson "offers a distinctive and promising approach to the whole issue of Christian presence in the world."[68] When the church, as the *totus Christus*, finally and fully embodies the gospel as her own culture, the result will be enough to bring about the eschaton:

> Were the gospel fully spoken, it would be a word about every item of reality that already is: every person, every atomic particle, every galaxy, every animal, and it would be an evocation of futurity, a creation of new language, infinite in its openness . . . it would therefore be a communication in which art and science were one. It would bind a community in which the disconnection of languages that divides our culture would be overcome . . . This is the aesthetic self-explication of the gospel-promise. Jesus will speak the word of love, to all men and to every incident of their lives and about every circumstance of their lives.[69]

A Critical Dialogue: Jenson and Gathercole on the Totus Christus and the Pre-Existent Christ

Jenson's treatment of the church as the *totus Christus* is not without its detractors. In an article entitled, "Pre-existence, and the Freedom of the Son in Creation and Redemption: An Exposition in Dialogue with Robert Jenson," Simon Gathercole challenges one of the formative aspects of Jenson's ecclesiology, namely his treatment of the *logos asarkos*.[70] The grounds on which Gathercole builds his argument are worth noting. Gathercole does not object to Jenson's rejection of traditional metaphysical language and welcomes his attempts to root all theology within the narrative of Scripture. However, Gathercole takes exception

68. Yeago, "Church as Polity?" 237. As Yeago suggests, and we are about to discover, few areas of doctrine prove as pressing or as problematic within the church's present context.

69. *S&P,* 77.

70. Gathercole, "Pre-existence, and the Freedom of the Son," 38–51.

to Jenson on the grounds that he either misinterprets, or ignores, certain key passages of Scripture. In dealing with the pre-existent Christ, Gathercole claims, Jenson's use of New Testament texts causes eschatology to ride "rough-shod over protology."[71] This flawed reading, he argues, results from Jenson's overt tendency "to load a great more theological freight on eschatology than is customary."[72] The problems commence with Jenson's alleged failure to deal with passages of Scripture assigned to the Son's activity in creation. Firstly, Gathercole proposes, Jenson avoids the Johannine texts whereby the Father and the Son are jointly identified as the *Alpha and Omega*. Secondly, he makes little reference to John's notion that the Son be seen as a co-agent in creation and thus, prior to earth's inauguration, exists on the creator's side of reality. Thirdly, Gathercole argues, Jenson fails to notice that the Son's pre-existence, along with his freewill, forms the entire presupposition of creation and the incarnation.[73] In Gathercole's reading, the Christ in whom we live, move, and have our being, appears absent in Jenson: "The second identity of the Son of God simply *is* the figure born of Mary who died on the cross. Jesus' sonship is constituted on two sides: on the one hand, Jesus' acknowledgement of God as Father *is* his sonship, and on the other, God's resurrection of Jesus determines his sonship."[74]

Jenson's attempt to expound Scripture in a trinitarian fashion rounds aground, as far as Gathercole is concerned, upon the notion of pre-existence. The implications of this critique should not be taken lightly. With Jenson's perennial insistence that trinitarian theology is the outworking of a grounded biblical Christology, large parts of Jenson's program are implicated by Gathercole's allegation. Referring to the importance of drama in Jenson, Gathercole continues: "It could be said that drama *is* the metaphysic which provides the framework for his system. It is in this territory that one can probe the internal consistency

71. Ibid., 50.

72. Ibid., 46.

73. Gathercole offers another category whereby Christ's pre-existence is viewed in the history of Israel. As witnessed in previous chapters, Jenson is himself keen to promote this position and subsequently receives praise from Gathercole in this regard. Ibid., 44–45.

74. Ibid., 43–44.

of that system. The key question here is: How can a character be said to write the play, to speak the drama into being, if his place in the drama is so radically confined to a particular act within it?"[75]

In her story, drama, and culture, Jenson asserts, the church exists as the *totus Christus*. As the people of God, this community enables the ongoing embodiment of God within time and space. However, as we discussed in the second and third chapters of this work, Jenson's notion of God demands an eternal embodiment through his Word, long before the existence of Israel or the church. If aspects of Jenson's theology undermine Christ's pre-existence, then this surely threatens our understanding of the triune God's eternal embodiment, and consequently, our understanding of the church. If the pre-existence of Christ is as insecure as Gathercole suggests, then talk of his embodiment appears somewhat dubious.

Given the breadth and scope of his theological output, we can concede with Gathercole, that the pre-existent Christ is under represented within Jenson's work. However, Jenson's lack of attention is not, in the main, the result of his mistreatment, nor avoidance, of certain New Testament texts. As we have often suggested, Jenson is unwilling to stake large amounts of theological capital upon what may or may not have occurred outside of the realm of creation. Given the fact that all of our arguments are constrained within the field of human history, Jenson is cautious about how far we can hypothesize as to what lies beyond this reality. It is this concern which drives him, firstly, to reject the metaphysical language traditionally on offer, and, secondly, to root his theological reflections within the biblical narrative. He is consequently reluctant to talk about the Son outside of the incarnation, Israel, and the church: "We may set a rule at the beginning, . . . Given the Incarnation, so that the human person Jesus is in fact the Son who lives with the Father in the Spirit, the distinction between the immanent Trinity and the economic Trinity holds only in the same way as does the distinction between two natures in Christ."[76]

As a New Testament scholar, it is hardly surprising that Gathercole demonstrates a greater textual dexterity than Jenson. However, more

75. Ibid., 48.
76. *ST* 2:173.

worrying is Jenson's supposed avoidance of the pre-existent Christ. Gathercole is again right to suggest that Jenson treats the realm of pre-existence as largely the Father's domain. "He is the 'pre-' of all being."[77] However, and Jenson is clear on this point, "he is this as the one who speaks the Word that grants purpose and so being to others than himself."[78] Here, we return to the doctrine of God's eternal embodiment within the Son, or the Word. In short, God's eternity, in Jenson, presupposes both the pre-existence of the Father *and* the Son, and subsequently of the Spirit. From here, Jenson once again reinforces the immanent connection between his Christology and ecclesiology. As the resurrected Lord, God's eternal embodiment is manifest in the church as the body of Christ. Along with Christ himself, this community constitutes the *totus Christus*: "That it is the man Jesus who is the Son is an event of decision in God; and that the church, with the very individuals who belong to the church, is the body of this person is the *same* event of decision. This event is the only act of election or predestination that occurs."[79]

Gathercole is also correct in his suggestion that Jenson's position owes more to eschatology than it does to ontology. For Jenson, the "pre-" in Christ's preexistence emphasizes the futurity of God to all other being, "and only so is the priority of his anteriority to being."[80] It is precisely this aspect of Christ's existence that enables him to reconcile the past and the future, and hereby rhyme hope with our history. While Gathercole commences with an ontological Christ who, in the Scriptures of the New Testament, takes on eschatological significance, Jenson works from the end backwards and establishes his ontology through God's futurity. While the approach may appear unconventional, the end result is certainly not unorthodox.

For Jenson, the pre-existent Christ represents God's own embodiment and thus becomes the free decision by which creation, incarnation, and redemption are made manifest in created time and space. In this eternal decision, all ontology and eschatology are reconciled

77. Ibid., 2:173.

78. Ibid.

79. Ibid., 2:175. Jenson here paraphrases Barth.

80. Ibid., 2:177.

within the "created time of the death and resurrection of Christ and of his audible and visible word in the church."[81] Most importantly, Jenson does not deny that Christ is ontologically prior to creation. What he questions is the terminological slippage that equates this doctrine with the notion that Christ is chronologically prior to creation. This use of "before" and "after" language contradicts our talk of pre-existence as, in using these phrases, we are immediately reverting to our notions of created time. Upon reflection, and contrary to his initial disclaimer, it is Jenson's metaphysics, and not his interpretation of the New Testament, which Gathercole fails to grasp. In response, Jenson suggests that Gathercole does "what folk often do to someone with a surprising idea." Having presupposed the conception that the idea was meant to replace, Gathercole "develops an argument against the validity of the idea using that traditional conception as a warrant."[82]

Having assessed one christological critique of Jenson's ecclesiology, we would do well to reflect further upon what many would consider the main weakness in his program. Being well acquainted with Jenson's immanent view of God and the world, his emphasis upon Christ and the church as the *totus Christus* is hardly surprising. As Richard John Neuhaus has said, "Jenson's radical realism in the identification of Christ and his church . . . is luminously evident."[83] However, the question arises as to whether such a unifying vision can be upheld. It is a question that we must pose with some haste, as the chapters that follow depend on its outcome. While it is one thing to suggest that Christ exists in the culture of the church, it is another to claim that this culture is his embodiment to the world. At this point, some of Jenson's most supportive colleagues

---

81. Ibid., 2:177. Unresolved within this are the ongoing theological tensions concerning God's eternal decision and freewill. Having often emphasised the former, Jenson opens the way for Gathercole, among others, to assert that he cannot account for the latter. The problem is not Jenson's alone. These issues have also been outlined by Paul Molnar in, Molnar, *Divine Freedom,* 61–72. Starting with Barth, Molnar appraises the attempts of a number of twentieth-century theologians to unify immanent and economic accounts of the Trinity. In the case of the *logos asarkos,* and ensuing doctrines of election and freewill, Molnar critiques Jenson's work alongside others, among them, Bruce McCormack and Douglas Farrow.

82. Correspondence with author, (24 Nov 2005).

83. Neuhaus, "The Public Square," 246.

distance themselves from his position. From a Reformed perspective, Colin Gunton suggests that Jenson exhibits "a stronger unifying drive than seems . . . acceptable."[84] And from a Catholic viewpoint, Susan Wood declares, "As deeply sympathetic as I am with Jenson's identification of the church as the risen body of Christ, I fear that he often makes this identification too directly."[85] In part, the problem occurs as a result of Jenson's unwillingness to deal in metaphor. Both in his critique of Aquinas, as outlined in the previous chapter, and in his subsequent denial of transubstantiation we witness a nervousness where this linguistic device is concerned. In Jenson's theology, it appears, metaphorical realities are *not real enough*. One possible resolution to these problems lies in the development of a use of metaphor that, while reinforcing the hard realities of sacramental language, avoids the perils of licentious literalism.[86]

The practical outworkings of Jenson's identification of Christ and the church as the *totus Christus* are certainly problematic. If there is no line by which to distinguish Christ from the church, how then do we explain the countless ecclesial crimes and misdemeanors of the ages? Who was at work when large parts of the Christian polity upheld the slave trade, validated Hitler's regime, or perpetrated religious genocide in Rwanda? Were these activities carried out by a church in error or the *totus Christus*? While it is one thing to identify Christ's presence within the culture of the church, it is another to conflate Christ into every churchly activity. Jenson's exposition of body language fails to bring closure to this controversy. For here we must muse as to whether the body of Christ can operate beyond the will of Christ himself. The resulting image of the body running away with the head is certainly puzzling.

84. Gunton, "Creation and Mediation," 92.

85. Wood, "Jenson's Ecclesiology," 182.

86. The challenge is not that Jenson denies the language of metaphor, but rather that he insists that certain description, such as the church as "the body of Christ," reach beyond metaphor and instantiate theological realities which are not to be meddled with. A further challenge arises as we attempt to differentiate between those descriptions that carry sacramental weight and others which are "mere" metaphor or analogy. The obvious example concerns the contrasting of body-language and nuptial-terminology within our discussion of the church. In Jenson, the former carries far greater weight than the latter, but is the emphasis wholly warranted?

While the work is yet to be done, the paradigm for the process may already be in place. In the next chapter, we will consider Jenson's thoughts on the efficacy of the sacraments. With his high view of Christ's presence, the same question arises as to the authentication of Jesus' bodily presence in these rites.

For Jenson, Christ's real presence in the sacraments is seen as a top-down movement. It is not our use of the sacraments that determines Christ's presence, but rather it is Christ's promised presence, will, and intention that guarantees his availability to us. In short, Christ is present in the church's story, drama, and polity by his own choice. Furthermore this perfect presence can withstand great heresy and error. For while it is uncontroversial to suggest that the church's character is threatened by her behavior, it is also an inescapable reality that she maintains her status despite the fallenness of her members. According to conventional ecclesiology, a divided church is not the church at all, for God's body cannot be dissected at the whims of his people. And yet the holy catholic church, in its present state, appears inexorably divided throughout the world. We have two conclusions on offer. Either, his presence has passed us by or, by some mysterious act of grace, Christ, by his Spirit, holds his body together and makes himself present in the church. Upon reflection, Jenson's ecclesiology is a product of hope. In this, it is as much the work of a faithful theologian awaiting, expecting, and anticipating the one true church, as it is an overly unifying scheme. This said, the drawing of ecclesial lines of demarcation is a necessary theological task. In short, at what point do we disqualify ourselves from membership of the *totus Christus*?

Throughout his thought this question remains largely unanswered. However, the dialogue with Gathercole may generate further possibilities in this regard. For Jenson, a chronological interpretation of predestination is the flawed legacy of the same misguided approach to Christ's own pre-existence. This misinterpretation identifies predestination with a one-off event in the outer reaches of eternity, or timelessness. In this domain, election occurs long before, and regardless of, the actual events of our lives. Consequently, our encounter of the gospel, conversion, baptism, and so on, are all but divorced from Christ's work in election. By drawing together Jenson's eschatological notion of Christ's pre-existence, and his treatment of the church as a polity, a solution becomes apparent. The line of demarcation between Christ and his body is simply not ours' to draw. For Jenson, all talk of what does and does not constitute the church is talk of election and is thus Christ's to dictate. For it is Christ and his followers, or the *totus Christus*, who form the object of Christ's election. As before, the election of the pre-existent Christ is framed both ontologically and eschatologically. Our membership of the body, as a result, has not been merely predetermined before time, but rather will be determined in the fullness of time, and thus has been determined through time:

> Only now may we come to God's drawing of the *boundary* between the polity of God and the world's polities, that is, to the predestination of individuals. The decisive consideration follows from all the preceding: the "pre-" in "predestination" must be the same "pre-" as in "preexistence of Christ . . ." Therefore it is not that God has already *decided* whether I am or am not of his community. He *will* decide and *so* has decided; and *has* decided and so *will* decide; and so *decides* also within created time.[87]

Having decided upon the nature and membership of the *totus Christus* at the end of history, Christ has subsequently made the same decision at the beginning of history and at every point in between. From hereon every encounter with the gospel and every embodiment of Christ within creation is an ongoing act of election. In Jenson's scheme, the story, drama, and polity of the church have become the method and result of Christ's own predestination.[88] As a result, the process by which we qualify or disqualify church communities becomes as shaky as our predictions over who may, or may not be saved. This is not to say that on occasions such discussions are not called for. While the subject attracts

87. *ST* 2:177.

88. By eschatologically conjugating his ecclesiology, Jenson leaves open the possibility that the body be perfected through time. The emphasis on body-language, over and above the use of nuptial metaphor, would seem to diminish the possibilities herein. However, in the same way that the church should be viewed as a bride being prepared for her wedding day, the Christian polity can surely also be seen as Christ's earthly body resurrected towards its own perfection.

little attention, Jenson is a firm believer in the possibility of apostasy and asserts the right, and indeed the necessity of the church to expel dangerous heretics. After all, it is the responsibility of the church to discipline her borders.[89] However, all that we have encountered above makes Jenson wary of an overly prescribed doctrine and plan for such situations. In the main, Jenson is beyond distraction. The church is chosen, charged, and changed by an act of Jesus, and is actualized through the power of his Spirit. Jenson summarizes it thus: "The Spirit *frees* an actual human community from merely historical determinisms, to be apt to be united with the Son and thus to be the gateway of creation's translation into God."[90]

Conclusion

With this quote fresh in our minds, one final question arises. It is a question that Jenson himself posed to Karl Barth, in response to the *Church Dogmatics*. In Jenson's grandiose portrayal of the church as the *totus Christus*, "one wonders where the Spirit went." Our discussion, concerning Christ and his body has been unavoidably christological. However, this is not to suggest, that Jenson is ignorant of the need for an adequate pneumatology. All that has been said and all that must be said occurs only in the power of the Spirit. As Francis Watson points out, in Jenson, the Spirit opens the triune conversation and enables our participation within it.[91] Furthermore, the story, drama, and polity of the *totus Christus*, "is intrinsically, . . . and historically, accomplished as pneumatology."[92] Therefore, the church's dialogue concerning her identity is also the discourse of the Holy Spirit.[93] It is this Spirit empowered converse which initiates the church as both story, drama, and polity: "'It is the proper work of the Holy Spirit, to make the church.' And we must

89. Ibid., 2:205.

90. Ibid., 2:179.

91. Watson, "America's Theologian," 218.

92. Jenson, *Christian Dogmatics*, 143.

93. Such an overarching pneumatology will, in time, draw similar praise and detraction as does Jenson's ecclesial Christology. Likewise, we could expect a very similar defence and rebuttal.

add: the Spirit does this by giving himself to be the spirit of this community, by bestowing his own eschatological power to be her liveliness. As Anglican-Orthodox dialogue put it: the church is the community 'which is filled by the Holy Spirit, and it is precisely for this reason that every human person has the possibility of becoming a partaker of the divine nature.'"[94]

By the power of the Spirit, the church is equipped to proclaim and enact, to build and to paint and to sing and to dance the gospel into the world. With Jenson's commitment to the *totus Christus,* all reality becomes inescapably tied to the church's life and mission. All words and language, whether spoken or gestured, require a body. In the case of the triune creator, God's address is made through Christ, as his body, or the *totus Christus.* The action and availability of the triune God within his creation is thus to be found in the very body-language of the church. His real presence is nothing other than the story, drama, and language of the *totus Christus.* From a heavenly perspective, the church constitutes the triune God's contribution to the human conversation, while on earth this community simultaneously comprises the people of God, the temple of the Spirit and the body of Christ.[95] The church is constitutive of creation's past, present and future and, to this end, rhymes all our hope and histories. The full eschatological and ontological force and importance of Jenson's ecclesiology can be grasped in one maxim: "no church—no big bang!"[96]

94. *ST* 2:197.

95. This threefold description of Jenson's ecclesiology, as Susan Wood has noted, summarizes the ecumenical breadth and inclusiveness of Jenson's ecclesiology. Wood, "Jenson's Ecclesiology," 178.

96. Schwöbel, "Christ and Culture," *TTC,* 120; *ETC,* 220.

5

Christianese Whispers:
Jenson and Theories of Culture

COMMENCING WITH THIS DISCUSSION on culture, the remaining chapters of this work explore the cultural outworkings of Jenson's theology and subsequent notion of the *totus Christus*. In part, these investigations will retrace old ground, as we ask whether culture can confirm Jenson's presuppositions of reality. In the main, however, we will explore the outworkings of Jenson's scheme within the cultural life of the church. In this chapter, we will discuss culture as both the language that human beings share about reality and the means by which Christ is present in the church.

Jenson's analysis and development of the *totus Christus* is among the boldest and most daring imaginings of his entire program. It is not enough for us creatures to confess the one God who has time, space, and language for us. For Jenson, the gospel is an invitation to be part of God's time, to live in his space and to speak his word. As the *totus Christus*, the church represents both the anticipation and fulfillment of this promise in the here and now. In the story, drama, and polity of the church, her members find themselves speaking a new language in a new time and place. In Christ, the church finds herself at the gates of heaven, identified as his resurrected body and partaking in the triune discourse. As the church draws creation into Christ through her culture, so too

Christ makes himself present in creation through the cultural language of the church.

When it comes to culture, Richard Neuhaus remarks, Jenson is "always and relentlessly, some might say incorrigibly, Jenson the theologian."[1] Jenson's multiple excursions into the world of culture are pre-empted by his singular belief that all realities are to be understood, first and foremost, theologically. As Neuhaus points out, Jenson's "thought on ethics, politics, culture, and other aspects of the public square is not theology *ad extra,* as distinct from theology, *ad intra.* The entirety of all that is is . . . *ad intra* to the life of God, the Father, Son, and Holy Spirit."[2] Once again, the implications of this are most readily witnessed within Jenson's ecclesiology. In the same way that history cannot be divorced from the life of the church, neither can the cultures of the world be detached from the culture of the *totus Christus.* As the mediator of creation, savior of mankind and the promised end of all existence, Christ is available to the world through the community of the church. Hence, in the life and community of the church we become fully human. As mentioned in the previous chapter, the church is constituted as the people of God, the body of Christ and the temple of the Spirit.[3] It is for this reason that the church is to be known as Christ as culture.

While Jenson's position is theologically courageous, a question arises as to whether his view can be supported in theory. Having identified the theory in this chapter, we will later observe Jenson's theory in practice. If Jenson's program is to stand, he must balance his theological presuppositions and ecclesiological pronouncements, with a substantial enough theory of culture. This theory must demonstrate a double utility. In the first place, it must confirm culture as the communal and theological language through which human beings come to terms with the realities of created time and space. And secondly, it must affirm the possibility of Christ's presence within the culture of the church, as

1. Neuhaus, "The Public Square," 238.

2. It is for this reason that, as Stanley Hauerwas has suggested, "Jenson does not 'do' ethics." For Jenson, "Christian ethical reflection does not belong uniquely to any of the loci of Christian theology. When Jenson does what looks like ethics, however, it is done as an aspect of his ecclesiology." Hauerwas, "Theology Overcomes Ethics," 252, 258.

3. Jenson, "The Church as Communion," 68.

the *totus Christus*. Our discussion will be enhanced by two additional voices. Richard Niebuhr's seminal work has long set the standard for theological discussions of culture, and will consequently provide our starting point. Our second interlocutor, Kathryn Tanner, provides a more contemporary formulation of the subject at hand. Her creative use of postmodern anthropological method offers a dynamic alternative to the Niebuhrian scheme.

The Orthodox Account: Niebuhr, *Christ and Culture*

Niebuhr's pioneering work on theology and culture has set the agenda for several generations of Protestant dialogue. His "view of culture is extraordinarily perceptive," Christoph Schwöbel observes, "and anticipates much of the discussion that gained a wider forum only with the rise of cultural anthropology."[4] It appears surprising then that Niebuhr avoided any close definition of culture itself. What's more, while many treatments of culture appear overly porous, weakened unassailably by their own omissions, Niebuhr's formulation faces the opposite challenge. In his groundbreaking work, *Christ and Culture,* the essence of culture eludes closer identification. Culture, Niebuhr argues, is manifested largely through its own effects. It is the subsequent observation and interpretation of these effects that the theologian must attend to if he is to take culture seriously. Among other things, Niebuhr suggests, it is possible to assert that culture is created, social, dynamic, temporary, and so forth. He continues:

> Culture is that total process of human activity and that total result of such activity to which now the name *culture* . . . is applied in common speech. Culture is the "artificial, secondary environment" which man superimposes on the natural. It comprises language, habits, ideas, beliefs, customs, social organization, inherited artifacts, technical processes, and values. This "social heritage," this "reality sui generis," which the New Testament writers frequently had in mind when they spoke of "the world," which is

4. Schwöbel, "Christ and Culture," 112.

> represented in many forms but to which Christians like
> other men are inevitably subject, is what we mean when
> we speak of culture.[5]

Underlying Niebuhr's expansive account, as John Howard Yoder suggests, "culture is almost indiscriminately . . . equivalent to 'anything people do together.'"[6] Culture is both the result of humanity's achievement and the complex reality of human existence. In short, it forms a language that human beings use to come to an understanding of their world. Or as Niebuhr himself puts it, the aim of culture is the "temporal and material realization of values."[7] Despite this, Niebuhr avoids the temptation to define culture theologically. His plan, having identified culture aside from theology, is to investigate the effects of theology upon culture. The interface between the two is to be negotiated by means of Niebuhr's Christology. However, his Troeltschian historical method divorces the Jesus of history from the Christ of faith and from hereon Niebuhr finds it impossible to re-establish a stable bridgehead between the two. This limitation holds grave consequences for the ensuing relationship between theology and culture. Not wishing to promote one aspect of his Christology over the other, Niebuhr attempts to hold both figures together through a retrospective appeal to the doctrine of Christ's dual natures: "The ancient church raised the question in terms of Jesus Christ's unity or duality and needed to decide for the latter, for there was an evident polarity between the Jesus of history and the Christ of faith which could not be resolved by the absorption of one into the other."[8]

Having identified a number of characteristics from the tradition, Niebuhr asks whether christological attributes can be simultaneously

---

5. Niebuhr, *Christ and Culture*, 32–33. Niebuhr borrows the concept of an "artificial, secondary environment" from social scientist Malinowski. Malinowski, "Culture," 621.

6. Niebuhr, *Christ and Culture*, xxii.

7. Ibid., 36. The annexing of the term "values," what with its Nitzchean roots, may provide some insight into the unavoidable divorce that occurs between Christ and culture within Niebuhr's work. Jenson's own prognosis concerning modernity's choice between nihilism and the gospel may find further confirmation here.

8. Ibid., xli.

located in the faith of the church and Jesus' history. Can the liberal's longing for love be found in Jesus' story? Can the eschatologist's hunger for hope be secured in the history of Christ? Can the faith that Protestants pursue or the humility that monastics maintain be traced back to the Jesus of history? In Niebuhr's account they can, and furthermore, through the connection of these realities, the "original portraits with which all later pictures may be compared and by which all caricatures may be corrected . . . are radicalized in such a way that they compliment one another in a profound theological sense."[9] As a result, in Niebuhr, the two complex realities of Christ and culture meet in a dialogue about Christ's identity within the church. In Niebuhr, as Schwöbel points out, the converse, which constitutes the church, "is not an amorphous never-ending tale in which all distinctives are blurred," but rather relies upon "a typology as a way of following the conversation more intelligently."[10]

Having framed the interaction between theology and culture, Niebuhr's typology locates all further discussion between two poles of thought. The first, posits theology and culture as separate from one another with Christ positioned either above or against culture, while the second synthesizes the two and thus locates Christ within culture. Between these polarities, Niebuhr identifies a possible middle ground, whereby Christ fulfills cultural aspirations, accommodates cultural deficiencies, or converts culture itself. Despite this, Niebuhr struggles to secure a stable connection between Christ and culture, and thus his overriding position situates Christ as above or apart from culture.

Niebuhr's earlier appeal to the doctrine of the two natures is merely a front for his relativistic view of history. This flawed methodology severely impacts his program. For Niebuhr's Troeltschian method, as Colin Gunton has argued, "suggests that all times and places are to be understood exhaustively in terms of their temporal context, with the result that no era or event can be distinguished from any other with respect to its significance."[11] As a result, the cultural Christ of faith can never be fully authenticated as the Jesus of history. For all its prom-

9. Schwöbel, "Christ and Culture," 109.

10. Ibid., 113.

11. Gunton, *The One, The Three and The Many.* 88.

ise, Niebuhr's program struggles to maintain its own presuppositions. While determined to connect the two realms, Niebuhr creates a chasm between the worlds of Christ and culture. Set adrift from culture, Christ becomes an overly abstract concept in search of evermore-elusive connections with his creation. The ensuing separation of Christ and culture results in a theologically unacceptable and ultimately unnecessary dissection of reality.

As humanity's attempt to grasp the complexities of reality, Niebuhr's definition of culture takes a similar starting point to that of Jenson. In Niebuhr we can confirm that culture forms a communal language by which human beings come to terms with their existence. We have, in part, answered the first question with which we commenced this chapter. However for all his attempts to the contrary, Niebuhr's Christology fails to deliver any real possibility that Christ can be unified and, as such, identified with the culture of the church. The unavoidable separation of Christ from culture struggles to provide the vocabulary for Jenson's christological and trinitarian description of reality, let alone his notion of the church as culture. All this suggests that a new theory is needed to deal with the complexities at hand. In 2003, Jenson gave a lecture entitled, "Christ as Culture." He admits that this heading was "a rather too obvious parody" of H. Richard Niebuhr's book.[12] Although indebted to Niebuhr, Jenson is determined to provide a fresh account of the issues at hand. He is certainly not alone. In his introduction to the latest edition of *Christ and Culture*, George Marsden goes so far as to suggest that, "despite its enormous influence in the past fifty years, . . . Niebuhr's analysis in its present form could be near the end of its usefulness."[13] The all-important categories, at their best, now appear misleading and, at their worst, are simply wrong. Likewise, Stanley Hauerwas and Will Willimon have argued that, "Few books have been a greater hindrance to an accurate assessment of our situation than *Christ and Culture*."[14] The question arises as to how Jenson's own theory will compare with

---

12. Jenson, "Christ as Polity," 323.

13. Niebuhr, *Christ and Culture*, xxi. Marsden's quote is from his Foreword to the latest edition of Niebuhr's work.

14. Ibid., xxi.

that of Nieubuhr. However, before we come to Jenson we will consider another new theory on the subject.

The Postmodern Alternative: Tanner, Culture and Christianity

Kathryn Tanner has made much theological use of the post-Niebuhrian developments in cultural studies and anthropological method. Given fifty years of further cultural analysis and theological enquiry, Tanner provides a far more progressive approach to the interface between theology and culture: "Although less than one hundred years old, the modern anthropological meaning of 'culture' now enjoys a remarkable influence within the humanistic disciplines of the academy and within commonsense discussions of daily life. In explanatory importance and generality of application it is comparable to such categories as gravity in physics, disease in medicine, evolution in biology."[15]

Armed with a closer anthropological definition, Tanner sets forth a series of distinctives by which culture can be identified. For Tanner, culture is both universal amongst humans and peculiar to them. It is anthropologically diverse and thus varies according to geography and community. It represents a whole way of life and relies upon a process of social consensus. It both consists of and constructs human nature, and in this guise produces the conventions that we, in turn, call culture. And finally, it is contingent and socially determining.[16]

Where Niebuhr's distinguished the theological and cultural realms, Tanner's study unites the fields from the start. Employing, what she calls, a postmodern anthropological method, Tanner addresses theology as an essential element of culture. Through her approach, "a postmodern stress on interactive process and negotiation, indeterminacy, fragmentation, conflict, and porosity replaces," the earlier conceptions of culture which are evident in Niebuhr.[17] Tanner's treatment of culture retains the broad scope of the Niebuhrian notion while instantiating a crucial theological advance. Repositioning theology within culture, Tanner is not forced to detach the main elements of her program but can rather

15. Tanner, *Theories of Culture*, ix.

16. Ibid., 25–37.

17. Ibid., 38.

focus upon the possible illumination of theology by cultural anthropology. From here, she questions whether the Christian faith instigates its own culture. Through her anthropological method, she attempts to uncover a uniquely theological pattern of behaviors, or series of rules, within Christian communities. If fruitful, the experiment would enable an interpretation of Christianity as a cultural language-game.[18]

Tanner's search for a Christian culture rests upon the answers to three specific questions. Firstly, she asks whether a Christian culture can be defined in social terms. Put another way, can the church, on the basis of her own distinct social practices, be understood as an alternative community? After much testing, the results appear to be negative. Tanner illustrates this in reference to the early church. While the lives of early church members may appear radically different from their contemporaries, the first Christians did not stop being Jews, Romans, or Greeks on account of their induction into this new community. Likewise, we could not expect the church to divorce herself from our own wider community and culture. As a result, Christians pay taxes, obey the highway code, read newspapers, work in office blocks and attend concerts, yet none of these could be marked out as uniquely Christian practices. On a theological note, if Christianity were to fully assume the role of a distinct and self-sufficient culture, then sin would have to be banished from its midst and grace would be withheld at its borders. Tanner continues: "Christian communities are neither self-contained nor self-sufficient. The character of Christian social relations is sustained . . . by some fairly isolated social activities . . . that involve in the main only Christians—for instance, church services. But Christians always bring with them on such occasions their social roles and commitments . . . Christians, moreover, remain in interaction with non-Christians . . . Their Christian commitments remain relevant to these spheres, too."[19]

With this route towards an exclusively Christian community coming to a dead-end, Tanner tries another approach. Here, she asks whether we can identify a Christian culture through the demarcation of

18. Note our earlier discussion on theology, language, Jenson and Wittgenstein in chapter 3.

19. Ibid., 152.

specific cultural boundaries through the ages. The search for these common denominators of Christian culture proves equally unsuccessful. To illustrate the point, another lesson from history will suffice. While the Christian community has, in the past, allowed its members to acquire and employ slaves, more recently the church has become defined by its defiant opposition to the practice. This neither confirms the latter day church as the ultimate Christian community nor does it depose the earlier community. Furthermore, while it maybe possible to create a long lasting dogmatic position on all manner of cultural issues, it is not possible for this record to authoritatively dictate what ultimately makes for a Christian community. Likewise, attempts to abstract a list of common themes and attributes from Christian behavior is equally unconvincing. Cultural values such as, "respect for human beings," "love for one another," or "equality, liberty and brotherhood," may express Christian truths but are hardly exclusive to the church. The challenge of historical relativism reoccurs once more. For Tanner, Christian culture and community cannot be defined by specific cultural boundaries through time, for these limitations are always relative to the context in which the church finds herself.

Pressing on, Tanner tries a third test. Here, she considers whether a Christian culture could be denoted through a set of continuous and common cultural practices. Once again the search proves unsuccessful. Not even the existence of established Christian rituals can provide Tanner with an affirmative response to her own question. Take, for example, the Eucharist. How is the efficacy of this ritual established and measured? Furthermore, is such a practice to be qualified and termed as Eucharist, Holy Communion, the Lord's Supper, or by another name entirely? And what are the final boundaries of sacramental activity that necessarily authenticate the ritual at hand? Can we truly identify one universal amidst the many particular and diverse meals that Christians celebrate? Once more, history undermines the plan. For throughout time, the Christian community has found it as easy to disagree, as it has to agree upon its own common concerns. The point is underlined by Tanner's turn to the tradition. Here, Tanner alleges that many cultural continuities are merely the result of hindsight and thus struggle to bear the scrutiny of anthropological method. Theologians, it is suggested, unravel history to weave their own common threads and to promote their preferred cultural practices and continuities: "While there are boundaries between Christian and non-Christian ways of life, those boundaries are fluid and permeable. Claims and values that are outside are brought inside (or, much the same thing, what is inside is brought outside) in process of transformation at the boundary. Christian identity is therefore no longer a matter of unmixed purity, but a hybrid affair established through unusual use of materials found elsewhere."[20]

With this, it becomes almost impossible to conceive of a Christian culture as a conventional language-game, for nowhere can we observe the rules of participation. On this occasion, however, Tanner's failure to identify the defining ingredients of a decidedly Christian culture, triggers an important breakthrough: "What Christians have in common, what unites them, is nothing internal to the practices themselves. What unites them is concern for true discipleship, proper reflection in human thoughts and deeds of an object of worship that always exceeds by its greatness the human efforts to do so."[21]

For her initial questions to be answered in the affirmative, Tanner argues, Christian history would have to be entirely subjugated as God's own history. Likewise, in a definitively Christian culture, church members would exist in an immediate relation to God to the point whereby they could directly apprehend and issue God's own determinations and decrees. However, Tanner suggests, with some theological allowance and openness, talk of a Christian culture is certainly possible in our own time and space. Here, Christian culture is not understood as a theological or societal hand-me-down, nor is it the church's birthright, but rather it is both her future aim and present mission. "In the end," Tanner concludes, "how the identity of Christianity should be summed up is an unanswerable question in that Christianity has its identity as a task; it has its identity in the form of a task of looking for one."[22] Tanner's study clears the way for this eschatological interpretation of culture. The church, then, is a work in progress, an ongoing conversation and, subsequently, a community in the act of becoming. Tanner proposes that the

20. Ibid., 152.

21. Ibid., 152.

22. Ibid., 154–55.

culture of the church is the communal embodiment of the language and converse of Christian theology. In this ongoing and open-ended cultural conversation the church is continually reformed in her own midst.

For all its eschatological possibility, Tanner's theory lacks the necessary ontological resources by which to confirm her breakthrough. The inability to constructively deal with history proves as much a flaw in Tanner's postmodern method as it did in Niebuhr's more orthodox formulation. Furthermore, while the move to identify theology within culture is welcome, Tanner struggles at times to prevent theology from disintegrating into yet another cultural construct. In this, Niebuhr has been proved right. For where Orthodox discussions often become stuck in the past, more progressive accounts of theology and culture become too tied to the future; we are either overly rabbinical, as in the case of Niebuhr himself, or overly eschatological, as with Tanner.[23]

Tanner's achievement is the construction of a theory of culture capable of containing a theological discourse as to the identity of the Christian community. Much of this resonates with Jenson's own instincts. The location of all theological language and material within the realm of culture, and the ensuing eschatological emphasis upon the nature of identity, bear significant promise.[24] However, the difficulties in identifying a Christian culture continue to restrict the pronouncements that Jenson urges us to make. If the verifiable nature of Christian culture is as illusive as Tanner suggests then surely the possibility of identifying Christ within and *as* a culture is receding from our grasp. What is more, having reduced theology to a sub-section of culture, Tanner's anthropological riches may come at theology's expense.[25] Through her commitment to anthropological method, Tanner runs the risk of recategorizing all theology as a spiritual subset of anthropology. Finally, in both Niebuhr and Tanner we face two complex realities namely, Christ

23. Niebuhr, *Theology, History and Culture*, 5–6.

24. There are parallels here with Jenson's eschatological interpretation of identity. For Jenson, human identity is primarily a question of what we are becoming.

25. The theological implications of her analysis are not far removed from Lindbeck's appropriation of Wittgensteinian language-games. As with Lindbeck, it is hard to imagine how theology might deal with extra-cultural entities. If this is the case then theology appears unable to articulate its own subject and thus becomes a fool's errand. See the previous discussion on theological language-games in chapter 3.

and culture. The difference between the two programs lies in the cause of separation. Niebuhr's Christ appears so high above culture as to be of limited earthly use, while Tanner's Christianity is so culturally earthed as to appear inseparable from it. However, despite their differences, both theories display the unique theological conversation that the language of culture facilitates.

Christ and Culture: Comparing and Contrasting
Niebuhr and Jenson

While the sheer scope of his definition is occasionally problematic, Niebuhr is surely right to suggest that culture consists of human activity, or the things that people do together. For Jenson similarly, culture is viewed as the total sum of all human activity, or the phenomena of the social. As with both interlocutors, Jenson is quick to utilize developments in social theory to bring a closer definition to his theological notion of culture. In Jenson, culture is, "The mutual behavior of a group in so far as this behavior is sustained by teaching and not only by genetics and physical ecology . . . Or . . . the mutual behavior of a group of persons in so far as this can be abstracted from those doing the behaving, as in itself a coherent system of mutually determining signs."[26]

Through this mutually determining system of signs, Jenson asserts, culture becomes meaningful and intelligible. Like Tanner, Jenson rejects Niebuhr's starting point, insisting that the very title, *Christ and Culture*, instantiates Christ as one thing and culture as another. Niebuhr's book, Jenson argues, concerns "possible prepositions to replace the non-committal conjunction," and as a result, Christ must be considered as against culture, above culture, or ahead of culture. Either way, he is clearly away from culture.[27] Rather than separate theology and culture, Jenson stresses their interdependence. However, instead of subsuming theology within culture, as in Tanner, Jenson insists that culture itself be construed within the domain of theology. Once again, the "Scripture and the theology of the church sustain the great maxim

26. Jenson, "Christ as Polity," 324.
27. Ibid., 323.

of the theology of culture, that the soul of every culture is a religion and the body of every religion a culture."[28]

Jenson's theological notion of culture is activated by his Christology. Having disguised his historical relativism beneath his commitment to the doctrine of the dual nature, Niebuhr's attempt to identify the Son as both the Christ of faith and the Jesus of history was doomed to failure. As Jenson has long acknowledged, attempts to emphasize Christ's duality over and above his oneness, are always costly for Christian theology. For the self-evident truth of the gospel discloses that the Son is one, both as the Christ of faith and the Jesus of history: "Since the gospel says of Jesus that he is risen from the dead, 'Jesus' itself must denote an accomplished human life; within the language of modernity or postmodernity, we will inevitably and rightly say that 'Jesus' refers to a historical figure, to a 'historical Jesus' or 'Jesus of history.'"[29]

In this, Jenson succeeds where Niebuhr fails. Niebuhr himself demonstrates his attraction to the position, only to be let down by his own impoverished view of history. "The Jesus Christ of the New Testament," Niebuhr declares, "is in our actual history, in history as we remember and live it, as it shapes our present faith and action."[30] Where Niebuhr resolved his own dualism by reference to the dual nature of Christ, Jenson displays his unifying tendencies once more by treading the opposite path. Jenson unifies the Jesus of history and the Christ of faith through his critique of the tradition's unhelpful preoccupation with the two natures. In Jenson, Jesus Christ is to be proclaimed as the one, unified Son of the Father.[31] Here, Christ is understood to have but one nature that incorporates elements that we appropriate as either human or divine. However, regardless of the number of categories we employ to expound the mysterious complexity of his personality, Christ's oneness remains.

28. *ST* 1:51–52.

29. Ibid., 165.

30. Niebuhr, *Christ and Culture*, 13.

31. Once again, Jenson is anxious to reappropriate the findings of Chalcedon by placing a greater emphasis on the oneness of Christ's personhood, as opposed to the duality of his natures. This causes George Hunsinger to declare Jenson as a monophysite. We will return to this accusation, along with Jenson's response, at the conclusion of this thesis. Hunsinger, "Robert Jenson's Systematic Theology: A Review Essay."

Furthermore, Jenson's unifying drive does not limit Christ's connection with culture. While Niebuhr utilizes Christ's dual nature to establish a connection with the diversity of culture, Jenson returns to his christological trinitarianism to achieve the same end. Here, the unity of the Son is one reality within the diverse life of the Trinity, which, in turn, creates an infinitely diverse community through the person of the Son: "That Christ has the divine nature means that he is one of the three whose mutuality is the divine life, who live the history that God is . . . That Christ has human nature means that he is one of the many whose mutuality is human life, who live the history that humanity is."[32]

As God's humanity, Jesus provides a permanent meeting point between history and eternity. Where Niebuhr's separation of Christ and culture preserves the Ptolemaic map of the universe, Jenson, as we discovered in chapter 2, rejects this outmoded cosmological cartography. If God is to create creatures for himself, Jenson insists, he requires a space where he can be with them. The traditional placement of heaven in the far reaches of the universe is too far off, restricting Christ's presence to one long cosmological commute. In Jenson's modification, God has created the whole universe in a single place in order that he can remain present to it. The implications of Jenson's spatial remapping prove significant where culture is concerned. In Jenson, the events of history occur within God's own life. While, in Niebuhr, the Father and Son may find a place in "the cultural complex, but only as elements in the great pluralism" of history, in Jenson, the "cultural complex" and the "great pluralism" are already to be found in the community of the Trinity.[33] The relational and conversational time and space that God has for his creation provide the platform for human communities and their subsequent converse concerning reality, or that which we call culture. As a direct result of the love that the Father shares with the Son through the Spirit, humanity represents the highest expression of creation and is thus christologically constituted and triunely fulfilled. For this reason, Christian theology offers the ultimate anthropology by establishing the inherent connection between divine and human personhood. In this formulation, the creator and creation are connected by the continual

32. *ST* 1:138.

33. Niebuhr, *Christ and Culture*, 39.

availability of Christ to his creatures. Schwöbel paraphrases Jenson on the point: "God's presence to creation is different in the word of the gospel and the sacraments and in the hearts of believers, different again in the creative presence that maintains the being of the whole of creation. However, all these modes of presence are not to be spatially differentiated; they follow the differentiation and relation of God's Trinitarian self-giving."[34]

Jenson's theory of culture is, once again, the outworking of his own Christology and trinitarian theology. Having deconstructed the inevitable Niebuhrian sequestration of Christ and culture, Jenson is now able to talk of Christ *in* culture. In the future, we may find ourselves able to talk of Christ *as* culture.

Christ *as* Culture: Comparing and Contrasting Tanner and Jenson

Jenson's determination to avoid dualism provides him with a similar starting point to that of Tanner. However, while Tanner is directed in this way by her reliance upon postmodern anthropological method, for Jenson the move is driven by his christological commitments. The extra-cultural realities of which theology speaks are not articulated by the theologian's ability to step outside of culture but rather are the result of the cultural revelation that God embodies in Christ. Therefore, in the same way that the theological language-game is made possible—with all its linguistic and extra-linguistic inferences—by God's embodiment as the Word, so too, the theological language, that we call culture, is activated by God's habitually cultural self-revelation.

Christians, Jenson reminds us, know Christ as a Jewish male, by the name of Jesus, who lived in Palestine in the first century and spoke Aramaic. Furthermore, "'Christ' is a title, and therefore is itself meaningful only within a particular culture, in this case the culture of Israel, The title 'Christ,' *Messiah,* has its use within Israel's politics, her cult, even her arts and architecture."[35] While Niebuhr himself noted that in Christology "there is no escape from culture," his mistrust of history

34. Schwöbel, "Christ and Culture," 118.

35. Jenson, "Christ as Polity," 323.

prevented him from making so direct a connection.[36] Jenson continues: "Thus it makes a logical tangle to speak of Christ 'and' culture abso-lutely, since by referring to Christ one is already invoking a specific culture, that of Israel. However Christ is related to other cultures or to the general human need to have a culture, the relation is *not* simply external; a relation between, say, Christ and Chinese culture is in itself a relation between Jewish cultures and Chinese culture."[37]

In Jenson thinking, God's people form an identifiable culture. Christ is identified in his incarnation, in the nation of Israel, in the church, and in the eschaton. All of these are cultural occurrences of God's identity in the person of Christ within a given community. These enculturations enable us not only to talk of Christ *in* culture but also of Christ *as* culture. While it may seem senseless to talk of "an indi-vidual person as himself a culture," Jenson reminds us that, "Christ's individuality is of a peculiar sort, indeed he is an individual at all only in a sense unique to him."[38] As the eternal Word of creation, God the Son becomes present in the words that his people share about him and thus, in the cultural converse which is the church, Christ is embodied as culture. Furthermore, under the scrutiny of Tanner's postmodern method, Jenson's theory holds up. Subjected to the questions posed earlier, Jenson is able to identify a distinctly Christian culture. Firstly, in Jenson, Christ has always been defined in social terms, or as an alterna-tive community. It is this communal identification that enables Jenson to give account of the pre-existent Christ within the Old Testament: "The pre-existence of Jesus Christ there belongs among other factors to his pre-existence in and as the nation of Israel. For Israel also is the human Son, whom God called out of Egypt as he would call Jesus the Son from the tomb."[39]

While as a community, Israel had much in common with her neighbors, no other culture could claim to be the "Son of YHWH," or a "light to the Gentiles." Jenson argues that our understanding of the Father's relationship with the Son is first rehearsed in the relationship

36. Niebuhr, *Christ and Culture*, 71.

37. Jenson, "Christ as Polity," 323.

38. Ibid., 325.

39. Ibid., 326.

between Israel and YHWH. In the gospel's defining moment, "what in Israel is scattered, both in the way of history and by sin, is gathered up in one Israelite," Jesus.[40] As Christ is defined socially in the people of Israel, so too, he can be identified in the culture of the church. As the body of Christ, the church represents the Son's availability to his creation in a culture he calls his own. "As Christ is the church, he is in the same or related sense a culture, the culture the church is."[41] As one culture among many, the church faces limits upon the extent of her assimilation. For instance, the Christian community cannot separate itself from the culture of Israel, for the church, by nature of its own distinct revelation and the one who it worships, is always a Jewish sect. To this end, the church has been impoverished and undermined when contemporary concerns have wedded her to the cultural zeitgeist. For example, Jenson notes the damage caused by the Western church's excessive and corruptive commitments to counter-ideologies. The Enlightenment's persistent drive towards autonomy, for instance, has often disintegrated the sociality vital to the church's cultural embodiment of Christ.[42]

Secondly, unlike Tanner, Jenson is able to assert Christ's cultural credentials in the behaviors and boundaries of the church. The earlier discussion concerning the Lord's Supper illustrated the difficulties thrown up by Tanner's questions; however, Jenson's position on the subject provides a far more helpful account. Prior to Jenson, the challenge concerned the lack of agreement over essential ingredients, the liturgical differences between the rites of different churches and the impact of these rulings upon sacramental efficacy. Jenson turns the problem on its head. It is not our remembrance or thanksgiving that authenticates the act in time but rather it is the promised presence of the Son. Jesus is present in the Eucharist, not through our own achievement or sacramental faithfulness and not through the boundaries that we have drawn up or adhered to, but rather through his promised presence by his Spirit.[43] In our remembrance of him, he remembers us and in this

40. Ibid.

41. Ibid., 325.

42. See the discussion on "The Church as Drama" in chapter 4 and Jenson's critique of Enlightenment perversions of the Eucharist.

43. This is not to say that these issues are unimportant to Jenson, "Eucharist" *dialog.*

act we become a truly Christian community. "The Eucharist promises: *there* is my body in the world, and you here eating and drinking commune in it. It promises: *there* is the actual historical church, and you are she. That the risen Christ is not present merely 'spiritually' is itself a vital promise of the gospel, and the one made specifically by the bread and cup."[44]

The authentication of our practices as Christ's body are simply not ours to give. The boundaries of Christian social practice are not, ultimately, the business of church councils, but rather rest with the one who can truly call himself the Head of the church. Christ has promised his presence to his church in order that his church might be available as his body in the world. In this, Christ exists as a culture amongst all other cultures. Once again, God is as good as his word. Thus, in the context of the Supper, when Christians ask about Christ's whereabouts, they can confidently proclaim that he has not left heaven to visit his people, and likewise neither have they left earth to join his heavenly host. In the Eucharist, insists Jenson, Christ is present and gives his body both to us and through us.

Jenson's portrayal of the *totus Christus* provides further insight into the boundaries between Christian and non-Christian cultures. While, in Jenson, Christ is permanently present to the church as his body, he is especially and momentarily present in certain acts in space and time, such as the sacraments. In the same way, although Christ is permanently present in the many cultures of the world as the creator and sustainer of all things, he is especially and momentarily present in the culture of the church, for this is his embodiment and availability to creation. Once again, the boundaries of such presence are God's to delineate. All this does not render the church passive in the authentication of her culture. For if Christ is made available in the community and culture of the church, then the considerations and decisions concerning the authentication of the church's practices is of critical importance to her mission. As Stanley Hauerwas has intimated, the specific mission that Jenson ascribes to the Christian community means that the church "must discipline her borders."[45] For to allow her members to disprove

44. *ST* 2:220.

45. Hauerwas, "Theology Overcomes Ethics," 262.

the church's mission would be also to deny her claim to the Spirit and thus undermine the ecclesial realization of Christ's body upon which the community is reliant. However, as in our last chapter, Jenson is reticent to assign great detail to his doctrine of apostasy. What we can say is that Christ, by his Spirit, remains the guarantor of God's presence within the culture of the church.[46]

Thirdly, in Jenson, Christ can be defined through the cultural continuities and commonalities of his people? As we have already witnessed in this chapter, theological accounts of culture often struggle to hold past and future together without favoring one or the other. Jenson's theory of culture, on the other hand, rhymes hope with history, the eschatological with the rabbinical, and the postmodern with the orthodox. Rather than contradict Tanner, Jenson confirms that the continuity of God's story is guaranteed retrospectively and with the benefit of hindsight. However, his thesis has little to do with theologians reconstructing revelation for their own purposes. For Jenson, God is to be found in the future and history is to be regarded as his own triune narrative. To this end, the story of creation is narrated by its subject from his own time and place of completion and perfection. This story is not open-ended, but rather awaits its full and certain grand finale. While eschatologically oriented, Jenson's theory of culture retains a comprehensive range of ontological referents. Experiments in establishing continuity, Jenson purports, are too caught up in relating the past to the present, and not concerned enough with transforming the present into God's future. The church is not merely a community of interpretation focused on ancient textual relics. The church is an eschatological community of liberation that "calls up as future the story of a particular man of the past."[47] Through his resurrection, Christ has transformed the church's congregants into citizens of the eschaton. We arrive once more at Jenson's ecclesial leitmotif: "Christ is eschatologically and so ecclesially what Augustine called the *totus Christus*: he is himself simply

---

46. As mentioned in the last chapter, Jenson's unexpanded notion of apostasy concerns his affirmation of the tradition's decision to excommunicate the heretics that threatened the very nature and mission of the church. *ST* 2:204–6.

47. *ETC*, 4.

as himself *and* he is himself one with his disciples, with the members of his body; and only as he is both is he indeed himself."[48]

Jenson's work makes talk of a distinctly Christian culture more viable. For Jenson, Christian culture is not merely a discussion concerning Christian identity but is, rather, a dialogue between the church and Christ and, consequently, between the Father, Son, and Spirit. In the *totus Christus,* the two complex realities of Christ and culture become one. In so doing, Jenson's program answers not one, but all three of Tanner's unanswered questions. In Jenson, the conversation that constitutes the church community represents both a christological embodiment of culture and the theological fulfillment of culture as a whole.

Conclusions

While Niebuhr, Tanner, and Jenson speak of theology and culture in different theological terms, all three theologians declare language, or converse, as the determining factor within their theories. In Niebuhr, we greet Christ and culture in dialogue one with another. In Tanner, the church has become a living discussion towards the nature of Christian identity. In Jenson, however, the discussion moves to a new level. Here, "culture is the mutual behavior of a group of persons in so far as in itself a coherent system of mutually determining signs."[49] In this guise, culture takes the form of a language-game played by human beings in their attempts to come to terms with, and experiment upon, reality.[50] Having earlier reflected upon the theological implications and insinuations of language, Jenson wastes no time in adopting culture within this overall scheme.

In Jenson, language and culture become joined. Language presupposes culture, and culture presupposes language. Thus, just as we cannot conceive of a form or mode of human existence without language, neither can we imagine an example of human community lacking in

---

48. Jenson, "Christ as Polity," 325.

49. Ibid., 324.

50. As we noted in the previous chapter, Jenson considers both linguistics and semiotics as part of one unified theory of language.

its own decipherable culture.[51] Within the temporal nature of reality, humans utilize the language of culture to orientate themselves within time. Likewise, humanity uses culture as a physical language by which to negotiate the realities of space. Through ceremonies, objects, signs, greetings, and symbols, culture provides visible words by which humans organize their experience.[52] Through the multiplicity of cultures and cultural forms, we give voice to the realities with which life presents us.

Jenson uses the connection between language and culture to close the circle. Here, culture has become the universal language used by humankind to identify and explain the world and our place within it. As all access to our past, present, and future is granted and achieved linguistically, so too it is mediated culturally. For Jenson, individual cultures and cultural-forms exist as reconstructions of, or experiments with, reality.[53] For example, in art we view a representation of reality through the pictorial imagination and spatial craft of the artist. In music, we apprehend the very temporal nature of reality in rhythm, tone, harmony, dissonance, tension, climax, and resolution. In theater, we witness a staging of reality through drama, narrative, plot, and personality. Likewise, locally determined and identified cultures use particular cultural forms to give voice to their own stories and situation. As Neuhaus suggests, in Jenson, "the cultural realities of the public square have their own integrity and legitimate urgencies, but they are not understood until they are understood theologically."[54] The theological implications of the view are prominent and have been identified by a number of prominent theologians. Among them is Paul Tillich: "Religion as ultimate concern is the meaning-giving substance of culture, and culture is the totality of forms in which the basic concern of religion expresses itself. In abbreviation: religion is the substance of all culture, culture is the form of religion."[55]

If culture is humanity's response to everyday questions and ultimate concerns, as rightly suggested by Tillich, then religion itself forms the substance of all cultural converse. While Jenson agrees that culture

51. Note our previous discussion of language and culture in chapter 3.
52. *ST* 2:58–61.
53. Jenson, "Christ as Culture 2," 69–71.
54. Neuhaus, "The Public Square," 238.
55. Tillich, *Theology of Culture*, 42.

is the form of an underlying religion, he is anxious to make a clear distinction between the religion (or ultimate concerns) expressed within culture and the christological cause and fulfillment of culture. In this, Jenson departs radically from the Tillichian notion of culture, a move that we will examine in far greater detail in our next chapter, on art. Jenson repeatedly reminds us that the most significant theological discovery of our own age rests in the identification and confession that the God of the gospel is not the god of whom human religion speaks. The impact of the discovery is important. For Jenson, the linguistic nature of culture is not the result of its connections with the human religion it embodies but rather is entirely contingent upon the one triune God who speaks creation into being. As the creative Word, the Son is God's speech in and to his diverse creation.[56] As we discussed in chapter 3, the words that humans use to address each other are both dependent upon, and an extension of, God's own creative word.[57] Having transposed this christological notion of language into his theory of culture, Jenson is able to reinforce his own view of the *totus Christus*. In the unique language-act, which is the gathering of the church, Christ himself is present as culture. At this point, we return once more to prayer. This founding and fulfilling language-act "leads us into what is perhaps the deepest mystery of" life within the community and culture that Christ embodies:[58] "'Thy Kingdom come soon,' we pray. 'Cure my child tomorrow,' we pray. Also believers have great difficulty believing that such giving advice to the Almighty is a sensible procedure. But we are to consider that when we pipe up 'Our Father . . .' it is not some group of hole-in-the-corner creatures speaking; it is the *totus Christus,* it is the second person of the Trinity addressing the first."[59]

The culture of the *totus Christus* is constituted in the living discourse of the church. In our stories and prayers, songs, and sermons, the church hears, shares, and proclaims the very Word of God. In these words, Christ is embodied in time and space as the creator, redeemer,

56. *ST* 1:165–66.

57. Note Jenson's correlation of humanity's morally obligating speech and God's creating speech in chapter 3.

58. Jenson, "Christ as Polity," 328.

59. Ibid., 328.

and perfector of reality. Through the theological utterance that comprises her communal life, the church joins the triune narrative within the time and space of history. These "utterances about God operate to posit an attitude to life exactly *as* narrative language."[60] As both the cause and content of the church's language-act, the Son, as the Word of God, provides the fulfillment of all language and culture. In him, and in the culture of his church, hope and history rhyme like nowhere else.

Towards the end of his life Niebuhr hoped that the dialogue between Christ and culture might refresh and reform the tired doctrines and symbols of the Christian church. "We note that the symbolism of the Scriptures is never static. In every age, among every people, old symbols are refreshed by the addition of new ones."[61] Niebuhr bemoaned the church's inability to say something new to those "who shake their heads when we speak to them in our foreign tongue."[62] In Jenson we have a new account of Christ as culture that may provide the kind of language that Niebuhr longed for. It falls to us now to examine the implications in the cultural life and language of the church and the world.

60. *KOTHF,* 108.

61. Niebuhr, *Theology, History and Culture,* 32.

62. Ibid., 30.

6

Changing Rooms:
Jenson on Art and Architecture

HAVING EXPLORED THE RELATIONSHIP between language and culture in our last chapter, we will now apply our findings to two particular cultural forms. In our discussion of art and architecture, we will consider how these cultural languages enable our grasp of space and reflect upon their importance within the life of the church as the *totus Christus*. For, just as space proved vital in understanding Jenson's account of God's relationship to the world, so art and architecture, the cultural employment of space, is vital in understanding the church as culture and, in this, the *totus Christus*.

Of all the art forms utilized by theology, and the cultural conversations instigated by the church, few have proved as significant as those of art and architecture. It is impossible to separate the theology of the church from the history of these disciplines. Over many centuries, the language of art and architecture has given voice to doctrine, brought Scripture to life, and provided a physical stage for the gospel's re-enactment. In return, as Jeremy Begbie points out, "Christian doctrine has profoundly affected the form, content, and development of the arts."[1] It appears surprising then that this language has been so neglected

---

1. Begbie, "Christ and the Cultures," 101.

by theologians. A point made with customary eloquence by Dorothy Sayers:

> The Church as a body has never made up her mind about the arts, and it is hardly too much to say that she has never tried. She has, of course, from time to time puritanically denounced the arts as irreligious and mischievous, or tried to exploit the Arts as a means to the teaching of religion and morals . . . And there have, of course, been plenty of writers on esthetics who happened to be Christians, but they seldom made any consistent attempt to relate their esthetic to the central Christian dogmas.[2]

Jenson's interest in art and architecture commences with the role that these art forms play in our grasp of space. If, as our second chapter suggested, creation is the space that God has for us, then the artist's interpretation of this reality is a supremely *theological* concern. For Jenson, all art and architecture is an experimentation upon created space. Having posited culture as our conversation concerning reality, we reflect now upon the place of art and architecture within this theological dialogue. Firstly, we will discuss the importance of fine art for our understanding of spatiality, and secondly, we will reflect upon the role of architecture in Christ's embodiment of the church as the *totus Christus*.

Alongside Jenson, we will also consider the work of Paul Tillich and Nicholas Wolterstorff. In Tillich we discover a bold account of the eschatological power of art, while in Wolterstorff we witness the multilayered ontology inherent any work. Having compared and contrasted these theories with Jenson's own observations, we will consider how art and architecture enable the church to become the changing room of reality. In addition to our three main interlocutors, our discussion will be enlivened by the insights of several other thinkers. Among them, are Jeremy Begbie, George Pattison, and Brian Horne.

---

2. Sayers, *Letters to a Post-Christian World*, 147–48.

Opening the Future: The Role of Art in Paul Tillich

"There must be few theologians," Jeremy Begbie suggests, "for whom art has been more important than Paul Tillich."[3] In addressing God as her lone subject of enquiry, Tillich declares, theology has confined secondary subjects, such as art and architecture, to the unnecessary or, even, the impossible. However, theology does not mean talk of God as one object alongside others but is rather, "talk of the manifestation of the divine in all beings and through all beings," and thus the language of art and architecture demands theological interpretation.[4] In his youth, Tillich dreamt of becoming an architect but by his late teens the call to philosophical theology had taken over. The space between these worlds is closer than we might imagine: "I decided to build in concepts and propositions instead of stone, iron, and glass. But building remains my passion, in clay and in thought, and as the relation of the medieval cathedrals to the scholastic systems shows, the two ways of building are not so far from each other. Both express an attitude to the meaning of life as a whole."[5]

Artistically enlivened during his time as a chaplain in World War I, Tillich's "concern with the concept of meaning," as James Luther Adams explains, "first came to the fore in connection with his interest in art."[6] For Tillich, the murals of the Sistine Chapel express a more eloquent interpretation of creation than is possible in the language of technical theology. Likewise, the Expressionists provide an insight into existence beyond that offered by analytical philosophy. For Tillich, art is a deeply theological language. Through the arts, he declares, this "meaning-reality, the ultimate, the deepest all-shattering and ever newly creating meaning reality" is made available to theology.[7] In every picture, Tillich proposes, "an ultimate concern is expressed, and . . . it is possible to

---

3. Begbie, *Voicing Creation's Praise*, 1.

4. Tillich, *On Art and Architecture*, 205–6.

5. Ibid., 221.

6. James Luther Adams is quoted in an essay "Tillich's Concept of the Protestant Era," published as an Afterword in Tillich, *The Protestant Era*, 298.

7. Ibid., 298.

recognize the unconscious theological character of it."[8] In this, Tillich's notion comes close to George Steiner's proposal that all art is dependent upon, and in some form projects, God's real presence: "Any coherent account of the capacity of human speech to communicate meaning and feeling is, in the final analysis, underwritten by the assumption of God's presence. I will put forward the argument that the experience of aesthetic meaning in particular, that of literature, of the arts, of musical form, infers the necessary possibility of this 'real presence.'"[9]

For both Tillich and Steiner, art equips people to recognize the transcendent nature of reality. Caught in the angst of our finitude, art emboldens our existence and enables us to reach towards the infinite. Art provides Tillich with a theological language for the description of reality. As the theologian deals with art theologically so too the artist deals with theology artistically. While the former analyzes and interprets the artist through words, the latter expounds theology through symbol. Through art, the human person realizes the complexity of his or her existence. Furthermore, caught between finite rest and infinite restlessness, the production of art becomes humanity's instinctive reaction to reality:

> The urge arises to express the essential unity of that which we are in symbols which are religious and artistic. Man creates the gods as symbols of that which has created him, the infinite from which he comes, from which he is separated and to which he is longing to return. In anticipation of the unity and the religious artistic expression of this anticipation, he wins the courage to take his finitude and the anxiety of his finitude upon himself. He wins the courage to be.[10]

According to Tillich, the artistic act comprises three specific tasks. Firstly, art opens up reality. Although science makes it possible to dissect and describe an object in atomic detail, its language cannot expound the object's inner meaning. While these hidden realities, Tillich

8. Tillich, *Theology of Culture*, 27.

9. Steiner, *Real Presences*, 3.

10. Tillich, *Art and Architecture*, 15.

suggests, resist the penetration of scientific cognition, they are power-fully probed by the artist. "When we look at the pictures of Van Gogh," Tillich argues, "We experience the power of being . . . We participate in it . . . Art makes us aware of something . . . which, without artistic intuition and creation, would remain covered forever."[11] Tillich's love of Expressionism is worthy of note. As Jeremy Begbie argues, his passion was driven by the movements' attempts to deconstruct a world of face-value appearances, and subsequently to reconstruct reality according to its own "spiritual values" and "inner truth."[12]

We arrive now at the second task of artistic activity in Tillich's thought, for having opened our eyes to reality, art goes on to *transform* it. The transformation is made possible by the two forms of reality contained within a work of art. The first represents the relative reality of normative experience, while the second comprises the absolute, or religious reality, which under girds our existence. The artist's "belief-ful realism" depicts this second underlying reality and thus transforms the viewer's previous perceptions. It is for this reason, Tillich suggests, that we frame historic eras by the artistic styles that accompanied them. To talk of the gothic, baroque, or renaissance period is not merely to recall the artistic trends of bygone days but rather to acknowledge the fact that art frames our vision of history. In Tillich's portrayal, the artist turns prophet, as he expresses, "the dynamics in the depths of society which come from the past and run toward the future."[13]

For Tillich, there is no imitation that is not transformation. An infinite gap separates the most imitative form of art from the reality it mimics, and subsequently, artistic form and natural form are never the same.[14] Through the artist's deeper depiction of reality, each onlooker becomes aware of his ultimate concern and transcends his previous lim-itations, finitudes and anxieties. In the art gallery, we become witnesses

11. Ibid., 15–16.

12. Begbie, *Voicing Creation's Praise*, 14–19. Begbie points out that Tillich's inter-pretation of expressionism is open to question.

13. Tillich, *Art and Architecture*, 29.

14. Ibid., 20.

of an "absolute reality in these relative things . . . they have become 'holy' objects," and art has become the media of divine revelation.[15]

Here, we arrive at the third role of artistic action in Tillich. The transformation of reality through the anticipation of "the absolute" enables the artist and his or her audience to transcend present possibilities. For while the spatial language of art reflects the many different realities of culture, one ultimate reality underlies every work. For Tillich, this inner meaning, which transcends both the artist and his object, is the power of art and the life-blood of metaphysics. This elaborate philosophy of meaning runs through the entire body of Tillich's work. Employing an important distinction between what he calls form (*Form*), import (*Gehalt*), and content (*Inhalt*), Tillich claims that all forms of existence are filled with a living import which points to the absolute as the ground of all being.[16] It is the synthesis of this form and import that constitutes the content of art, and hence each work of art conveys something of the theological nature of reality itself: "There is one element in every cultural creativity which is not an element beside others, but the substance of all the others, namely, religion . . . I speak of religion as a state of being ultimately concerned. Religion in this universal sense is valid of religion, as well as of non-religion, and it is the substance of culture. It gives meaning to all cultural creations."[17]

The revelatory power of art directs us towards the meaningful beauty and unconditional nature of absolute reality. For in Tillich, each work of art contains the meaning of the particular and the universal. It is this ability to mutually portray finite and infinite realities that generates art's offer of transcendence. The claim holds a soteriological significance. "I was standing before one of the round Madonna paintings of Botticelli," Tillich reflects. "In a moment . . . there was opened to me the meaning of what a painting can reveal. It can open up a new dimension of being."[18] In its unique expression and projection of ultimate concern, art anticipates the possibility of salvation.[19] To anticipate

15. Tillich, *Protestant Era*, 299.

16. Ibid., 298–99.

17. Tillich, *Art and Architecture*, 22.

18. Ibid., 204.

19. Ibid., 21.

such salvation is, for Tillich, to lay hold of it. But how, one might ask, does Tillich square this artisitic soteriology with his Christian faith? As Begbie argues, in Tillich, there lies a central mimesis between the artist's projection of the absolute and the portrayal of Christ within the New Testament. In theological terms, the Gospels provide a gallery of christological portraiture.[20] In these depictions of Jesus of Nazareth, the gospel portrayal of the incarnation takes on the form of an expressionist painting. For here, Tillich suggests, Jesus' surface traits are not imitated naturalistically nor reproduced as in photography. Neither are they idealized by the painter's own notion of beauty, but rather they express an encounter with Christ.[21]

In Tillich, we witness a compelling account of the eschatological power and possibilities of art. However, as pre-empted in our preceding chapter, an effective formulation of the language of culture requires both eschatological vision and ontological support. For Tillich, this element is provided by the artist's use of symbolism. The artistic language that transforms and transcends reality comprises a complex vocabulary of artistic symbols.[22] As with a sign, artistic symbols point beyond themselves. More than signs, they participate in the very meaning and power that they symbolize. These symbols, he suggests, cannot be invented, as they are reliant upon pre-existing connections with reality. It is the internal ontology of symbolism, Tillich suggests, which provides art with its unique revelatory status and eschatological possibility. As employed by the artist, these symbols pries open our souls in order that we might experience their absolute content: "Symbols with these four characteristics have a double-edged character, or a double-edged function. The one function is to open up, to reveal something which otherwise does not enter into our consciousness. The other side is to use some aspects of reality . . . in order to provide material for the symbolization of that which transcends everything finite. In doing so, symbols at the same time draw the realm from which they are taken into the realm of the unconditional which they symbolize."[23]

20. Begbie, *Voicing Creation's Praise*, 54–56.

21. Tillich, *Systematic Theology*, 2:133.

22. Tillich, *Art and Architecture*, 31–38.

23. Ibid., 37.

For Tillich, the artist has limited power where the language of symbol is concerned. For, in most cases, symbol is intuitively projected onto his work. While symbol provides art with an ontology, there appear few means by which we can analyze or verify these aspects in detail. At this point, a problem arises. If the eschatological reality which art conveys is not verifiable through a set of identifiable ontological referents, then how can art's claim upon the ultimate be secured? The implications for a theology of artistic language appear particularly undesirable. For while an eschatological vision of reality is inherent to the Christian faith, we are also provided with a series of ontological inputs by which to evaluate any eschatological claim or occurrence. Without these adequate checks and balances, the very heart of Christian theology comes under threat. For instance, what is to prevent the discovery of a religion that perfectly supports Tillich's theory of art and ultimate concern, while simultaneously denying Jesus as Lord? Within the Tillichian artistic domain, pantheism and natural religion would both seem to offer themselves as adequate, if not preferred alternatives to the Christian faith.[24]

In, *Art Modernity and Faith,* George Pattison calls upon theologians to ponder "the strange miracle . . . of visual art, and spend time in the space which this strange miracle opens up."[25] Few theologians have responded to this call like Tillich. Despite the flaws in his program, Tillich has performed a pioneering service in his identification of art as a theological language. In Tillich, we discover a grand unifying vision, a profound appreciation of art, an elaborate metaphysical system, an expansive eschatology, an impoverished ontology and a calamitous view of history. The overlap between this and our critique of Hegel in chapter 1 is notable. Later, we will discuss the theologian whom Tillich himself

24. Tillich's problem in this regard is as much to do with his Christology as it is to do with his theory of art. Like Niebuhr before, Tillich fails to fully establish the Son as both the Christ of faith and the Jesus of history and, as a result, struggles to maintain Christ as the absolute ground of all being and ultimate concern. As Begbie has pointed out, the "weakness in Tillich's Christology . . . has serious consequences for his view of art." Begbie, *Voicing Creation's Praise,* 56.

25. Pattison, *Art, Modernity and Faith,* 176.

introduced to Hegel.[26] However, before we consider Robert Jenson's theory of art, we will turn to another.

Unveiling the Past: The Place of Art in Nicholas Wolterstorff

In *Works and Worlds of Art,* Nicholas Wolterstorff outlines his own theory. Since the eighteenth century, Wolterstorff argues, Western society has increasingly limited the arts to the domain of aesthetic contemplation; a move first instigated by the Romantics, or the "first secular analysts and critics of modernity."[27] The unifying tendencies of Romanticism defied the cursed fragmentation of instrumental rationality and boldly proclaimed life as an imitation of art. As "socially other," the artist's work came to be considered solely for its own sake. However, as Wolterstorff points out, "aesthetic contemplation is neither the invariant purpose behind the creation of works of art, nor always what is most worth doing with them."[28] The restriction of art to the realm of aesthetic contemplation, Wolterstorff suggests, has privatized the discipline, exalted high art above all other forms, favored the wealthy and educated, and failed to recognize the full cultural importance of art itself. Pushed to its furthest limits, and in this aesthetic guise, art becomes an object of salvation. To quote Max Weber: "Art becomes a cosmos of more and more consciously grasped independent values which exist in their own right, Art takes over the function of a this-worldly salvation . . . It provides a *salvation* from the routines of everyday life, and especially the increasing pressures of theoretical and practical rationalism."[29]

In this, Wolterstorff suggests, art has become a surrogate god. When the secular religions of political revolution and technological advance fail, the modern secular cultural elite take refuge in the religion of aestheticism.[30] With this, Wolterstorff attacks that which Tillich held dear. For the Romantics, art transports us from the dusty reality of daily

26. Jenson has remarked that his first encounter with Hegel occurred at a lecture given by Tillich. Interview with author, (Princeton, 16 June 2005).

27. Wolterstorff, *The Theological Significance of Going to Church and Leaving.*

28. Wolterstorff, *Works and Worlds of Art,* xii.

29. Weber, *Essays in Sociology,* 342.

30. Wolterstorff, *Art in Action,* 50–51.

living to the sublime heights of aesthetic exaltation. Having shut down our human interests and arrested our memories and anticipations, we are free to experience new life. In the mode of aesthetic contemplation fine art offers an alternative route to redemption and worship, and thus forms a fully functioning religion. The quest for an ontology of art now assumes an even greater urgency: "The Protestant view which sees every work of art as expressing the Religion (i.e., ultimate concern) of its maker, will not do as a comprehensive approach to the arts. Yet there is something of fundamental importance to be learned from this view— namely, that there is always *a world behind* the work, of which the work is an expression; and that often the religion of the artist, or his particular version of secularism, has a central role in that world."[31]

Wolterstorff's argues that all art be understood as an instrument of action. Wherever it occurs—and as Wolterstorff reminds us, it occurs everywhere—art manifests intent, purpose, response, and action. Furthermore, in its commission, creation, and reception, art provokes action. In every time and place, Wolterstorff suggests, we can identify styles and forms of art that are particular to that context. Works of art are, in this regard, an embodiment of the society in which they occur. The activities employed in the production of these artifacts, Wolterstorff argues, are therefore characteristic of the community that produced them.[32] The argument appears lost among many contemporary art theorists. However, the placing of art among the "practical virtues" of scholasticism, as Brian Horne points out, underlined that "its orientation is towards doing, not to the pure inwardness of being. Art is concerned with 'making.' We might call this craft."[33] Along similar lines, Jenson argues that a rightful "understanding of artistic activity is recognition that an artist must labor to construe his possible world, that he cannot just decree it; he must work on something."[34] It is for this reason that the products of this process are called, "works" of art.

31. Ibid., 88–89.
32. Ibid., 21.
33. Horne, "Divine and Human Creativity," 138.
34. Jenson, "Christ as Art," 71.

Through his labor, Wolterstorff asserts, the artist creates a world. But what lies behind this world?[35] All works of art, Wolterstorff argues, exist as real worlds in that they present a "state of affairs." These states of affairs are anchored to entities in the world, making the artist's projection ontologically verifiable. For example, Monet's paintings of the Palace of Westminster rely upon the existence of such a building and location. Yet, Wolterstorff's hypothesis is not limited to realist artworks, for while the overall effect of a surrealist painting by Salvador Dali may appear confounding, the work still exhibits references to recognizable realities. With some certainty we can make out a clock that has melted, or an elephant with the legs of a giraffe. These verifiable entities are unavoidable, as no artist can present an idea or object that is external to his spatial experience. From this, Wolterstorff concludes, that all art conforms to a fundamental ontological principle:[36] "*There being unicorns* did not belong to the pictorial situation of the south-western Indians; but *there being condors* did. *There being such a god as Olmec* did not belong to the pictorial situation of the European medieval painters; but *there being unicorns* did."[37]

As Steiner points out, even the most unrecognizable depiction conforms to Wolterstorff's ontological principle. "All representations, even the most abstract, infer a rendezvous with intelligibility."[38] For Wolterstorff, the world projected in a work of art not only includes a state of affairs but is in itself a state of affairs. This state of affairs may be considered possible, as in Monet's paintings of Westminster, or impossible, as in the surrealist depictions of Dali. However, each work projects a reality, even if it rejects actuality. It is this interpretation of reality that connects art so closely to religion: "[In a work of art] we are confronted with the obvious fact that the artist is not merely projecting a world which has caught his private fancy, but a world true in significant respects to what his community believes to be real and important. Since in most communities it is the religion of the people which above all is

35. Wolterstorff, *Worlds and Works*, 200.

36. Ibid., 126. Surrealism: The title of the genre confirms Wolterstorff in his thinking. The artist here, projects a reality on top of the reality already perceived.

37. Ibid., 303.

38. Steiner, *Real Presences*, 139.

important in the their lives, this implies that much of the world's representational art is explicitly *religious* art."[39]

Artists continually import, both consciously and unconsciously, their experience of spatial reality into the worlds they create. As a result, even the most fictitious and fantastic work of art betrays its ontology. It is this ability to retain and project the real world that enables art to concretize the identity and spirituality of a community. Humanity, as Wolterstorff suggests, rarely restricts religious belief, historical remembrance, or political aspiration to the noetic realm, choosing instead to substantiate these realities in stories and dramas, in song and dance, and in painting and sculpture.[40] "If the spiritual dimension in art is related first of all to its form," as Richard Harries points out, "it is secondly due to art's capacity to put before us what simply is."[41] Where Tillich's eschatological theory of art is illustrated by the Expressionists, Wolterstorff's ontological approach is exemplified by the artists of the Renaissance: "It was consistently their goal . . . to construct their paintings that we would see the objects as *behind* the plane of the painting's surface rather than in front of it. The picture was to be seen as a window onto the reality beyond. In that way they differed from the Byzantine artists, who wished their designs to be seen as objects in front of the plane of the surface."[42]

Wolterstorff rejects the semiotic approach, taken by Tillich, choosing rather to develop a theory of art as speech, or language-acts, thus categorizing art as a cultural language-game.[43] In this, he stands alongside a range of philosophers, art theorists, and theologians, including Wittgenstein, Austin, and Searle. Drawing also on the work of Kendall Walton, Wolterstorff suggests that the objects and images used by the artist and audience, act as pictorial props by which prospective players engage in this spatial language-game.[44] Acknowledging the limitations of a purely symbolic or semiotic approach, Wolterstorff's theory pro-

---

39. Wolterstorff, *Worlds and Works*, 358.

40. Ibid., 360.

41. Harries, *Art and the Beauty of God*, 107.

42. Wolterstorff, *Works and Worlds*, 289.

43. Ibid., 200. See the earlier discussions of language-games in Jenson and Wittgenstein (chapter 3) and cultural theories in Jenson and Tanner (chapter 5).

44. Wolterstorff, *Works and Worlds*, 318.

vides visual art with a more sophisticated array of linguistic resources. He illustrates his theory with reference to an altarpiece by Jan van Eyck.[45] The painting in question features a lamb at its center, but Wolterstorff points out that the reality projected is that of Christ. However, no one would infer from this that Christ has the physical properties of a lamb but rather that the artist is projecting both a literal lamb and the real Christ. In this, the move from mysterious symbol, as the utterance of the unutterable, to metaphor, as the existence of a complex reality within in a special language-act, offers the artist and the audience a far greater range of grammar and vocabulary by which to interpret the world at hand: "If the artist then produces a design which can be seen by his audience as a three-sided empty box but which they will tend to see as a cube, and if the artist knows about this tendency on their part and does nothing to try to counteract it, then what he does is to be counted as picturing a cube . . . Essentially the same thing holds for language."[46]

In art, we are drawn into a unique language-game that cannot be played with words.[47] While Wolterstorff's language of art is ontologically weighted, his theory bears eschatological implications. In Wolterstorff's theory, the artist assumes a prophetic role, for she or he "is to describe, not the thing that has happened, but a kind of thing that might happen."[48] As in Tillich, the language-games that artists and their audience engage in transform our own perceptions of reality. Wolterstorff concludes:

> I have been pointing out some of the ways in which the action of world-projection is involved in the lives of us human beings, both artists and beholders. The artist, by virtue of projecting a world, alters or confirms us in our beliefs, this in turn having ripple-effect throughout our lives. He alters or confirms us in our abilities and tendencies. He evokes emotions in us. He gives to us aesthetic

45. The altarpiece is to be found in St Bavo, in Ghent.

46. Ibid., 304.

47. Harries, *Art and Beauty,* 110. Following on from the dialogue concerning his appropriation of language and timelessness in chapter 3, it should be stated that for Wittgenstein, works of art draw their perspective of reality from eternity. Wolterstorff is not explicit to this extent.

48. Wolterstorff, *Works and Worlds,* 155.

satisfaction, and delight in observing how well he has met the demands and resolved the problems of his craft. He gives expression to his own self.[49]

Aside from the comments above, Wolterstorff devotes little time to the eschatological nature of artistic language. Although not blind to the possibility, Wolterstorff remains decidedly reticent in assigning any revelatory qualities to the worlds that artists project. Where in Tillich we encounter a profoundly artistic eschatology at the expense of ontology, in Wolterstorff the dilemma is inverted. Having provided us with useful foundations, a closer comparison of the work of Tillich and Wolterstorff with that of Jenson, may provide a way forward.

Space for Time: Architecture and Eschatology in Jenson and Tillich

Having appraised the work of Tillich, we come now to Robert Jenson's treatment of art and architecture. In comparing their work, a range of common traits and commitments come to light. Both are Lutheran theologians from the Hegelian tradition, both were trained in Europe and have worked, mostly, in the United States. Both have made use of philosophy in the development of a distinct and wide ranging style of systematic theology, and both can rightly claim the title, "theologian of culture." Of particular significance to our present study is their shared concern for the concept of time. Like Jenson after him, Tillich considers the classical subordination of time to space to be the calamity of cosmology. For when time becomes secondary to space, teleology is sacrificed for materiality.[50]

Prioritizing time over space, Tillich, like Jenson, relocates space as the presence of time. Consequently, Tillich concludes, "If one has found space, that is, presence, then the power of time, the power with which

49. Ibid., 367.

50. Tillich forces us to choose from three equally unattractive realities. Firstly, Paganism—the eternal battle for territory between countless inferior gods. Secondly, Nationalism—the equation of our god with the god of our nation, place, and race. Thirdly, Mysticism—the final resting place of Greek philosophy and a consequent imprisonment in the ever turning cycle of history. Tillich, *Theology of Culture*, 31–35.

human beings create time for themselves, drives one into the future."[51] When the tradition reverses this, demoting time under space, the latter becomes the container in which things exist rather than the context in which living things find their existence. For Tillich and Jenson, the language of art and architecture does not only project objects in space but rather communicates the temporal-spatial nature of reality itself.

The church's tendency to negate time is illustrated by Tillich's critique of Protestant architecture. Here, architects forsake artistry for its polar opposite, namely imitation. When the temporal and teleological nature of reality is forgotten, the church settles for the cyclical repetition and re-creation of familiar spatial objects. Rather than anticipating a new creation, our stayed architectural forms are an attempt to deny time's passing and to contain the old world. However, in this rejection of the temporal reality of artistic language, not to mention the eschatological expectation of the kingdom, the church becomes artistically and theologically dishonest. "The failure of imitation," Tillich declares, "is that it is not born out of the creative inspiration of the builders of the original work. Imitation comes out of the scientific study of things done in the past. They are produced without the unconscious, symbol-creating side of the artistic process."[52]

As the meeting place of artistic theory and philosophical theology, Tillich demands that Christian art and architecture reveal what is coming as opposed to what has been. He rails against the church's perversion of the "beautiful," for this is often defined by the evocation of the past, as opposed to the promise of the future. In one drastic pronouncement, Tillich calls upon his sainted Expressionists to provide art's redemption: "I believe that the word *expressiveness* must, at least for thirty years from now, replace the desecrated word *beautiful*, desecrated most by religious art at the end of the nineteenth century."[53]

While initially resonating with Tillich, Jenson soon turns on his colleague. The divergence concerns the relationship between art, architecture, and ultimate concern. Jenson agrees that a predilection for imitative art has caused the church to dwell in her past and has thus

51. Tillich, *Art and Architecture*, 85.

52. Ibid., 223.

53. Ibid.

risked the rejection of God's future. Architectural imitation, he insists, has resulted in the erection of mini-mock-Gothic cathedrals jarring against the background of a contemporary world. At best, the choice between modern and traditional architecture has become a matter of personal taste or communal preference. In confusing art with imitation, the church has exchanged her defining teleological drive for iteration and repetition. Jenson's dislike for imitation stretches beyond his distaste for much church architecture.

Jenson's précis of the eighth-century controversy concerning icons within in the Orthodox Church proves enlightening at this point. The theological road to iconoclastic art and imitation is, Jenson states, paved by Origen and the image-concept by which he "serves to express faith in creation and salvation through Christ."[54] The problem here concerns Origen's philosophical sources: "Where did Origen get this key concept of image? Ultimately, of course, it is a fundamental myth quite probably co-temporal with the human race. But the historical source was Plato."[55] In Origen's characterization, God becomes the divine craftsman who manufactures reality according to his timeless pattern. Thus, the world becomes a work of art, or an imitation of the divine. From here, all earthly artistry is perceived as the imitation of the divine and timeless image branded invisibly upon creation. Jenson illustrates the point by emphasizing the lack of perspective and the golden environment utilized in Eastern icons of the Christ. While Tillich might well interpret such reconstruction as an attempt at honest expression, for Jenson the move is driven by a Platonic portrayal of Christ as "sheer being," rather than "historical reality." Jenson vehemently protests against this timeless quest and its consequent promotion of a pagan conception of deity. As before, theological formulations which contract God outside of time, place the church in an ontological and eschatological deficit and thus she commences her descent into the realms of religion.[56] Jenson here returns to his favorite parable, comparing the man who built more barns in a vain attempt to defy time, with the church's cultural investment in

54. Jenson, "Christ–Dogma and Christ-Image," 147.

55. Ibid., 148.

56. Wolterstorff also points out that, like Tillich, Protestant accounts of art often use religion as their starting point. Wolterstorff, *Art in Action*, 84–85.

a similar insurance policy. Initially reassured by familiar buildings and imitative art, we forget that we have been fooled out of our trinitarian faith by the timeless gods of religion.

The irony for Jenson, as he points out in an essay entitled, "God, Space and Architecture," is that the god of human religion has little in common with spatial art-forms. For he himself is not experienced as a spatial reality. Rather, he "is experienced as the one in whom we find what we vainly seek in things in space, as the fulfillment of spatiality. He is the posit of the existential meaning of space."[57] He is changeless and therefore exists only as a pure and perfect presence. Likewise, this pagan deity is not a temporal reality for he lives outside of time and, as such, is an "unassailably present being." All this, declares Jenson, "is the solution of religion—and the God of religion is therefore the Absolute Presence. His mode of life is the *nunc simul,* the all-already-now-at-once of eternity."[58]

Despite his lack of spatial embodiment and temporal manifestation, the god of religion is often experienced analogously to spatial-temporal relations. Hence, we experience his presence as closeness and his transcendence as distance. Much church architecture follows this ill-advised pattern. Roman Catholic churches function as theaters for the holy, structured around a table with bread and wine that, with the architecture, provides stage for Christ's presence. During the Mass one finds oneself far off, almost lost in the transcendent heights of a vaulted ceiling. Later, in the Eucharist, we draw near enough to touch and taste the one who seemed beyond us only moments ago. Protestant churches, on the other hand, function as lecture halls for the word. This scene is set for sounds, rather than sight. The building is structured for a sacred discourse for, here, faith comes by *hearing.* Lutherans, Jenson confesses, have made a clumsy combination of the two. Like Tillich before him, Jenson calls on the church to foster new forms and styles of architecture. In particular, he argues, church architecture should mark Christianity out as the polar opposite of human religion. Something that her propensity for Gothic architecture makes it hard to do: "In Gothic churches the structure itself draws us through God's distance to his presence. Gothic

57. *ETC,* 11.
58. Ibid., 11.

architecture synthesizes all the means we have discussed for providing spatiality for the God of religion; it is the perfect religious architecture, and our hankering for it in religious moments is a sound, if reprehensible, intuition."[59]

From hereon, the conflict between Jenson and Tillich mounts. In fact, Jenson's theology of the arts could be construed as an outright attack upon Tillich's notion of ultimate concern. In each age, Jenson argues, the church discovers something new and peculiar about the gospel. "The discovery of our age is that the God about whom the gospel speaks is not simply the same as the God of religion—indeed, that he is his antithesis."[60] Christian worship often appears empty because the building in which it occurs is structured around a god whose existence is demolished by the gospel. For Jenson, the gospel is a call to faith in the future, and hence the God of this gospel is not an absolute or changeless presence, but rather the one who is always coming to us. "The present reality of this God, his being *now* for us, is therefore not a quasi-spatial nearness but rather the *event* of this word that opens the future being spoken."[61] The God of the gospel does not exist in the now, as analogous to things in time and space, but rather happens in time and space. As a result, God's separation from us is not determined spatially, but rather temporally and as such his presence is exactly what we do so that his space is not a different space from the one we occupy as we worship him:[62] "The space provided for the worship of this God, for his present, must be a space for this action, for the telling and acting out of the gospel. It must, that is, be wholly a stage. And there must be no auditorium, for here there are no spectators, here the telling and acting out is done not for the worshipers but between the worshipers; here the place of God is not a different place from that of the worshipers."[63]

Jenson calls upon church architects to design new church buildings in line with the theological discovery of our era, and challenges

59. Ibid., 12.

60. Ibid., 12.

61. Ibid., 13.

62. See the discussions concerning God's space for creation in chapter 2 and Christ's subsequent embodiment of the church as the *totus Christus* in chapter 4.

63. Ibid., 13.

church leaders to continually reshape the environments in which they lead worship. In this way, the church is transformed into a changing room, where each week the temporal reality of the gospel is spatially present through the endless variations of its own enactment. This use of space, Jenson claims, should not direct the congregation to a holy location but to each other. For it is here, in the community who are called his body, that Christ is made present among as. Jenson continues: "The whole idea of a common focus . . . is exactly what we must overcome in our church architecture. For God's present is exactly the moment of our action; the space that action takes up. A space for worship is the capsule of a moment."[64]

For Jenson, the reality that Christian art and architecture must project is not that of an ultimate concern but rather the temporal-spatial embodiment of the resurrected Christ.[65] While Tillich's theory leaves us caught between Christology and existential natural theology, Jenson provides a more solid grounding for the theology of art and architecture. Furthermore, his christological approach may resolve the Tillichian problem. Were we to understand ultimate concern as the creating word that God has revealed in Christ and his church then Tillich's theory may well obtain an adequate ontology by which to secure its position within Christian theology.

The Real World: Art and Ontology in Jenson and Wolterstorff

In analyzing the ways in which works of art project reality, both Jenson and Wolterstorff utilize language. A closer comparison with Wolterstorff's theory of art proves beneficial at this point. As in Wolterstorff, Jenson's linguistic account stresses the importance of ontology. "A concern for communication in the arts is a concern that the arts remain language, that is, that in stretching forward to the future, they do not lose hold of the past, do not cease to talk about the world that already is."[66] Jenson's concern betrays a deep-seated mistrust of the

64. Ibid., 14.

65. Had he discovered a more christological interpretation of religion as ultimate concern, Tillich's own theology of art might, have retained a more Christian character.

66. Ibid., 3.

avant-garde. His discomfort in this is not dissimilar from Wolterstorff's. Wolterstorff uses this genre as an illustration of the easy obfuscation of, "so called," high-art. In its constant craving for novelty, innovation, and new language, Wolterstorff suggests, the art world bewilders its audience with a rapid promotion of discontinuity.[67]

Art, in Jenson, takes the form of a linguistic exercise concerning the nature of time and space. Hence, the language of art enables the artist to experiment with reality and to posit a possible world. Prior to the modern artistic era, Jenson proposes, fine art focused upon a world of objects salient in space and thus well adapted to different subjects. In this Cartesian domain, space can be grasped, contained, acted upon, and manipulated by the artist. More recently the postmoderns have deconstructed this world as an unnecessary and oppressive bourgeois construct. As Jenson points out, the deconstruction of reality that we attribute to postmodern philosophy was first attempted artistically by modern artists such as Picasso.[68] Through their experiments, twentieth-century artists taught the Western world that the Cartesian "depiction [of reality] was only one possible world, for if it had been simply the 'real' world, it could not have been deconstructed," in the first place.[69] "Modern art was from the beginning," according to Pattison, "engaged in the . . . critique of established reality."[70] As the product of a revolutionary age, modern art provided a multifaceted reconstruction of the world. However, as Jenson himself points out, this process of radical artistic reconstruction is no new phenomena:

> Looking perhaps at a seventeenth-century portrait, one often has . . . the feeling that if one could contrive to move a bit sidewise . . . one could see behind the figure . . . But, of course, pictorial representation, even sculpture, can locate

67. Wolterstorff, *Art in Action*, 28–29.

68. Jenson helpfully points out that what is referred to as "modern art" relates more directly to the philosophies of postmodernity than it does to those of modernity. Jenson, "Christ as Art," 70. For Jenson, artists such as Picasso and musicians such as Schöenberg, anticipated the philosophical breakthrough ahead of their philosopher contemporaries.

69. Ibid., 70.

70. Pattison, *Art, Modernity, Faith*, 1.

figures in space in quite other ways than as salient objects
in a space projected as a subject's field of vision . . . Thus
the figures in a medieval window are all confined to their
flat surface, and are determined to remain so in despite
of any maneuvers by an apprehending subject; nor will it
do to explain this with an inability of the artisans . . . as
the impressionists were to teach us, the world can, seemingly . . . be construed with only the haziest of internal
boundaries.[71]

The possible worlds construed in art are not simply limited by, or
contained within, the work's frame. The worlds projected by the artist, Jenson argues, mediate our own vision of spatial reality. Jenson is
anxious to affirm the ontological reality of these experimental worlds.
As possible worlds, these experiments rely upon a complex set of contingencies imported from the artist's own experience. In the case of
modern art, the artist's autonomous drive to create new language can, at
times, render her work as linguistically bankrupt. If the artist loses her
grip on the past, she loses the ability to communicate meaningfully and
thus her activity is no longer language.[72] As a result, Jenson declares,
much of the "art sold or exhibited . . . in the last thirty years . . . is the
product of deliberate metaphysical nihilists, who . . . if they can be said
to construe an alternative world, construe a void."[73] The question arises
then as to how we come to validate, or verify the realities projected
within art? "One should note the congruence of this question with that
posed by postmodern theorists of *language*, who argue that texts fail
to mediate any 'presence' other than themselves, so that finally a text is
only the indefinite set of its interpretations, there being no standard by
which to rate them."[74]

Jenson's ontology drives us further back than Wolterstorff's, trans-
ferring us from a philosophical analysis to a theological formulation.

71. Jenson, "Christ as Art," 69–70.

72. *ETC*, 7.

73. Jenson, "Christ as Art," 71. In this vein, both Jenson and Wolterstorff make
reference to Duchamp's exhibiting of a urinal as the antithesis of art. Wolterstorff, *Art
in Action*, 62; Jenson, "Christ as Art," 72.

74. Ibid., 71.

Within all works of art, Jenson suggests, there lies a "standard world." This world represents creation as the creator views and intends it. As the ultimate and accurate view of reality, the standard world constitutes the sum of created time and space, of divine and human activity and of hope and history. Access to this world is only available directly to the creator. While artists do not enjoy unmediated access to it, the very language they use to project reality ontologically presupposes this standard world. In his attempt to understand and expound the world presented to him, the artist projects a possible version of the creator's own blueprint. In this act, we witness reality as mediated through human activity and as mandated by the creator. For if "the standard world were immediately available to us, there would be no possibility of our making art—God the Artist, . . . would be the only artist."[75] All art, then, becomes a sacred and timely experiment with created space. In relation to current philosophical and artistic theories, Jenson's point is unfashionable, to say the least. "The attempt to sever the connection between the realm of art and that of the sacred," Horne suggests, dates back to the start of the eighteenth century and is now so accepted that even mention of the fact appears 'trite.'"[76]

There is one thing upon which all three of our subjects are agreed and that is the existence of a real or standard world that, while only immediately present to God the creator, forms the only basis from which all art proceeds. Henceforth, the initiation of a secular-sacred divide in the realm of the arts, by which any reference to absolute reality is refused, is both theologically and artistically fatal. It is along these lines that Philip Sherrard proclaims the impossibility of the "avant-garde". "There can be no such thing," he argues, "for the simple reason that there is nothing of which one can be *avant* or in the rear."[77] The classification is bankrupt. Harries reinforces the point saying, "The capacity to attend to what is before us, to attend to the quiddity—the very essence of a thing as it makes itself visible to us—is basic to the [whole] artistic enterprise."[78]

75. Ibid., 71.

76. Horne, "Art: A Trinitarian Imperative?," 80.

77. Sherrard, *The Sacred in Life and Art*, 49.

78. Harries, *Art and Beauty*, 106.

The denial of reality, Jenson argues, although common in contemporary thought, runs contrary to Judaeo-Christian theology. With this revelation, we have reason to believe in a standard world supplied by the creator, and consequently our artistic experiments proceed in one way or another from his reality. This confession significantly affects our notion of human creativity: "Christians and Jews . . . know there is God, and even what he is like. And so they know there is a standard world, the one he, as we uniquely say, 'creates.' Or, looking from the other side, Christians and Jews know that artists are not creators, not even co-creators—whatever such beings might be."[79]

Jenson's differentiation between what are standard and possible realities provides us with a sophisticated theological explication of the artistic process. Through the arts, Jenson exposits a postmodern account of reality while upholding a realist epistemology. By working on the world that actually *is*, the artist experiments with *possible* worlds. These worlds remain only possible because the artist is not God, and thus cannot create out of nothing. As a result, each aspect of the language-act or experiment that we call art is irrevocably tied to creation in its mediated form. While the "real world" maintains its presence within the projection, it eludes the immediate apprehension of anyone save God himself. It is, as Horne notes, this mediated experience of creation which forces humans into the act of artistry in the first place. As God alone exists in a state of absolute freedom, he is the only being who has the option not to create. "His creature, on the other hand, . . . possesses only relative freedom and is subject to the necessity of creation. Not to do so would be to refuse the conditions of his very being."[80] Wolterstorff illustrates the point:

> [The artist's] . . . business is to bring forth an expression of himself in the form of a new creation. In distinction from God, however, that requires struggle. God creates in sovereign, untrammeled freedom. But confronting the artist is an actuality which exists apart from his will, threatening him with constriction: the constricting actuality of aes-

79. Jenson, "Christ as Art," 71.
80. Horne, "Art," 85–86.

thetic norms, the constricting actuality of artistic and social traditions, the constricting actuality of the institution
of high art itself, the constricting actuality of materials, the
constricting actuality of the fact that unless the artist finds
acceptance for his work he cannot live.[81]

The paper that we have quoted in the paragraphs above is not entitled, "Christian Art," or "Christ in Art," but rather, "Christ *as* Art." As
with culture, Jenson's theology of art is yet another demonstration of his
trinitarian Christology and immanentist ecclesiology. For Jenson, the
Son, through whom all things were made, represents the Father's artistic
experiment with a possible world. As temporal-spatial creatures within
this possible world, our knowledge of the real world is mediated to us in
the gospel of the Son, as the experiment of the Father. The "real world"
will elude us 'til our dying day, however in the mean time, we are free
to experiment upon this world through our own artistic activities and
cultural conversations. A direct application of Jenson's notion is found
in an essay devoted to the use of images in Christian worship entitled,
"Christ–Dogma and Christ–Image."[82] Firstly, Jenson purports that Jesus
is the legitimate subject for works of art. Unlike Tillich, Jenson's justification is historically grounded in the incarnation. Artistic portrayals
of Jesus, and the Christ-event, are to be considered as extensions of the
depictions through which God has chosen to reveal himself. Like the
baking of bread for the Eucharist or the translation of the Bible, this
work is essential to the continued conveyance of Christ as the ground of
all reality. What is important, according to Jenson, is the artist's attempt
to capture the unity of Christ's humanity and divinity. And furthermore,
that the artist acknowledge that his subject is beyond the scope of his
imagination.[83] This by no means makes futile the artist's effort, as the
efficacy of the work is not purely predetermined by the painting's form
and content, but rather by its use in the church's enactment of the gospel. For it is in this moment, when the language of art is drawn into the

81. Wolterstorff, *Art in Action*, 52.

82. Jenson, "Christ–Dogma and Christ–Image," 147–51.

83. Ibid., 148–50.

entire cultural discourse of the *totus Christus*, that Christ is embodied among us:

> The "human nature" which the Son of God is said to take on . . . fits a story much better than a thing. It is the concrete personality and history of Jesus that God the Son makes his personality and history. Our representations of the man Jesus ought, therefore, to be representations of events from the evangelical history, rather than portraiture. The typical "head of Christ" does not belong in a house of worship. It is the crucifix, the manger-scene, the cleansing of the temple, etc., which are the "human nature" we are allowed to depict.[84]

This established, Jenson must now press on, for as Horne rightly suggests, "a theory of art cannot be merely christological."[85] Jenson's christological conception of art finds its fullest exposition within the notion of the triune drama.[86] In an essay entitled, "Beauty," Jenson provides a trinitarian framework for all artistic activity.[87] Beauty, Jenson asserts, is in the eye of the beholder: "Perhaps my eye unifies what it sees and calls the unity beautiful . . . or perhaps the fit . . . is purely serendipitous. Either way, the beauty is there where my eye, following its own dictates, puts it. The alternative is that what I find beautiful is beautiful antecedently to my finding, because it is first beautiful in the eye of God, who somehow shares his perception."[88]

The arbitrary nature of our own artistic adjudications is forced upon us by the singularity of our judgments. Similarly, while a "merely unitary god could perhaps create a world possessed of being and truth; it would not, however, be beautiful."[89] As we discovered at the very start of this chapter, the beauty of an artwork is the work and consideration

84. Ibid., 151.

85. Horne, "Art," 89.

86. According to both Horne and Jenson, a more robust Christology would not be enough to fully Christianize Tillich's theory of art. Only a trinitarian formulation could guarantee this.

87. *ETC*, 147–55.

88. Ibid., 148.

89. Ibid., 149.

of the artist's community, as much as it is the work of the artist himself. The truth, goodness, and beauty of the space which we denote as creation, as Jenson would remind us, and Horne verifies once more, is at the same time, a communal effort and the opening of a most beautiful conversation: "God speaking Himself in His Word and hearing Himself in His Spirit: expressing Himself in His Son and receiving Himself in His Spirit. It is not by any other action that the world is brought and sustained into being. The answer the creatures make is, like prayer, not so much a reply to God . . . but a participation in a dialogue which already exists—the eternal conversation of God himself."[90]

With this, we arrive once more at the notion of triune discourse and our own prayerful participation within the dialog. Jenson would surely approve of such an eloquent description. In Jenson, the Son—or the Word in which the triune conversation is constituted and by which creation is spoken into being—is the Father's experiment with a possible world. In his being lies the sense of all created things, for without him there would be nothing. In so far as the world conforms to knowable laws and patterns, it does so through axioms known only to God himself. As a result, the Son is not merely the sense that the world makes but rather is the sense of the experiment itself.

Having taken its place within the wider converse of culture, as the theological dialogue concerning the nature of spatial reality, art awaits its fulfillment within the life and community of the church. The artist's perception of standard reality is not necessarily heightened by his personal faith commitment. Likewise, the connection between churchly art and standard reality is not guaranteed by the content of the work nor by the devotion of its artisan. As throughout history, so also with the church, art is an instrument of action. Stripped from the broader language of culture and constrained within the realm of aesthetic illation, art's connection with the real world is threatened. However, as enacted by human communities in their exploration and discussion of their own realities, the language of art moves closer to its own fulfillment. Within the life, community, and culture of the church, art and architecture become instruments of divine action and provide a window into the life of the creator. However, within our present time and space, the church

90. Horne, "Art," *Trinitarian Theology*, 87–88.

embraces this reality in the mode of anticipation: "No created artist can ever be satisfied with any of his or her actual experiments . . . and with us that is a good thing despite the threat of futility that hangs over our creations, for when *we* are satisfied we stop. God however *is* satisfied with his experiment; he pronounces it good; . . . for with him there is no dissonance between standard and experiment."[91]

Conclusion

Having earlier declared the church as Christ's cultural embodiment in the world, Jenson was quick to remind us that culture exists as an attempt to act upon and change nature. With this in mind we come to a new declaration. "Christ is art," implores Jenson, and is embodied within the community that is the *totus Christus*. As the Father's own experiment with reality, the Son is to be found in the cultural life and converse of the church. Here, the very presence of Christ as God's unfolding experiment with reality transforms the church, along with her buildings and artifacts, into the world's own "changing room." In this moment, the church is actualized as God's experiment with a possible world. Within the cultural converse of the church, the creator becomes available to his creatures and calls forth new creation. In the very buildings that stage our gatherings and the art forms that provide their backdrop, God is enacting the latest developments of his experiment with the Son that is our world. For this reason, the arts have proved essential to the cultural activity of the church, and the church has likewise been central to the development of Western culture. The church artist, as Jenson points out, may have no greater access to the standard world than his non-Christian counterpart, however "by faith a churchly artist lives the movement of the very Experiment which posits creation."[92] The last word belongs to Jenson:

> If the church's artistic working takes place within and indeed moves with the Experiment . . . then we have another insight into why prayer and sacrifice work: the

91. Jenson, "Christ as Art," 74.
92. Ibid., 75.

Experiment that posits all things and their movements is the *totus Christus*, Christ as he embraces us. When we utter, "Save us from the time of trial," or "Give us this day our daily bread," within the whole sweep of the church's great "work," our piping belongs to the free movement—the chorus, the mural-in-progress, the ballet . . .—by which the creation occurs.[93]

93. Ibid., 76.

7

Variations on a Theme in Time:
Jenson and Music

IN THE PREVIOUS CHAPTER, we discussed art and architecture as cultural languages that human beings utilize in their attempts to understand reality. As with all other language-acts, these cultural-forms are
predicated upon God's own creative Word. For it is the Son who embodies and fulfills the Father's experiment with a possible world, namely
creation. In the culture of the church we witness this experiment at
first hand and become participants within it. These languages are thus
central to the life and culture of the Christian community, in that they
inform our conversations about reality and create the backdrop for our
re-enactment of the gospel. Subsequently, in the dramatic production
that is the life and culture of the church, congregants are transformed
into the very body of Christ.

While undoubtedly spatial, Christ's presence in this community, as
our account of art and architecture suggests, is primarily temporal.[1] For
this reason, this book finds both its close and its climax in the concept
with which we commenced our discussions. In Jenson, reality is the
story of a God who has time for us, and the culture of the church is the
dramatic fulfillment of his promised presence. In this final chapter, we

1. Note the discussion of art and architecture in the work of Jenson and Tillich,
in chapter 6.

come to the language of music and its specific relationship to time. As in the previous chapters, we will begin by assessing the role of music in our perception of reality. If Jenson's temporal presuppositions are correct, then surely a temporal art form, such as music, can significantly inform and enhance our notions of reality. Furthermore, if Christ embodies the cultural language and spatial art forms of his people, what is to stop him from becoming temporally available in music?

The first section of this chapter will explore Jenson's treatment of music as the language of time.[2] From hereon, we will introduce two dialogical partners. Having considered Augustine's reflections on the art form, we will introduce Jeremy Begbie's account of the relationship between music, theology, and time. In conclusion, we will explore the implications of Begbie's program within Jenson's own theology of culture. As in our previous chapter, our discussion will be punctuated and propelled by other cultural commentators ranging from theorists, such as, George Steiner and Theodore Adorno, through to notable musicologists, such as, Jonathan Kramer, Susanne Langer, and David Epstein.

One final methodological note and disclaimer is important. Those familiar with Jenson may register surprise at the subject of this final chapter. The early essay, "Worship as Word and Tone," along with a selection of paragraphs from the more recent lecture on "Christ as Art," represent Jenson's only publications on music to date.[3] While passing references demonstrate a love for the art form, nowhere do we find a formal reflection on the role of music. However, it remains my position that music provides a most fitting finale to this study. To a theologian who proclaims time as the primary presupposition of reality, music's experimentation with temporality provides the languages of theology and culture with a unique meeting point. Jenson's occasional comments support the supposition. "Could there be a culture that did not . . . make any kind of music?" he asks.[4] In this closing chapter, I will argue that

---

2. The notion is obviously not original. "This is precisely the unique thing about music: it speaks a language that is understood without learning, understood by everyone, not just the so-called musical people." Zuckerkandl, *The Sense of Music*, 4. We will, however, avoid the all too easy pronouncement of music, as "the universal language." Opinion as to the truth of the statement is considerably divided.

3. Jenson, "Worship as Word and Tone," 175.

4. Jenson, "Christ as Drama," 197.

a properly theological account of the language of music can form the fulfillment to Jenson's theology of culture.

Theme: Music and Language according to Jenson

"In the face of music," George Steiner writes, "the wonders of language are also its frustrations."[5] While the art form, in one sense, represents pure communication, discussions as to the content and message of music often defy description. This said, can we then include music within the theological language called culture? In an essay entitled, "Worship Word and Tone," Jenson outlines his thoughts on the subject. As the medium by which humans experience existence, the articulated sounds of speech or language open and maintain the temporal and structural relations necessary for human consciousness. Not limited to spoken words and sentences, these linguistic experiments extend to song and instrumental music. These organized sounds, Jenson concludes, form the "chief material for artifacts made as communication," or, language.[6] Furthermore, it is "impossible to draw any clear *a priori* line between speech and song; the line can be drawn only pragmatically and for a given language and linguistic situation."[7]

In Jenson, music and speech form the two poles of human communication. Jenson's "spectrum of utterance," ranges from the mono-toned, mono-rhythmic reading of scientific prose at one end, to the perfect performance of a Bach partita at the other.[8] From here, Jenson can effectively incorporate music into the theological converse of culture. Subdivided into many different attempts at language, each individual music-act performs an experiment upon reality and thus projects a possible world. Jenson explains: "For the world of a fugue is a different sort of world than the world of a sonata-movement, to say nothing of a

5. Steiner, *Real Presences*, 65.

6. All human efforts to intentionally construct sounds are to be considered language. Jenson further notes that while we can shut out the visual world by our eye lids, we have no natural respite from our audible reality. Jenson, "Christ as Art," 72.

7. Jenson, "Word and Tone," 175.

8. Already we witness the potential of music as the fulfilment of both the cultural and theological discourses concerning the nature of reality.

raga. It surely suggests something that . . . Beethoven was a contemporary of Hegel; or that the vogue for 'other musics' coincides with the rise of a sort of popular pantheism."[9]

As with art and architecture, it becomes impossible to separate musical language from the wider cultural converse. However, if music is to be understood as language, what, and how does the art form communicate? At first, music appears powerless to communicate any meaning whatsoever, leaving Jenson to suggest that music "communicates the sheer possibility of meaning, the mere and all-encompassing occurrence of our self-transcendence."[10] Specific attitudes, thoughts, and proclamation are not the property of musical language. Rather, music is the remarkable possibility of these attitudes and their communication to another. In Jenson, as in Steiner, to be addressed through speech and to encounter music is to experience the freedom of another and thus to wager upon transcendence.[11] As Steiner argues, in place of asking, "What is music?" we might better postulate as to "What is humanity?" for it is humans that make and, it seems, cannot help making music.[12] As Jeremy Begbie argues, "It is not sound-patterns alone which mean but people who mean through producing and receiving sound-patterns in relation to each other."[13]

Jenson, like Begbie, remains skeptical of the notion that particular musical modes or materials carry innate meanings. All such communication is surely the import of musicians and the export of their audience; it is not the property of the tones themselves. Jenson points out that J. S. Bach, as the founder of Western music, did not rely on the theological content of the notes and rhythms themselves, but rather "shaped songs and dance-forms to a sophisticated, even scholastic eschatology."[14] Far from undermining the claim to language, this admission strengthens music's claim. "Composers can deliberately . . . write music which expresses particular meanings," Jenson asserts. "When this is done it is the

9. Jenson, "Christ as Art," 72–73.

10. Jenson, "Word and Tone," 177.

11. See discussion concerning language and transcendence in chapter 3.

12. Steiner, *Real Presences*, 4–7.

13. Begbie, *Theology, Music and Time*, 13.

14. Jenson, "Christian Civilization," 2005.

same as if the music were written to a text."[15] Likewise, to one conversant in its vocabulary and grammar, a musical text can be read in much the same way as a poem or a novel. In this, Jenson echoes Roland Barthes.[16] "There is a progressive movement, from the language to the poem, from the poem to the song, and from the song to its performance. Which means that the *mélodie* has little to do with the history of music and much with the theory of the text."[17]

Music's purchase upon language is constituted in its appropriation of time. Through themes, both old and new, the musician holds his or her audience in a prolonged and heightened state of remembrance and anticipation. Music creates a temporal frame of reference within which a composer, performer, and listener can locate themselves. In his *Philosophy of Modern Music*, Theodore Adorno illustrates this essential connection between music and the temporal process. In this survey of twentieth-century music, Adorno presents a dialectical comparison between two of the era's most influential composers.[18] The first, Arnold Schöenberg, along with the 2nd Viennese School of his founding, personifies the abandonment of old language forms in search of the new. The second, Igor Stravinsky, eschewed such experimentation to concentrate on more primitive musical language-acts. For Adorno, the complete rejection of history, on the one hand, and the utter denial of the future, on the other, results in an irresolvable crisis of artistic language.

Jenson attempts to resolve this crisis with his own account of music. In this depiction, all music relies upon the mutual possibility of recollection and expectation. For to strip the art form of either of these is to forego its claim to language and subsequently to undermine its own existence. If the temporal language of music is to retain the possibility of meaning, composers must utilize the language which history affords them, otherwise, Jenson quips, the performer might as well "turn several radios on and off at random, calling whatever sounds result music."[19] However, while the past cannot be ignored, neither can the future. As

---

15. Jenson, "Word and Tone," 178.

16. Barthes, *Image, Music, Text*, 153. See also, Goodman, *Languages of Art*, 178.

17. Barthes, *Image, Music, Text*, 186.

18. Adorno, *Philosophy of Modern Music*.

19. *ETC*, 7.

in speech, each musical address is the creation of new language and the interruption of our lives with some new possibility, for while in our words we share our desires for the future, in our music we share futurity itself.[20] If music has any special meaning, Jenson muses, it is "the openness to the future in which all particular meanings occur."[21] With this, the possibilities of music for Jenson's theology become apparent. With music, Jenson argues, language steps closer to fulfillment and thus the metaphor of resurrection is given the edge of felt conjecture: "What then do we communicate by the nonsemantic articulation of our utterances? By its music, rhetoric, rhythm, etc.? I suggest that we thereby bespeak to each other the openness of the future merely as such, the sheer possibility of things being the way things are not, the sheer hope of somehow overcoming the facts. By the music and rhetoric and utterance, our world-sharing moves, we communicate freedom, we share spirit."[22]

In Jenson, language is the many "things we do to come to an understanding with each other in a world."[23] Music certainly fits within this definition. Furthermore, if every human deed is, as Jenson suggests, a failed or successful attempt to rhyme the past and the future, then few language-acts can claim to achieve this as directly as music.[24] As a result, it is simply not enough to assert that all discussion of music is also a discussion about language. If language is the combination of word and tone, then all subsequent dialogues concerning language must include some reference to music.[25] As intimated above, music provides Jenson's theories of language and culture with a new eschatological edge. The musicologist, Victor Zuckerkandl, notes the theological implications of this point:

---

20. As we discussed in chapter 3, a greeting such as, "Good morning," can constitute someone new breaking into our lives.

21. Jenson, "Word and Tone," 178.

22. *VW*, 57.

23. *ETC*, 1.

24. *S&P*, 105.

25. Jenson purloins Schleiermacher's terminology at this point. Jenson, "Word and Tone," 175.

Who is man that this almost-nothing, this "nothing but tones?" could become one of his most significant experiences . . . All transitory things have the character of metaphor, that is, point beyond themselves, have meaning. Could it be that tone, because it is the most transitory of all things, is therefore the most meaningful? These are clearly no longer musical problems; they are problems of a theory of meaning, problems of philosophy. They cannot be approached, however, except on the basis of an understanding of the elementary nature of musical phenomena.[26]

Recapitulation: Music and Time according to Augustine

Having devoted an entire treatise to music, the importance of the art form for Augustine is most prominent within the *Confessions*. Unmentioned early on in the work, music plays a crucial role in Augustine's journey towards faith and eventually accompanies his conversion.[27] The absence of music in the first seven books is not without note, but is rather symptomatic of Augustine's struggle to resolve the contradictions between time and eternity, and the physical and spiritual world.[28] Augustine considers this predilection for physical reality as the great hindrance to faith.[29] When it comes to music, J. J. O'Donnell notes, Augustine's circumspection is conditioned by the art form's prominence within Pagan ritual.[30] While eschewing music's inherent physicality, Augustine welcomed the form's innate spirituality. For Augustine, music holds the capacity to stimulate both body and soul, and where music is concerned, his preference is for soul.[31] Having spent years wrestling rationally with the Almighty, the final prelude to Augustine's conversion occurs in a mystical moment when the simple song of a small girl, or

26. Zuckerkandl, *Sense of Music*, 246.

27. Augustine, "De Musica."

28. Augustine, *Confessions*, 85.

29. Ibid., 115.

30. Augustine, *Confessions: Introduction, Text and Commentary*, 3:218.

31. Note the outworkings of Augustine's Platonic inheritance. As a result, while music may provide us with access to the religious nature of reality, its connections with physicality and fallenness prove problematic.

possibly an angel, penetrates his most heavy imaginings. In this moment, Augustine's theological contortions are interrupted by a revelatory event made possible by music. Augustine relays the story:

> I was asking my self these questions, weeping all the while with the most bitter sorrow in my heart, when all at once I heard the singsong voice of a child in a nearby house. Whether it was the voice of a boy or a girl I cannot say, but again and again it repeated the refrain "Take it and read, take it and read." At this I looked up, thinking hard whether there was any kind of game in which children used to chant words like these, but I could not remember ever hearing them before. I stemmed my flood of tears and stood up, telling myself that this could only be a divine command to open my book of Scripture and read the first passage on which my eyes should fall.[32]

In the following scenes, Augustine's spiritual growth is often accompanied by music. "Although I was not yet fired by the warmth of your Spirit, these were stirring times," he declares. "It was then that the practice of singing hymns and psalms was introduced . . . to revive the flagging spirits."[33] Of another incident, Augustine recounts how a companion resolved unbearable tensions as he performed a psalm of mercy and justice. Within a few moments, the whole household had stopped to join with his refrain. Later, Augustine awoke in the night, disturbed by faith and disbelief. As he lay alone, a popular hymn came to him and with it, the truth that his imaginings had sought:

> *Deus, Creator Omnium*
> Maker of all things! God most high!
> Great Ruler of the starry sky!
> Who, robing day with beauteous light,
> Hast clothed in soft repose the night,

---

32. Augustine, *Confessions*, 177.
33. Ibid., 191.

That sleep may wearied limbs restore,

And fit for toil and use once more;

May gently soothe the careworn breast,

And lull our anxious griefs to rest.[34]

For Augustine, music is experienced as a theological converse concerning the transcendent goal of human existence. The art form opens us up towards the potential fulfillment of our lives. While able to stimulate the sensual and fallen nature, music can also transcend this and lead to redemption. But what is the key to music's theological potency? The answer to this question can be found in Augustine's treatise, *De Musica*. Augustine's initial definition of music resonates with Jenson's own starting point. As both a language and a "practical science," music is our attempt to make meaningful communication through the production of controlled variations in sound.[35] Hence, the ability to speak and enjoy language are, for Augustine, the two marks which distinguish mankind above the animal kingdom.[36]

In *De Musica*, Augustine attributes music's power to its ability to measure the immeasurable, namely time. For Augustine, time, or the present, arrives out of that which does not yet exist, passes through the now, without duration, and immediately becomes non-existent.[37] To satisfactorily account for time, Augustine must find an explanation for this slippery process. Convinced that different periods of time are somehow mathematically related, Augustine looks to music for a resolution. He soon observes that music is able to account for, and measure, the passing of time.[38] From this deduction, he establishes an elaborate scheme relating time's movement to musical rhythm, meter, and verse. Rhythm enables the subdivision of time into equally divisible periods of

34. Ibid., 202. These verses are taken from St. Ambrose's "Evening Hymn."

35. Jackson Knight, *St. Augustine's De Musica*, 11–12.

36. Augustine, "De Musica," 12. Note our previous discussion concerning Jenson's identification of Adam and Eve as the first featherless bipeds to address one another through language, in chapter 3.

37. Augustine, *Confessions*, 269. See discussion on Augustine and Jenson on time, in chapter 1.

38. Augustine, "De Musica," 17.

duration. Each section of time and each passing beat provide a measure of time's movement. For this reason, a song is not measured by pages or volumes, for this is an irrelevant spatial calculation. Rather a song is measured by the number of beats and bars that it contains: "Take the line *Deus Creator Omnium,* which consists of eight syllables, alternately short and long . . . I say confidently that one is single and the other a double quantity, of course, I mean their duration in time. I can only do this because they are both completed and are now things of the past. So it cannot be the syllables themselves that I measure, since they no longer exist. I must be measuring something that remains fixed in my memory."[39]

In its most basic form, time is measured by the physical in-take and out-flow of breath. Beyond this biological process, Augustine proposes six progressive accounts of music's use of time. At the summit of the scheme, Augustine highlights the importance of memory when marking time in a musical performance.[40] In singing a song, we begin in a state of expectation, knowing that the whole piece is ahead of us. As we sing each part of the song, our expectations transition through the present into the past and simultaneously into our conscious memory. As the song progresses, our expectations lessen and our memory extends. When we reach the end, the entire work has become a memory and remains within our soul. Thus, in the mode of memory, music moves the soul and, in so doing, the soul takes hold of time itself. In this moment all physicality is negated by sheer spirituality. "*Deus creator omnium,*" Augustine declares, "has a pleasant rhythm for the ear, but the soul loves the sequence the more for the health and truth in it."[41]

For Augustine, music's capacity to account for the temporal nature of reality is educed from the inherent connection of time to consciousness. Melody and harmony are heavenly realities leant only fleetingly, yet ever remembered and always anticipated. While music fades in the ear, for the soul it plays on. The mysterious language of music thus equips mankind to stretch beyond all spatial and temporal limitations, and reach for the absolute reality of the eternal. The art form's power to

39. Augustine, *Confessions,* 275–76; Augustine, "De Musica," 85.

40. Ibid., 88.

41. Ibid., 123.

transcend the present, to recollect the past, and to anticipate the future is derived, firstly, from its ability to project the reality of passing time, and, secondly, through its vindication of the immortal soul's immunity to time itself. In this moment, temporality, physicality, and fallenness become suspended, leaving only the human person's eternal soul.

In Augustine, the potential of music is simply infinite: "The purpose of it [*De Musica*] is to lead young people of ability, and perhaps, older people too, gradually, with reason for our guide, from the things of sense to God, in order that they may cling to Him who rules all and governs our intelligence, with no mediating nature between . . . That is not because we choose to linger in association with such minds, but because we wish to travel by way of them."[42]

Like Jenson after him, Augustine proposes that God comes to us with the question of time.[43] It appears unsurprising then that *De Musica* should be Augustine's sole treatise on any art form. Augustine is convinced that the art form's distinct appropriation of time is enough to form the basis of a natural theology within culture. In its fusion of art and science, music both connects and calculates the movement between our timeless souls and the temporal world in which we now live. This process is thus joined to God in his own self-determination; a point noted by Catherine Pickstock: "Musical measurement is applied by Augustine even to God, on account of the relationality between the persons of the Trinity, the supremacy of arithmetic as *transcending* measure is implicitly surpassed. In this way, music becomes the science that most leads towards theology."[44]

In our first chapter, we considered Jenson's critique of Augustine on time. It is now helpful to rehearse the main points. The great flaw in Augustine's argument, argues Jenson, is his definition of God as sheer presence. If God's eternal being determines the existence of temporal beings and if God is simply presence then temporal realities cannot find their being in past, nor future, but must rather seek some form of permanent present in which to locate themselves. In this case, "It is not entirely appropriate to say, 'There are . . . past, present, and future.'

42. Ibid., 85.

43. Ibid., 123.

44. Pickstock, "Music: City, Soul and Cosmos after Augustine," 243.

It would be better to say, 'There are . . . the presence of past things, the presence of present things, and the presence of future things.'"[45] In their struggle for existence, past and future must maintain presence, or risk non-existence. Furthermore, if time itself is only distinguishable as the permanence of present, what prevents it from becoming eternity?[46] "Thus throughout his discussion Augustine is pressed to the verge of answering, 'What is time?' with a flatly Neoplatonic 'Nothingness.'"[47] The implications for music are severe.

Augustine is not alone in attributing timeless qualities to music. In the attempt to safeguard ourselves against the threat of the future, these temporal escape mechanisms appear attractive. However, as we have long discovered, such notions are ultimately self-deception. As a result, Jenson declares, music is often seized by human religion as one route towards a permanent present. In this transaction, we have exchanged a theological language about the reality of the triune God, for a religious discourse concerning our participation in divine being: "Thus, for example, in the Upanishads the first creation is a middle realm, which is still eternity but also already time, and which thus mediates our flight from time to eternity. This realm is a world made of music: its substance is tone and its articulation is melody and rhythm."[48]

In religion's flight from temporality towards the outer limits of timelessness, the specificity of meaning disappears along with the importance of historical reference and content. Such Gnosticism, according to Jenson, is evident in the church when textless music is promoted as language independent of the historical narrative and eschatological promise of the gospel. As we were reminded at the outset of this work, Christianity's distinction lies in its rejection of the God of timeless being and its confession of the triune God whose timely story is told in his history with creation.[49] To state otherwise is to risk a pagan capitulation. As Brian Horne points out, the mistake is not unique to Augustine:[50]

45. *ST* 2:30.
46. Augustine himself ponders this question.
47. Ibid., 30.
48. Jenson, "Word and Tone," 179.
49. See discussion on time and timelessness in chapter 1.
50. Considering earlier comparisons, Adorno's critique of Hegel's treatment of

"George Steiner's theories . . . remain, at best, paradoxical, and at worst, intellectually dubious—lacking in logical coherence because they are operating, in all their theological language, with a concept of God as undifferentiated being."[51]

Augustine comes unnervingly close to proposing his own brand of soul music as the Christian version of the Upanishadian middle realm. The recapitulation of Augustine's flawed notion of time lends music a somewhat pagan tone. Ironically, it was this worldview from which Augustine had sought to liberate music all along. As a result, music does not provide Augustine with an effective natural theology, but reinforces his own problematic view of a time. The problem is not merely theological. Augustine's scheme also runs into a musicological dead end. Susanne Langer reminds us of music's time-boundedness stating: "Music unfolds in time. Time unfolds in music. Music makes time audible."[52] Similarly, Jonathan Kramer asserts, the meaning of music is not to be found primarily in the emotional and intellectual investments of composers, performers, and listeners, nor in its ability to transport the listener beyond the boundaries of time itself, but rather in its own appropriation of time: "Since time in music not only communicates syntactic meanings but also presents symbolic meanings, it must be studied both theoretically and aesthetically."[53] In a similar vein Victor Shepherd writes: "Temporality, then, is not the environment in which music occurs; it is a crucial part of what music *is*—of what *everything* is. Music is meaningful, then, not because of its representational power (unlike some forms of painting it largely lacks this) but rather through the interplay between music's temporal processes and the manifold temporal processes that shape our lives."[54]

---

motion is worthy of note in this regard. Adorno suggests that the idealist's reliance upon Absolute Spirit as the utter immanence of presence and being, leads to the reduction of music to an "absolute monad," ossifying the form and damaging its innermost content. Adorno, *Modern Music*, 16–18.

51. Horne, "Art," 83.

52. Langer, *Feeling and Form*, 110.

53. Kramer, *The Time of Music*, 4.

54. Shepherd, Review of "Theology, Music and Time," 243.

A musical retreat into timelessness undermines the art form it-self and further negates its role in our apprehension of the temporal nature of reality. Jenson would surely approve of the observation. Far from escaping temporality, as Marvin Minksy argues, music forms the best available tool for our consideration of time. Commenting on our various musical experiments with temporal and spatial reality he states:

> Each child spends endless days in curious ways; we call it "play." He plays with blocks and boxes, stacking them and packing them; he lines them up and knocks them down. What is that all about? Clearly, he is learning Space! But how, on earth, does one learn Time? Can one Time fit in-side another, can two of Them go side by side? In music we find out!
>
> Many adults retain that play-like fascination with making large structures out of smaller things—and one way to understand music involves building large mind-structures out of smaller music-things. So that drive to build music-structure might be the same one that makes us try to understand the world.[55]

At first, Minsky's thesis does not appear far removed from that of Augustine. However, pushed to its logical conclusion the divergence is decisive. If music enables us to grasp temporality as the presupposition of reality, then all attempts to contract ourselves out of time—by music or other means—are ventures towards unreality. The attempt to erase time presents a clear and present danger to our experience of reality itself. Psychiatrist Frederick Melges, in his book, *Time and the Inner Future,* reports the account of a highly intelligent physicist suffering from acute paranoia: "Time has stopped: there is no time . . . The past and future have collapsed into the present, and I can't tell them apart."[56] While genres such as, plain song, minimalism, and aleotoric music have all been employed by composers in a bid to stall or suspend time, Kramer rightly points out that the temporal contexts in which an audi-ence listens to music means that the composer can only ever achieve a

55. Minsky, "Music, Mind, and Meaning," 5.

56. Melges, *Time and the Inner Future,* xix.

blurring of temporality. "However much we become part of the music, we do not totally lose contact with external reality," and, for this reason, music cannot enforce a schizophrenic experience of time upon its listeners.[57] While music may radically alter our own notion of temporal reality it cannot erase it. Jenson's instinctive notion that musical language enables our grasp of temporal reality resonates with musicologists. In this, Zuckerkandl himself pushes the boundaries of theological application: "A God enthroned beyond time in timeless eternity would have to renounce music . . . Are we to suppose that we mortals, in possessing such a wonder as music, are more privileged than God? Rather, to save music for him, we shall hold, . . . that God cannot go behind time. Otherwise what would he be doing with all the choiring angels?"[58]

Music's distinction is not that it transports us into the timeless but rather that it forces us to rethink time. It is, in part, Augustine that we have to thank for this determination. Augustine rightly apprises us of the potent possibilities of theological language as presented in music. His recognition of music's unique ability to contain and project the temporal nature of reality represents a vital contribution to both theology and music. However, his perennial tendency to dichotomize time and eternity undermines the very assumptions under which he operates.

Development: Music and Time according to Jeremy Begbie

In his exploration of the interface between music and theology, Jeremy Begbie exhibits an almost Jensonian mistrust of theories that ascribe timeless characteristics to the language of music. His misgivings, as we have already discovered, are well founded. Begbie's own proposal centers upon a reassertion of music's temporality. "When we ask *how* music is temporal, we are confronted by an enormous range of temporal . . . processes."[59] From here, Begbie utilizes the timely nature of music to construct a theological explication of time itself. As both musician and theologian, Begbie outlines the complexities of musical time. The standard philosophical and theological accounts of temporality simply

57. Kramer, *Time of Music*, 376.
58. Zuckerkandl, *Sound and Symbol*, 151.
59. Begbie, *Theology, Music and Time*, 6.

do not do justice to the experience of time which music affords. Musical time, Begbie claims, transcends standard formulations in six different ways. Firstly, music rejects simplistic and singularly linear concepts of time. This is not to say that music lacks direction, in fact the opposite is true. A piece of music is subject to concurrent and multifarious developments of theme, harmony, instrumentation, rhythm, etc. However, while *"directionality is one thing,"* Begbie argues, *"one-dimensional linearity is another.* This distinction will be crucial to much of the theological discussion which follows."[60] Once again, as David Epstein points out, it is the distinct appropriation of time that provides the possibility of meaning in music: "Thus time, motion, tempo, . . . and the host of other qualities of musical speech, coalesce in the service of controlled affective statement . . . These neural propensities have an affective aspect related to the satisfaction, or pleasure/displeasure that we experience in our temporal anticipations and expectations, and in the fulfillment of these expectations."[61]

Secondly, according to Begbie, music transcends the largely quantitative model of time preferred by modernity. This is not to say that musical time is not quantitative; as we have seen in Augustine, music is more than capable of measuring temporality. However, Begbie points out that music also has the ability to "'take our time' and give it back to us, enriched, [and] re-ordered."[62] The use of background music in restaurants, waiting rooms, and other public spaces provide practical examples of this. This second aspect of musical time reflects the central aspect of Epstein's program:

> [Musical] time has value well beyond the mere tracking, or "telling," of time. Scientists, engineers, artisans recognized ages ago that if energy were to be transferred to a given body by means of force . . . then a "rhythmic" application of force would be one of the most efficient ways of achieving this . . . Three people trying to move a heavy object, for example, will coordinate their efforts in a rhythmic way,

60. Ibid., 59.

61. Epstein, *Shaping Time. Music, the Brain, and Performance,* 481.

62. Begbie, *Theology, Music and Time,* 19.

chanting "One-two-three-HEAVE!" to focus everyone's energies at the same moment.[63]

Thirdly, Begbie suggests, music transcends the overly simplistic progressivism that all too easily gains credence as time's interpretation. While certain musical forms do exhibit this, many do not. The song provides the most obvious example. The form of a song is rarely oriented towards a single "collecting goal."[64] As with most forms of music, songs rely upon repetition and recapitulation for their identity and development. In music, the progressive tendency to reject the past as unrepeatable is entirely lacking. "[Good] music, is highly repetitive," proclaims Shepherd, "never cloyingly so but always [as] 'sameness with a difference.'"[65] Beethoven's Fifth, and most famous, Symphony provides the perfect example. Along similar lines, Barbara Barry argues, "Musical time is dialectical in being simultaneously structured and transcendent. The structuring of time harnesses and orders repetitive physical rhythm, not by erasing its repetitions . . . but by organizing them into a coherent design combining repetition with variation, anchorage with departure, into a formal scheme which both satisfies the need for order and organizes its time span."[66]

Fourthly, in Begbie, music transcends the notion that time is only to be interpreted through a series of continuities. Musical time relies upon elements of surprise and discontinuity. Where linear models tend to downplay discordant interruptions, such "indirect routes and ruptures are an inherent and enriching part of" the musical process.[67] In one beat a major theme is dropped, never to return, while in another, a momentary motif, unnoticed in its first articulation, arises from nowhere dragging all else in its wake. "The combination of musical structure and affective potentiality," suggests Barry, creates a "highly ordered time-organization . . . [that] actively displaces events which might

---

63. Epstein, *Shaping Time,* 135.

64. Begbie, *Theology, Music and Time,* 60.

65. Shepherd, "Review, *Theology, Music and Time,*" 245.

66. Barry, *Musical Time,* 250.

67. Begbie, *Theology, Music and Time,* 60.

otherwise have filled its duration."[68] There is an indubitable connection here between music's ability to surprise us and Jenson's own notion that God's persistence, as a temporal infinity, does precisely this.

Fifthly, Begbie claims that music contradicts the notion that all futures are an extension of the past. At any point, a composer is at liberty to introduce radically new schemes or materials to a work. While these may have little or no bearing upon what the audience have experienced so far, they may yet prove decisive to the final destination of the work. Having no past of their own, these novel devices are the inventions of the future. In this way, music reminds us that fulfillment and completion comes to us from the future. In this, Begbie insists, music once again promotes "quality time."

> [Overly] linear metaphors have often had the effect of *minimising the place of radical and qualitative novelty,* encouraging a view of the future as proceeding inexorably from the past through the present governed . . . by a deistic "God," or by the laws of Newtonian mechanics, or sometimes by both. This can have the effect of curbing due recognition of the place of contingency and intrinsic unpredictability. There is little room for acknowledging that past and future are experienced as qualitatively (not just quantitatively) different.[69]

Sixthly, Begbie proposes, music transcends our simplistic notions regarding the process of time. An overly linear view of time leads to a masking of transience by mortality. Time's seemingly inexorable and inevitable advance absorbs and overcomes everything within its wake, thus luring us once more towards a false sense of futurity and eventually to timelessness. As Jenson himself insists, time is more than "one damned thing after another."[70] The sense of music resists and transcends such a notion of time. For all its glorious orderliness, music fails to mask its transience, perpetually amplifying the birth, death, and resurrection of themes and tones: "The tones which die to give way to others are

---

68. Barry, *Musical Time*, 250–51.

69. Begbie, *Theology, Music and Time*, 60.

70. Jenson, *Story and Promise*, 105.

related, not externally by being placed on a straight line but internally by virtue of waves of tension and resolution, such that the tones' past, present and future are, in some sense, interwoven. Music, in other words, subverts the assumption that transience is necessarily harmful, that fleetingness is intrinsically irrational."[71]

Through Begbie's model of time, these musical realities combine to illustrate the complex temporal process in which we find ourselves. Begbie envisions a musical work as encapsulating a series of ever-widening time bands, or waves. In microform, these intervals account for the minutiae of musical material. These microwaves can determine the distance between two semiquavers, or the period of a single down beat of the conductor's baton. However, no wave exists outside of the time of the piece and thus each wave is encompassed within a broader wave. The waves extend throughout the work, encompassing each bar, phrase, section, movement and, finally, the entire work as a whole. Begbie's musical exposition of the temporal process, with its resultant theological content and implication, is remarkable. Here, no moment of time is relegated to the unimportant, and no movement of time is considered arbitrary. Each note relates to every other note in the composition. Likewise, every bar brings meaning both to the next bar and, simultaneously, to the one that came before. Familiar phrases are perpetually rephrased in the form of repetitions, transpositions, and inversions. Finally, every musical fragment, whether noticed or unnoticed, remembered or forgotten, expected or unexpected is summoned to a vital role in the creation of the one huge and complex temporal event. In musical time, at least, remembrance and anticipation, hope and history are destined always to rhyme.

For Jenson, a model of time must account for two simultaneous processes if it is to successfully negotiate the temporal nature of reality.[72] Firstly it must provide, "a la Augustine, the 'distention' of a personal reality," through which we can grasp the temporality of our own human existence. Secondly, it must equip us with an "external metric of related events." Time, in Jenson, is not the distended soul stretched into

---

71. Begbie, *Theology, Music and Time*, 61.

72. See discussion of Jenson on time, in chapter 1.

eternity, but the "infinite enveloping consciousness" of the triune God.[73] Begbie's model of musical time provides an effective account of this dual process. While offering human experience a unique and rounded presentation of the temporal nature of reality, music both enables the external measurement and comparison of moments within time, and finally, provides the assurance that each and every temporal movement is embraced and guaranteed by a wider wave of temporal events. The waves of time in which we live and move and have our being are finally, and fully, embraced within the temporal infinity of God himself.

Jenson's own account of time and history fits well with Begbie's musical formulation. For Jenson, created time is not to be disconnected from the reality of God's own person and activity. Such a move would surely comprise a retreat into deism. Rather, in Jenson, time and history presuppose the eternal drama that is the triune God. In this guise, time retains its drive and direction, and can both confirm and confound our expectations of reality. The temporal realities of predictability and surprise, remembrance and anticipation, and tension and resolution find their instigation, climax, and resolve within the life of the triune God. In his bracketing of all time and history within God's triune life, Jenson himself resorts to music. For Jenson, the act of creation is enacted in the rhythm of God's speech. Through the word, God's "upbeats" and "downbeats" conduct the created order into being. The continued "ordering of all events," he adds, "is their coherence by logical and musical appropriateness within God's thinking of them."[74] Finally, music heralds the final outcome of God's divine action, and his eternal life with his people. Quoting Edwards's, Jenson proclaims: "The 'exquisite spiritual proportion' that will be the eschatological perfection of creation and that is now its inner meaning is . . . that of a 'very complex tune, where respect is to be had to the proportion of a great many notes together.' If we try to conceive the Kingdom, the 'society in the highest degree happy,' we should 'think of them . . . sweetly singing to each other.'"[75]

Begbie's musical exposition of time provides a potent application of Jenson's own notion of the temporal nature of reality. Here time is

73. *ST* 2:34.
74. Ibid., 44.
75. *ST* 1:235

neither an oppressive mechanism nor a human construction. Rather time, in Jenson, forms our primary presupposition of creation and thus mediates the creator's own revelation. This notion is evidenced and explicated by music. This cultural language enables human beings to experience, evaluate, and experiment with time. In so doing, musicians project a possible world and posit their own theological account of reality. In Begbie, all human existence is preceded by a time signature, and our grasp of reality necessitates a theological interpretation of the temporal framework in which we find ourselves. In Begbie's model, music not only reflects the time-filled realities of music and culture in general, but offers new resources for a theological understanding of the created order.

Finale: Time for Music in Jenson and Begbie

In our discussion of music, the interface between theology and culture has shifted to a new level. It is no longer enough to claim music as a cultural language requiring theological interpretation. In Begbie, we witness the unique contribution which music makes to theology. While his publications on culture have largely ignored the form, Jenson's work bears witness to the importance of musical language for his theology as a whole. Throughout his systematics, Jenson uses musical concepts and terminology, such as "harmony" and "musicality," to describe God's actions and attributes. At his own insistence, we are to consider the descriptions as more than simply metaphor, the implication being that music itself provides a unique and essential exposition of the life of the triune God with his creation.[76] There is no reason, Jenson proposes, to suggest that the language of Greek philosophy is better primed for the exposition of reality, than the language of music: "Such words as 'harmony' are here conscripted to be metaphysically descriptive language more malleable to the gospel's grasp of reality . . . That we are used to the metaphysical concepts of Mediterranean pagan antiquity and its Enlightenment recrudescence does not mean they are the only

76. Note the earlier discussion concerning Jenson's use of metaphor. Jenson is either mistrusting of the concept or anxious to push theological language beyond the bounds of metaphor.

ones possible; there is no *a priori* reason why, for example, 'substance'—which after all simply meant 'what holds something up'—should be apt for conscription into metaphysical service and, for example, 'tune' should not."[77]

The question arises as to whether music can effectively bear such a metaphysical burden? While Jenson's musical instinct is not sufficiently scrutinized within his own theology, Begbie provides a number of test cases for his hypothesis. Having demonstrated the art form's utility in the interpretation of temporal reality, Begbie proposes a musical exposition of the incarnation and the Trinity. In relation to the former, Begbie invites us to consider the classic formulation of Christ's nature, or natures:

> If I play a note on the piano—say, middle C, the note fills the whole of my heard "space." I cannot identify some zone where the note is and somewhere it is not. I do not say "it is here, but not there." Unlike the patch of red on a canvas, it is, in a sense, everywhere. Of course, I can identify the source of the note (the vibrating string), and its location ("it is over here"). But what I *hear* does not occupy a bounded space. It fills the entirety of my aural space. If I play a second note—say, the E above middle C—along with middle C, that second note also fills the whole of my heard space. Yet I hear it as distinct. The notes "interpenetrate," occupy the same "space," but I hear them as two notes.[78]

When played on a piano, a major third produces a unique and unified musical effect. Sounded simultaneously, the two notes that produce this interval cannot be mistaken for another harmony. No matter how the conditions alter, the interval does not transmute into a minor third, a major seventh, an augmented fourth, nor any other combination of tones. Furthermore, within the harmonic singularity of the major third, we are clearly aware of two distinct sonic realities and yet both tones fill the same audible space. With these notes ringing in our ears, Begbie

77. *ST* 2:39.

78. Begbie, *Beholding the Glory*, 144–45.

reminds us of an age-old challenge: What does it mean to suggest that the incarnate Son is both man and God? In what aspects, moments, and events do we consider him to be "just a man?" Likewise, where and when does his presence and activity identify him as God? According to Begbie, the challenge of Chalcedon invites musical illustration. Jesus is both divine and human. However, the mystery of this divine personality does not offer itself for a simple mathematical evaluation. Having asked, in which time and space Christ is human? The church responds, "In every space!" Likewise, when we look to determine at which points Christ is divine, she replies, "At every point!" When asked how Christ can embody such distinct natures and remain unified as one person, we answer, that such an interpenetration is the very essence of his personality: "Here in Jesus Christ we witness the divine Son eternally in communion with the Father, engaging with our world so closely so as to assume humanity, flesh and blood; and far from being compromised, humanity here reaches its intended destiny in union with the Son—here *is* human existence as it was meant to be. In this person, we witness the closest interaction of divine space and human space ('without division, without separation') without either being compromised ('without confusion, without change')."[79]

Begbie's model offers a musical illustration of Jenson's own Christology. Having argued for a more unified understanding of the Son's personhood, Jenson suggests that we abandon the traditional emphasis on Christ's separate natures, preferring instead to talk of one nature comprising divinity and humanity combined. As before, Jenson's position seeks not to deny the two elements of the classical formula, but rather emphasizes that the interpenetration of these characteristics is what defines the Son as a unique and singular person in his own right. As a result, the space that we know as the incarnation is mutually filled by Christ's divinity and humanity. From here, it becomes easier to envisage Jenson's treatment of Christ's bodily presence. The unique mutual embodiment of the Son in heaven, the church, and creation does not create a problem if understood as equivalent to a musical interval.

As Brian Horne points out, "a theory of art cannot be merely christological, one cannot account for art by pointing to the person of Jesus

79. Ibid., 147.

Christ," for while the propriety of art is lodged in the incarnation, the necessity of art must originate in the creative life which is the triune God.[80] With this in mind, Begbie offers an additional note. If a "G" is added to the "C," and the "E," then the major third becomes a major chord. The three-way interpenetration that occurs in a musical triad. Here, three notes occupy the same space without negation and thus offer a unique illustration of triune reality. Begbie's model further illustrates Jenson's trinitarian formula at this point. The major chord, while existing in its own right, has no means of existence other than through the interpenetration of the three individual notes. Should one note drop out then the chord disappears. Likewise, left to their own resources, the two remaining notes are unable to recreate the effect in any way, shape, or form. The major triad is reliant upon three distinct yet interdependent musical entities. In the same way, God is both the sum of the triune cast and the individual persons themselves.

There is, however, one significant limitation with Begbie's triadic analogy. While the three note formula offers a range of possible orders and inversions, the model also implies a stasis; the C major chord being static in nature. This limitation is unacceptable to both Jenson and Begbie. It is now Jenson's turn to come to Begbie's aid. As J. Augustine Di Noia rightly asserts: "Jenson is convinced that, more effectively than a metaphysics of substance in its classical or modern forms, the metaphysics of music and harmony can support our efforts to give theological expression to what is otherwise inexpressible: the 'harmonious life of the triune God.'"[81]

Moving from harmony to melody, we are confronted with a new range of possibilities. It is this move that enables the climaxing motif of Jenson's systematics. "God is a fugue," he declares.[82] In a fugue, each individual subject retains its own, unmistakable character and personality, yet continually reappears, reshaped and redirected as a result of its exchange with fellow subjects. This dramatic musical converse relies upon the perpetual distinction of individual, yet mutually reliant, sub-

80. Horne, "Art," 90.

81. Di Noia, "Three Responses," 99.

82. This maxim forms the climax of both volumes of Jenson's *Systematics*. *ST* 1:236, 2:369.

jects, while endlessly facilitating their future variation, response, and development. The art of fugue illustrates music's ability to articulate the temporal process, once more. Through fugal form, the composer experiments with ontology and eschatology, forever attempting to rhyme the past and the future. Once more, it is not enough to suggest that theology has something to say about music, for music also has something to say about theology. It is hardly a surprise then that Jenson utilizes this musical language to describe the triune God. Begbie provides a useful commentary at this point: "Instead of a chord, might it not be more appropriate to speak of God's life as three-part polyphony, even, as Robert Jenson intriguingly suggests, a fugue? This more readily suggests response, giving and receiving, particularity of the persons, even the joy of God . . . The incarnation is not a theory, or a picture, or a concept—but essentially a drama of interpenetration between the triune God and humanity."[83]

The fugal drama which is the triune God reaches a climax, not in self-interpretation or self-reliance, although such realities are necessary, but in the invitation for other subjects to join his musical drama. A fugue, unlike a chord, is unlimited, in the number of notes, or subjects, it contains. In Jenson's work there is always the invitation for others to join the divine music of the triune God. For human kind is ultimately wrapped up in God's own time and in the melodies and harmonies that he has for us:

> We must therefore here abstract from the semantics of the divine conversation and so think only of its sheer musicality. To be a creature in specific relation to the Father is to be a motif in the orchestration that occurs when God's musicality opens *ad extra*. We might say: the Father hums a music "of the spheres," the tune of the creating triune conversation, and precisely so and not otherwise there are

83. Begbie, *Beholding the Glory*, 150. Begbie is thoroughly conversant with Jenson's work. Begbie wrote *Theology, Music Theology and Time* at the Center for Theological Inquiry in Princeton. Aspects of the book, according to Begbie, were influenced by, Jenson's *Unbaptized God: The Basic Flaw in Ecumenical Theology*. The CTI would later appoint Jenson as a senior scholar and provide an opportunity for both theologians to come together. Interview with author, (St. Andrew's, 20 Jan 2006).

the "spheres." Nor is it merely that there are creatures who are then harmonious with each other; to be a creature *is* to belong to the counterpoint and harmony of the triune music.[84]

Begbie supports and expounds Jenson's musical instincts, suggesting that music has the power to liberate, refresh, and extend the language of theology. The perpetual conundrum concerning the spatial reality of the Trinity may be assisted by a musical appropriation of time. When considered as three subsisting subjects within one temporal reality, as in the case of a fugue, the classic trinitarian formula appears more conceivable. Begbie's theological account of music provides the necessary resources by which to support Jenson's triune notion of temporal eternity.[85] The church, as Begbie suggests, views the Trinity as a mathematic puzzle that demands resolution. In our ecclesial sums we endeavor in vain to turn three into one, and visa versa, only to miss the fact that the triune God is first and foremost a reality to be experienced and enjoyed. All this, Begbie suggests, is the result of our desire to see reality, as opposed to listen to it. If we sit back and listen, we may find that other theological conundrums can be resolved through music.

Jenson's appropriation of musical language for theology does not end with his explication of the triune God. For Jenson, God's fugal nature is not only a description of his own life, but also forms the basis of his relationship to creation. In the first chapter of this work we discussed the timeliness of God as the presupposition of his creative and salvific acts. The God who has time for us, invites and enables us to participate in the triune event that he himself lives. The eternal God can thus invite all creation to join the heavenly music that constitutes his own life and discourse. Caught up in this fugal recital, each subject retains his or her own distinct and unique character and history, while becoming fully joined in the eternal communion. As in a fugue, the work is not a perpetual tone, nor a monotonous round of repetitions, but continually transcends itself with endless variations and develop-

---

84. *ST* 2:39.

85. The move may also herald the final abnegation of space in favor of time. We will come to this discussion in due course.

ments. It is for this reason that Jenson adopts Edwards' own maxim that "The End is Music."[86]

The practical importance of music within the life of the church hardly needs stating at this point. However, Jenson's thought is evidenced by the perennial musical accompaniment of church life. The whole world over, the church community gather to participate in, perform, and listen to music in one way or another. This unifying theme is neither accident nor coincidence. For Jenson, music teaches us something unique about God's character and enables us to anticipate our participation in his own triune life. Through the resurrected Christ, we are invited to join the heavenly music of the triune fugue, both once, and for all. Jenson envisions the church as the *totus Christus*, or Christ with his church situated at the gates of heaven. In this moment, word and tone come together, and the dramatic dialog that constitutes the Christian community's hope and history is transformed into the divine music of the triune God. This music is the very life and converse of the Trinity. It is the very present possibility that our hopes and our histories will, one day, rhyme. Finally, it appears Jenson is fully aware of the theological promise which music brings. "Now that I come to think of it, done properly, I suspect that a theological analysis of music might provide the most enlightening study of culture itself, and that likewise a musical exploration of theology might produce the a profound and complex exposition of the possibilities of theological language."[87]

Whether Jenson will follow his own instincts and formally set out his theology of music is unlikely. However, Augustine, Begbie, and others besides have done much to reinforce Jenson's musings on the matter. Most importantly, we can conclude that Jenson is justified in staking so much of his theology upon the nature of music. Music provides a language through which we can grasp the temporal nature of reality as the triune presupposition of all existence. In music, we hear first hand of the God who has time for us. In the ensuing cultural dialog we begin to interpret and understand the eternal personality and infinite drama of the triune God. Furthermore, in the culture of the church, this God

---

86. Jenson, "End is Music," 171.

87. Interview with author, (Princeton, 16 July 2005).

inhabits the music of his people within created time and space. In these moments, we experience his promised presence with us and anticipate our own end in the eternal and infinite music that constitutes his triune life.

Encore

WHILE MUSIC MAKES FOR a fitting finale, it would be naïve to suggest that it resolves all potential problems in Jenson's work. The conclusion of this book functions as something of an encore. This is not the result of hubris but rather an attempt to deal with any unfinished business. In these final pages, we will return to temporality for one last time and ask whether Jenson's theological distinctive supports or undermines his program. Before we come to this, we would do well to rehearse the main themes of the book.

In created time and space, human beings utilize language to take hold of their reality. Through the story of the resurrected Christ, we acknowledge these themes as the presuppositions of our existence and as aspects of the triune life. The time, space, and language which God has for his creation is an extension of the temporal infinity, eternal embodiment, and triune converse of Godhead. This eternal reality is revealed to us by the second person of the Trinity. As the creative Word of the Father, the Son holds open the time and space of creation and, by his Spirit, invites humanity to realize its existence within the triune discourse. This invitation is issued by the church as God's word to the world. In the story that she tells, the drama she enacts, and the language that she speaks, the church is Christ's embodiment *for* and *in* creation. It is this immanentist vision that drives Jenson's notion of the *totus Christus*, or Christ with his church. Unified in the time, space, and language of the Christian community, Christ *is* culture. The church's dependence upon the language of culture reinforces her own understanding of created reality and makes Christ present available within the time and space of history. Through her art and architecture, the church experiments with created space and consequently constructs a space in which Christ is present to the world. Likewise, in her use of music, the church plays with the reality of time and thus anticipates her inclusion in the perfected time of the triune life. Finally, Christ, as the culture of the church, transforms nature and calls forth new creation.

A discussion that had its beginnings in time, has music for a finale. Music provides Jenson with a linguistic meeting point for theology and culture. In addition, the art form returns us to the first principle of our investigation and, with it, Jenson's "pet subject." At the commencement of this study we set down Jenson's notion of time as the foundation for his theology. This reworking of time remains one of the most creative and controversial aspects of his program. While music does much to confirm his thinking on time and his subsequent theology of culture, it certainly does not drown out all of Jenson's critics. With this, one final question demands our attention. Does the preference for time as the presupposition of reality, and as manifested by Jenson's theological appropriation of music, provide a sound footing for his substantive account of theology and culture?

Having characterized God as a fugue and heaven-in-song, it appears that Jenson may be in danger of collapsing space into time. With the critical role that these categories play in his thought, a failure here could undermine the entire program. One particular question has already been raised on numerous occasions to this end. We must now draw some conclusions. While careful to deal with time and space together, Jenson's persistent promotion of time comes, inevitably, at space's expense. In all of his dealings, whether in created space, the nature of language, the *totus Christus,* theories of culture, or the language of art, temporality is prioritized above spatiality. As Jenson himself argues, space's primary importance lies in the temporal-spatial notion of presence, or presentness.

While the implications of this ordering play out in Jenson's entire body of work, the full force of his ideas are felt by the Christian community. As the centerpiece of his theology, the church, as the *totus Christus,* remembers and anticipates the God who has time and space for us. In this community, we are invited to take our place in the roominess of God's temporal infinity. It is here that hope and history rhyme once and for all. However, while Jenson's sacramental ecclesiology provides a compelling account of Christ's embodiment in the church, his presence within this community is primarily temporal, and only after that is it spatial. With this, Jenson's hard fought gains appear under some threat. We are left to ask one of Jenson's favorite questions: "Where has the body gone?" In almost every aspect of Jenson's work, there lies a tension between the temporal and spatial implications of the program. Whether intentional or unintentional, explicit or implicit, Jenson's high view of temporality has serious implications for space. At various points, the physical body of the resurrected Christ becomes almost irrelevant; he needs no such physical entity as the church provides him with his risen body. Likewise, when left to consider the nature of human embodiment in heaven, Jenson leaves us with a most vague account of our future physicality. In Jenson, our resurrected bodies are physical, yet inorganic.

It is of little surprise then that music fits the Jensonian scheme so perfectly. While careful never to abrogate space through time, the pre-eminence of the latter is indubitable. It is this inclusive ordering of time before space which draws Jenson's program towards its musical conclusion.[1] Music provides Jenson with a language capable of conveying the eternal pre-eminence of time over space. For while music is both temporal and spatial—the art form relies upon physical factors such as bodies, breath, pressure, action, and vibration—each musical experiment results in its own form of temporal embodiment. This said, our discussion on music presents us with two divergent conclusions. On the one hand, we may accept the inference that music provides a unique illustration of Jenson's ground-breaking treatment of time and its importance for trinitarian theology. Or, on the other hand, we may return to our initial discussion and decide that Jenson's notion of God's temporal infinity is theologically implausible. Should Jenson's promotion of time prove unjustifiable then rather than provide the fitting finale that we had hoped for, music may simply amplify a theological dissonance.

1. In his publications on the subject of culture, Jenson has devoted far more time to spatial art forms, such as art and architecture, than he has to temporal art forms, such as music or dance. Furthermore, the art form in which Jenson has most immediate experience is drama. A resolution to the problem of time and space at the end might be solved by an attempt to construe the triune converse through music, speech and drama. As Stephen Holmes has suggested, heaven may be better conceived as "opera," rather than fugue.

The importance of Jenson's work for contemporary theological debate is marked by the reviews and responses to his *Systematic Theology*. In 2002 the larger part of an issue of the *Scottish Journal of Theology* was devoted to this work. The critiques of George Hunsinger and Francis Watson, and subsequent response from Jenson, provide a useful framework for this final debate. Hunsinger commences his review by proclaiming Jenson's two-volume work as the "twentieth century's most accomplished systematic theology written in English."[2] This positive precursor belies much that follows. Hunsinger commences his elongated attack with an insinuation that Jenson has moved outside the bounds of Christian orthodoxy and closes with a barrage of the most serious allegations. Having neglected the cross and the atonement, Hunsinger declares, Jenson's work flirts with Arianism and Monophysitism, before finally settling for a subordinationist, monist, and tritheistic account of trinitarian reality.[3] Having attempted to expound an unbaptized God, Hunsinger argues, Jenson pays "the steep price of God's total Hegelian immersion."[4] In each wave of opposition, we witness one driving force. Underlying Hunsinger's affront there lies a deep suspicion of his colleague's treatment of time. It is Jenson's emphasis upon the resurrection, for example, which causes Hunsinger to doubt his orthodox credentials concerning the atoning work of Christ on the cross. His reliance upon the temporal implications of the event, Hunsinger declares, causes Jenson to underplay the physical sacrifice of the Son at Calvary. Once more, space is misplaced by time. Furthermore, Hunsinger alleges, Jenson's preference for the timely nature of Christ as the fullness of God the Son in the incarnation, and his subsequent association of Christ's

2. "It has few peers in any language," Hunsinger adds. Hunsinger, "Jenson's Theology," 161.

3. The dialogue underlines, once more, the indispensable role of culture in all theology. In addressing what he sees as the underlying fault line within Jenson's thought, Hunsinger's attack is carried out on Jenson's home ground. Having attributed the traditional doctrine of divine to the extraneous influence of Greek philosophy and culture and subsequently ruled against the formula's usage within Christian theology, Jenson has sought to replace the model with a more radically theological conception of time. However, Hunsinger suggests, Jenson's proposed alternative is irrevocably wed to the postmodern zeitgeist and should thus be ruled out on the exact same grounds. Ibid., 187–90.

4. Ibid., 188.

Sonship with the resurrection, displays a disavowal of the pre-existent Christ.

With the historical Jesus exhausting the identity of the eternal Son, Hunsinger aligns Jenson with Arius. It is his commitment to God's temporal infinity and subsequent denial of timelessness, impassibility, and immortality, which Hunsinger identifies as the root of these problems. This discomfort is not eased by Jenson's trinitarianism.[5] According to Hunsinger, Jenson's work is undermined by its author's unstinting commitment to a Hegelian "metaphysical historicism."[6] It is this element of the program that leads to the accusations of panentheism which we discussed in chapter 1.[7] Jenson's dialectical use of time and eternity limits the Trinity to the bounds of created history. The result is a relationship of mutual dependency between God and his creation: "God and the world are metaphysically one . . . [in] the *telos* of history," and subsequently, the historical narrative of the triune identity is, according to Hunsinger, unavoidably progressive.[8] The result is a simultaneously subordinationist, monistic, and tritheistic conception of the Trinity. With the second charge, Hunsinger strikes at the very heart of Jenson's reflections upon the *totus Christus*. In Jenson's depiction of the church as Christ's resurrected body, Hunsinger declares, we witness "a gesture to Hegel's idea that the Spirit is concretely actualized in the cultus of the religious community, except that the logical space Hegel assigned to the Spirit is now taken by Christ's risen body."[9] The church now appears simultaneously as both a cultus and a body. In Jenson, the unification of God with his creation through Christ and his church, or the *totus Christus*, forms the crowning moment of all history. However, as far as Hunsinger is concerned, we are now faced with the dual threat of monism and panentheism.

5. Jenson, Hunsinger asserts, is troubled by his own gifting as a systematician. His consistency in this regard, results in singular errors repeating and multiplying throughout his work. Ibid., 162.

6. Ibid., 175.

7. See the discussion concerning Jenson, Hegel, pantheism, and panentheism in chapter 1.

8. Ibid., 179. It is Jenson's dialectic, Husinger declares, which prevents God from becoming the same as the world.

9. Ibid., 196.

> Wonderful as they are in themselves, neither of Jenson's
> two metaphors for this final goal—conversation and mu-
> sic (the great fugue)—necessarily excludes a panentheis-
> tic, and therefore monistic, reading of his position . . . As
> viewed from above, the risen Christ fuses with the church
> to form an overly homogenized *totus Christus*, even as
> through the *totus Christus* God finally fuses, in effect, with
> the world. As viewed from below, . . . the *totus Christus*
> fuses . . . with second person of the Trinity.[10]

So where does Hunsinger's critique leave us? Firstly, as with previous interlocutors, Hunsinger cannot help but place words in Jenson's
mouth. As with Farrow, Gathercole, and others before, critics who wish
to explore the implications of Jenson's theology outside of the economic
realm of creation and history, face perennial difficulties. While never
denying the existence of the immanent and economic realms, Jenson
resists theological speculation upon the former. Consequently, for those
wishing to explore the role of the pre-existent Christ within Jenson,
there is little material to work with. The only option left, is to create
a secondary, synthetic account of his position from the few resources
available. While Jenson's treatment of Christ's history in the incarnation, Israel, and the church offer some usable assets, the projection of
these ideas onto an ahistorical realm is something of a fool's errand.

In Hunsinger's case, his chosen method of critique consists of a
dubiously proof-texted account of Jenson's theology that, at many
points, bears little accurate resemblance to the theologian's work. As
with Gathercole before him, Hunsinger's accusatory prose concerning
Jenson's denial of the pre-existent Christ constitutes a major misreading. The allegation is false. It may be fair to suggest that Jenson does
not devote enough attention to the concept, however it is inaccurate to
suggest that he lives in denial of the doctrine itself.

In his rebuttal, Jenson turns the theological tables on Hunsinger,
charging that it is his critic who has lost sight of orthodoxy. Hunsinger's
review, Jenson suggests, confirms that he too has inherited the metaphysical mistake that time and eternity exist as polar opposites. "It is
that very assumption," Jenson declares, "that engendered all the christo-

10. Ibid., 197–98.

THAMES CLIPPERS

THE 02, PENINSULA SQUARE
LONDON

N:*68813   TID*****9840
AID : A0000000031010
VISA DEBIT

VISA DEBIT

****.****.*.** 8711
ICC   PAN.SEQ 00

SALE

CARDHOLDER COPY

PLEASE KEEP THIS RECEIPT
    FOR YOUR RECORDS

AMOUNT   £2.30

Verified by PIN

THANK YOU
16:42 05

AUTH CODE

tive' of Scripture, from creation to eschaton, but also to the individual components of that narrative."[17]

As opposed to Hunsinger, Watson welcomes the subsequent elimination of the *logos asarkos* in Jenson's work. This "shadowy figure . . . [and] disincarnate divine Son who can be considered in abstraction from Jesus of Nazareth," to Watson's mind, is an unnecessary philosophical threat to biblical theology.[18] As in Jenson, "the doctrine of the Trinity tells us nothing about an empty space above the narrative," and hence, the second person in this divine communion is none other than Jesus.[19] However, while Watson supports Jenson's eschatological weighting of the triune revelation contained within the gospel, he is quick to suggest a scriptural development for the scheme:

> Since the New Testament speaks of eschatological futurity primarily by way of a narrative about the past, it opens not with a collection of apocalypses but with the fourfold canonical gospel in which what will be and what is are defined only in terms of what has been. While the four Gospels do indeed speak of the future and the present as they speak of the past, their past tense verbs are not to be straightforwardly translated into future ones. The Gospels mean what they say.[20]

In conclusion, Watson points out that his critique concerns Jenson's *tendency* to interpret Scripture, first and foremost, futuristically. The use of the word "tendency" is key. While they share many disagreements about Jenson's work, Hunsinger, Watson, and others agree on Jenson's tendency to promote time, and the teleological drive of an eschatological God, over and above the concept and substance of space. At times, this tendency leads commentators to follow implicit aspects of his program to, what they consider, their logical and problematic conclusion. We are then confronted with the possibility that time has sublated space, temporality has overcome embodiment, and music has drowned

17. Ibid., 220.
18. Ibid., 221.
19. Ibid., 221.
20. Ibid., 222.

out all other art forms. In our discomfort, we are left to contemplate the impossibility of a pre-existent Son, the absorption of Christ into the community of the church, the declension of the Trinity into an historical process, the problematic conception of an inorganic afterlife, and the promotion of the world as a pantheistic deity. While none of these can be said to be explicit within Jenson's work, his tendency towards temporality leaves him exposed towards such interpretation. However, as Watson suggests, the solutions to implicit problems may also be implicitly present within Jenson's program.[21] While Jenson himself may yet seek to propose new formulations of his own work, the tendencies outlined in this thesis have become ingrained over the past decades.

The importance of Jenson's work, along with these pressing issues, will, no doubt, create debate and discussion for years to come. Through Watson's characterization of Jenson's *Systematic Theology*, we are reminded, once again, of Jenson's compelling and creative vision for theology and culture. In Jenson's theology of culture we witness one of the discipline's most imaginative and systematic attempts to expound an orthodox trinitarian theology within a postmodern context. Jenson's focus upon story as the key to identity, and subsequent attention to words and language as the tools by which we negotiate the temporal and spatial realities of creation, provide him with both a philosophically plausible account of human experience and a biblical platform on which to posit the triune God as the only possible explanation of reality. His historical insistence upon the resurrection of Christ as the temporal and spatial Word event by which the triune God is identified, distinguishes the Christian faith from the realm of human religion while simultaneously confirming the gospel as the hope of all mankind.

As a lifelong theological theme of Jenson's life's work, the resurrection is the key to understanding God's own futurity. It is in this event that we witness first hand the openness of God and the goal of all creation. In the triune implications of this event, we discover that reality is a triune conversation that we are both caught up in and invited to join. Having been spoken into being by the godhead, we come to know and our future unity with him in the language that we share with and about one another. Through each other, we have overheard the voice

21. This is exactly Jenson's response to the allegation. Jenson, "Response," 225.

of the creator. This converse stretches far beyond those activities that we participate in with the use of a dictionary. In almost every aspect of human life, mankind seeks to give voice to the reality with which he is presented. This totalized conversation is the stuff of culture.

Finally, there is one Word in time and space that provides humanity with access to the reality of the creator himself. As the embodied Word of the Father, Jesus is made present in the world, by his Spirit and in the church. Bound together by the eternal language-act of the Trinity, the church addresses the Father and is filled and directed by the Spirit towards her own fulfillment in Christ. Watson paraphrases Jenson perfectly at this point: "When the gospel of Christ's resurrection is proclaimed and heard in the church, it is the Father's address to the Son that we hear. That life is the harmony of the triune perichoresis—a fugue in which we are permitted to double the parts. That life is our future and present dwelling place, our eternal home."[22]

In the Spirit-enlivened converse of the church, whether through speech or music, art or architecture, or other cultural languages besides, Christ is embodied in time and space. In this moment, hope and history rhyme for evermore.

22. Watson, "America's Theologian," 208.

Bibliography

Works by Robert W. Jenson

Books by Robert R. Jenson

Jenson, R. W. *Alpha and Omega: A Study in the Theology of Karl Barth.* New York: Nelson, 1963.

———. *America's Theologian: A Recommendation of Jonathan Edwards.* New York: Oxford University Press, 1988.

———. *Essays in Theology of Culture.* Grand Rapids: Eerdmans, 1995.

———. *God after God: The God of the Past and the God of the Future Seen in the Work of Karl Barth.* New York: Bobbs-Merrill, 1969.

———. *The Knowledge of Things Hoped For. The Sense of Theological Discourse.* New York: Oxford University Press, 1969.

———. *On Thinking the Human. Resolutions of Difficult Notions.* Grand Rapids: Eerdmans, 2003.

———. *A Religion against Itself.* Richmond, VA: John Knox, 1967.

———. *Song of Songs.* Louisville, KY: John Knox, 2005.

———. *Story and Promise A Brief Theology of the Gospel about Jesus.* Philadelphia: Fortress, 1973.

———. *Systematic Theology: Volume One, The Triune God.* New York: Oxford University Press, 1997.

———. *Systematic Theology: Volume Two, The Works of God.* New York: Oxford University Press, 1999.

———. *The Triune Identity. God according to the Gospel.* Eugene, OR: Wipf & Stock, 1982.

———. *Unbaptized God: The Basic Flaw in Ecumenical Theology.* Minneapolis, MN: Augsburg Fortress, 1992.

———. *Visible Words: The Interpretation and Practice of Christian Sacraments.* Philadelphia: Fortress, 1978.

Bibliography

Books Co-Authored by Robert R. Jenson and Carl E. Braaten

Jenson, R. W., and Carl E. Braaten, *Biblical and Theological Perspectives on Eschatology.* Grand Rapids: Eerdmans, 2002.

———. *The Catholicity of the Reformation.* Grand Rapids: Eerdmans, 1996.

———. *Christian Dogmatics.* 2 vols. Philadelphia: Fortress, 1984.

———. *The Ecumenical Future.* Grand Rapids: Eerdmans, 2004.

———. *Either/Or: The Gospel or Neopaganism.* Grand Rapids: Eerdmans, 1995.

———. *The Futurist Option.* New York: Newman, 1970.

———. *In One Body through the Cross.* Grand Rapids: Eerdmans, 2003.

———. *Jews and Christians: People of God.* Grand Rapids: Eerdmans, 2003.

———. *The Last Things: Biblical and Theological Perspectives on Eschatology.* Grand Rapids: Eerdmans, 2002.

———. *A Map of Twentieth-Century Theology: Readings from Karl Barth to Radical Pluralism.* Minneapolis, MN: Fortress, 1995.

———. *Marks of the Body of Christ.* Grand Rapids: Eerdmans, 1999.

———. *Mary, Mother of God.* Grand Rapids: Eerdmans, 2004.

———. *Reclaiming the Bible for the Church.* Edinburgh: T. & T. Clark, 1996.

———. *Sin, Death and the Devil.* Grand Rapids: Eerdmans, 1999.

———. *The Strange New World of the Gospel: Re-Evangelizing in the Postmodern World.* Grand Rapids: Eerdmans, 2002.

———. *The Two Cities of God: The Church's Responsibility for the Earthly City.* Grand Rapids: Eerdmans, 1997.

———. *Union with Christ: The New Finnish Interpretation of Luther.* Grand Rapids: Eerdmans, 1998.

Books Co-Authored by Robert R. Jenson and E. W. Gritsch

Jenson, R. W., and E. W. Gritsch. *Lutheranism: The Theological Movement and its Confessional Writings.* Philadelphia: Fortress, 1976.

Essays and Shorter Works by Robert W. Jenson

Jenson, R. W. "About Dialog, and the Church, and some bits of the Theological Biography of Robert W. Jenson." *dialog* 11 (Autumn 1969) 38–42.

———. "An Attempt to Think about Mary." *dialog* 31 (Fall 1992) 259–64.

———. "Aspects of the Doctrine of Creation." In *The Doctrine of Creation*, edited by C. E. Gunton, 17–28. Edinburgh: T. & T. Clark, 1997.

———. "Beauty." *dialog* 25 (February 1986) 250–54.

———. "The Body of God's Presence: A Trinitarian Theory." In *Creation, Christ and Culture: Studies in Honour of T. F. Torrance*, edited by R. W. A. McKinney, 82–91. Edinburgh: T. & T. Clark, 1976.

———. "A Call to Faithfulness." *dialog* 30 (Spring 1991) 90–97.

———. "Can American Community Sustain Itself Without Common Faith." *dialog* 15 (Fall 1976) 270–79.

———. "Christ as Culture 1: Christ as Polity." *International Journal of Systematic Theology* 5.3 (2003) 323–29.

———. "Christ as Culture 2: Christ as Art." *International Journal of Systematic Theology* 6.1 (2004) 69–76.

———. "Christ as Culture 3: Christ as Drama." *International Journal of Systematic Theology* 6.2 (2004) 194–201.

———. "Christ–Dogma and Christ–Image." *dialog* 2 (1963) 146–51.

———. "The Church as Communion: A Catholic-Lutheran Dialogue-Consensus-Statement Dreamed in the Night." *Pro Ecclesia* IV.1 (1995) 68–78.

———. "The Church and the Sacraments." In *The Cambridge Companion to Christian Doctrine*, edited by C. E. Gunton, 207–25. Cambridge: Cambridge University Press, 1997.

———. "Christian Civilization." In *God, Truth and Wirness: Engaging Stanley Hauerwas*, edited by L. G. Jones, R. Hütter and C. R. V. Ewell, 153–63. Grand Rapids: Brazos, 2005.

———. "Creation as a Triune Act." *Word and World* 2 (1982) 34–42.

———. "Creator and Creature." *International Journal of Systematic Theology* 4.2 (2002) 216–21.

———. "Does God Have Time? The Doctrine of the Trinity and the Concept of Time in the Physical Sciences." *The Center for Theology and the Natural Sciences* 11.1 (1991) 1–6.

———. "Mr. Edwards' Affections." *dialog* 24 (1985) 169–75.

———. "The Elusive Bottom Lines." *dialog* 29 (1990) 111–18.

———. "The End is Music." In *Edwards in Our Time: Jonathan Edwards and the Shaping of American Religion*, edited by S. H. Lee and A. C. Guelzo, 161–71. Grand Rapids: Eerdmans, 1999.

———. "Eschatology." In *The Blackwell Companion to Political Theology*, edited by P. Scott and W. T. Cavanaugh, 407–20. Oxford: Blackwell, 2004.

———. "Eucharist: Its Relative Necessity, Specific Warrant and Traditional Order." *dialog* (1975) 122–33.

———. "The Eye, the Ear, and Lutheranism." *dialog* 29 (1990) 174–77.

———. "The Father, He . . ." In *Speaking the Christian God: The Holy Trinity and the Challenge of Feminism*, edited by A. F. Kimel Jr., 95–119. Grand Rapids: Eerdmans, 1992.

———. "Film, Preaching and Meaning." In *Celluloid and Symbols*, edited by J. C. Cooper and C. Skrade, 41–50. Philadelphia: Fortress, 1970.

———. "The Hauerwas Project." *Modern Theology* 8.3 (1992) 285–95.

———. "An Hermeneutical Apology for Systematics." *dialog* 4 (1965) 268–73.

———. "Jesus, Father, Spirit: The Logic of the Doctrine of the Trinity. *dialog* 26 (1987) 245–49.

———. "Justification as a Triune Event." *Modern Theology* 11 (1995) 421–27.

———. "The Kingdom of America's God." *dialog* 15 (1976) 12–21.

———. "A Lenten Sermon." *dialog* 21 (1982) 229–31.

———. "The Mandate and Promise of Baptism." *Interpretation* 30 (1976) 271–87.

———. "The Measure of Meaning in Reading Texts." *dialog* 28 (1989) 247–56.

———, with J. Bale. "Odysseus, Ulysees, and the Wanderer." *dialog* 3 (1964) 179–84.

———. "Once More: The Jesus of History and the Christ of Faith." *dialog* 11 (1972) 118–24.

———. "On Seminaries in Long Retrospect." *dialog* 28 (1989) 87–90.

———. "On the Coming of the Bigger Church." *dialog* 18 (1979) 166–67.

———. "On the ELCA's Ecumenical Choices." *dialog* 35 (1996) 222–23.

———. "Orpheus, the Buttonmaker and 'Real Community.'" *dialog* 10 (1971) 32–38.

———. "Proclamation Without Metaphysics." *dialog* 1 (1962) 22–29.

———. "Response to H. Paul Santmire's review of *A Religion Against It Itself.*" *dialog* 7 (1968) 229–32.

———. "Religious Pluralism, Christology and Barth." *dialog* 20 (1982) 31–38.

———. "The Religious Power of Scripture." *Scottish Journal of Theology* 1 (1999) 89–105.

———. "Response to Watson and Hunsinger." *Scottish Journal of Theology* 55.2 (2002) 225–17.

———. "Review Essay." *Pro Ecclesia* XIV.2 (2005) 235–38.

———. "A Sermon Preached in the Chapel of Gettysburg Seminary." *dialog* 19 (1980) 141–43.

———. "The 'Sorry' State of Lutherans." *dialog* 22 (1998) 280–83.

———. "Theosis," *dialog* 32 (1993) 118–12.

———. "Toward A Christian Theory of the Public." *dialog* 23 (1984) 191–98.

———. "Toward an Understanding of 'Is Risen.'" *dialog* 19 (1980) 31–36.

———. "What Academic Difference Would the Gospel Make." *dialog* 18 (1977) 24–28.

———. "You Wonder Where the Spirit Went." *Pro Ecclesia* 2.3 (1993) 296–304.

Works by Other Authors

Abbott, H. P. *The Cambridge Companion to Narrative.* Cambridge: Cambridge University Press, 2002.

Adorno, T. W. *The Culture Industry: Selected Essays on Mass Culture.* Edited by J. M. Bernstein. London: Routledge, 1991.

———. *Philosophy of Modern Music.* Translated by A. G. Mitchell and W. V. Blomster. New York: Seabury, 1973.

Augustine, *Confessions: Introduction, Text and Commentary.* 3 vols. Commentary by J. J. O'Donnell. Oxford: Clarendon, 1992.

———. *Confessions.* London: Penguin, 1961.

———. "De Musica." *The Fathers of the Church.* Edited by R. C. Taliaferro. New York: Schopp, 1947.

Austin, J. L. *How To Do Things with Words.* Oxford: Oxford University Press, 1975.

Barry, B. R. *Musical Time: The Sense of Order.* New York: Pendragon, 1990.

Barth, K. *Church Dogmatics 1.1: The Doctrine of the Word of God.* Translated by G. Bromiley. Edinburgh: T. & T. Clark, 1936.

———. *Church Dogmatics 1.2: The Doctrine of the Word of God.* Translated by G. T. Thomson and H. Knight. Edinburgh: T. & T. Clark, 1956.

———. *Church Dogmatics 2.1: The Doctrine of God.* Translated by T. H. L. Parker, W. B. Johnston, H. Knight and J. L. M. Haire. Edinburgh: T. & T. Clark, 1957.

———. *Mozart.* Grand Rapids: Eerdmans, 1986.

——— *Protestant Theology in the Nineteenth Century. Its Background and History.* Translated by B. Cozens and J. Bowden. London: SCM, 1972.

Barthes, R. *Image, Music, Text.* Translated by S. Heath. London: Harper Collins, 1977.

Beardsley, M. C. *Aesthetics from Classical Greece to the Present: A Short History*. New York: Macmillan, 1966.

Begbie, J. *Beholding the Glory: Incarnation through the Arts*. Grand Rapids: Baker, 2000.

———. *Music in God's Purposes*. Edinburgh: Handsel, 1989.

———. *Sounding the Depths: Theology through the Arts*. London: SCM, 2002.

———. *Theology, Music and Time*. Cambridge: Cambridge University Press, 2000.

———. *Voicing Creation's Praise*. Edinburgh: T. & T. Clark, 1991.

Berman, D. *George Berkeley: Idealism and the Man*. Oxford: Clarendon, 1994.

Bockmuehl, M. *The Cambridge to Companion Jesus*. Cambridge: Cambridge University Press, 2001.

Bunnin, N., and E. P. Tsui-James. *The Blackwell Companion to Philosophy*. Oxford: Blackwell, 2003.

Caygill, H. *A Kant Dictionary*. Oxford: Blackwell, 1995.

Cell, E. *Language, Existence and God: Interpretations of Moore, Russell, Ayer, Wittgenstein, Wisdom, Oxford Philosophy and Tillich*. New Jersey: Humanities, 1971.

Clifton, T. *Music as Heard: A Study of Applied Phenomenology*. New Haven: Yale University Press, 1983.

Cobb, K. *The Blackwell Guide to Theology and Popular Culture*. Oxford: Blackwell, 2005.

D'hert, I. *Wittgenstein's Relevance for Theology*. Bern: European University Papers, 1975.

Ebeling, G. *Introduction to a Theological Theory of Language*. Translated by R. A. Wilson. London: Harper Collins, 1973.

Eco, U. *Mouse or Rat? Translation as Negotiation*. London: Weidenfeld & Nicolson, 2003.

Eco, U., and J. V. Wertsch. *The Aesthetics of Thomas Aquinas*. Massachusetts: Harvard University Press, 1988.

Edwards, J. *The Works of Jonathan Edwards*. New Haven: Yale University Press, 1980.

Epstein, D. *Shaping Time: Music, the Brain and Performance*. New York: Schirmer, 1995.

Fackre, G. *The Doctrine of Revelation: A Narrative Interpretation*. Edinburgh: Edinburgh University Press, 1997.

Farrow, D., D. Demson, and J. Augustine Di Noia O. P. "Robert Jenson's Systematic Theology: Three Responses." *International Journal of Systematic Theology* 1.1 (1999) 89–104.

Fiddes, P. S. *Participating in God: A Pastoral Doctrine of the Trinity*. London: Darton, Longman & Todd, 2000.

Foster, M. B. *Mystery and Philosophy*. London: SCM, 1957.

Gathercole, S. "Pre-existence and the Freedom of the Son in Creation and Redemption: An Exposition in Dialogue with Robert Jenson." *International Journal of Systematic Theology* 7.1 (2005) 38–51.

Gay, P. *The Enlightenment: An Interpretation, Vol. 2: The Science of Freedom*. London: Wildwood House, 1973.

Goodman, N. *Languages of Art: An Approach to a Theory of Symbols*. Indianapolis, IN: Hackett, 1976.

Gunton, C. E. *The Doctrine of Creation*. Edinburgh: T. & T. Clark, 1997.

———. *Father, Son and Holy Spirit: Toward a Fully Trinitarian Theology*. Edinburgh: T. & T. Clark, 2003.

———. *The One, The Three and The Many: God and the Culture of Modernity*. Cambridge: Cambridge University Press, 1993.

———. *The Promise of Trinitarian Theology*. Edinburgh: T. & T. Clark, 1991.

———. *Theology through the Theologians*. Edinburgh: T. & T. Clark, 1996.

———. *Trinity, Time, and Church: A Response to the Theology of Robert W. Jenson*. Grand Rapids: Eerdmans, 2000.

———. *The Triune Creator: A Historical and Systematic Study*. Edinburgh: Edinburgh University Press, 1998.

Hauerwas, S. *Resident Aliens: Life in the Christian Colony*. Nashville, TN: Abingdon, 1989.

Harries, R. *Art and the Beauty of God: A Christian Understanding*. London: Mowbray, 1993.

Hart, D. B. *The Beauty of the Infinite: The Aesthetics of Christian Truth*. Grand Rapids: Eerdmans, 2003.

Hart, T. *Faith Thinking: Dynamics of Christian Theology*. London: SPCK, 1995.

———. *Regarding Karl Barth: Toward a Reading of His Theology*. Carlisle: Paternoster, 1999.

Hegel, G. W. F. *On Art, Religion, Philosophy*. Translated by B. Bosanquet. New York: Harper and Row, 1970.

———. *Hegel and the Human Spirit: A Translation of the Jena Lectures on the Philosophy of Spirit with Commentary*. Translated by L. Rauch. Detroit: Wayne State University Press, 1983.

———. *Lectures on the Philosophy of Religion. Volume I: Introduction and the Concept of Religion*. Edited by P. C. Hodgson. Translated by R. F. Brown, P. C. Hodgson, and J. M. Stewart. Los Angeles: University of California Press, 1984.

———. *Lectures on the Philosophy of Religion. Volume II: Determinate Religion*. Edited by P. C. Hodgson. Translated by R. F. Brown, P. C. Hodgson, and J. M. Stewart. Los Angeles: University of California Press, 1984.

———. *Lectures on the Philosophy of Religion. Volume III: The Consummate Religion*. Edited by P. C. Hodgson. Translated by R. F. Brown, P. C. Hodgson, and J. M. Stewart. Los Angeles: University of California Press, 1984.

———. *Phenomenology of Spirit*. Translated by A. V. Miller. Oxford: Oxford University Press, 1977.

———. *The Philosophy of History*. Translated by J. Sibree. New York: Dover, 1956.

———. *Theologian of the Spirit*. Edited by P. C. Hodgson. Minneapolis, MN: Fortress, 1997.

Helm, P. *The Divine Revelation*. London: Marshall, Morgan and Scott, 1982.

Hepburn, R. *Christianity and Paradox*. London: Watts, 1958.

Holmes, S. R. *God of Grace and God of Glory: An Account of the Theology of Jonathan Edwards*. Grand Rapids: Eerdmans, 2001.

Horne, B. "Art: A Trinitarian Imperative?" In *Trinitarian Theology Today: Essays on Divine Act and Being*, edited by C. Schwöbel, 80–91. Edinburgh: T. & T. Clark, 1995.

———. "Divine and Human Creativity." In *The Doctrine of Creation: Essays in Dogmatics, History and Philosophy*, edited by C. E. Gunton, 135–48. Edinburgh: T. & T. Clark, 1997.

Hudson, W. D. *Wittgenstein and Religious Belief*. London: Macmillan, 1975.

Hunsinger, George. "Robert Jenson's Systematic Theology: A Review Essay." *Scottish Journal of Theology* 55.2 (2002) 161–200.

Inge, J. *A Christian Theology of Place*. Aldershot: Ashgate, 2003.

Inwood, M. J. *Hegel*. London: Routledge, 1983.

————. *Hegel*. Oxford: Oxford University Press, 1985.

————. *A Hegel Dictionary*. Oxford: Blackwell, 1992.

Jackson Knight, W. F. *St. Augustine's De Musica: A Synopsis*. London: Orthological Institute, 1949.

Jasper, D. *The Sacred Desert: Religion, Literature, Art and Culture*. Oxford: Blackwell, 2004.

Keightley, A. *Wittgenstein, Grammar and God*. London: Epworth, 1976.

Kerr, F. *Theology after Wittgenstein*. Oxford: Blackwell, 1986.

Kramer, J. D. *The Time of Music: New Meanings, New Temporalities, New Listening Strategies*. New York: Schirmer, 1988.

Küng, H. *Art and the Question of Meaning*. Translated by E. Quinn. London: SCM, 1981.

————. *The Incarnation of God: An Introduction to Hegel's Theological Thought as Prolegomena to a Future Christology*. Translated by J. R. Stephenson. New York: Crossroad, 1987.

————. *Mozart: Traces of Transcendence*. Translated by J. Bowden. London: SCM, 1992.

Kramer, J. D. *The Time of Music: New Meanings, New Temporalities, New Listening Strategies*. New York: Schirmer, 1988.

La Croix, R. R. *Augustine on Music: An Interdisciplinary Collection of Essays*. New York: Mellen, 1988.

Langer, S. K. *Feeling and Form*. London: Routledge, 1953.

Lindbeck, G. A. *The Nature of Doctrine: Religion and Theology in a Postliberal Age*. Philadelphia: Westminster, 1984.

Lee, S. H., and A. C. Guelzo. *Edwards in Our Time: Jonathan Edwards and the Shaping of American Religion*. Grand Rapids: Eerdmans, 1999.

Maritain, J. *Art and Scholasticism*. Whitefish, MT: Kessinger, 2003.

McCarney, J. M. *Hegel on History*. London: Routledge, 2000.

McCutcheon, T *Religion within the Limits of Language Alone: Wittgenstein on Philosophy and Religion*. Aldershot: Ashgate, 2001.

Melges, F. T. *Time and the Inner Future: A Temporal Approach to Psychiatric Disorders*. New York: Wiley, 1982.

Minsky, M. "Music, Mind, and Meaning." *Computer Music Journal* 5.3 (Autumn, 1981) 28–44.

McKim, D. K. *The Cambridge Companion to Martin Luther*. Cambridge: Cambridge University Press, 2003.

McKinney, R. W. A., ed. *Creation, Christ and Culture: Studies in Honour of T. F. Torrance*. Edinburgh: T. & T. Clark, 1976.

Molnar, P. *Divine Freedom and the Doctrine of the Immanent Trinity*. Edinburgh: T. & T. Clark, 2002.

Neuhaus, R. *The Naked Public Square: Religion and Democracy in America*. Grand Rapids: Eerdmans, 1984.

————. *American Apostasy: The Triumph of "Other" Gospels*. Grand Rapids: Eerdmans, 1989.

Newbigin, L. *The Gospel in a Pluralist Theology*. London: SPCK, 1989.

————. *Signs Amid the Rubble: The Purposes of God in Human History*. Edited by G. Wainwright. Grand Rapids: Eerdmans, 2003.

Niebuhr, R. H. *Christ and Culture*. San Francisco: Harper, 1951.

——. *Theology, History and Culture: Major Unpublished Writings.* Edited by W. S. Johnson. New Haven: Yale University Press, 1996.

Nielsen, K. "Wittgensteinian Fideism." *Philosophy* 42.161 (1967) 191–209.

Pannenberg, W. *Anthropology in Theological Perspective.* Translated by M. J. O'Connell. Edinburgh: T. & T. Clark, 1985.

Pattison, G. *Art, Modernity and Faith.* London: SCM, 1998.

Pickstock, C. "Music: City, Soul and Cosmos after Augustine." *Radical Orthodoxy: A New Theology.* Edited by J. Millbank, C. Pickstock, and G. Ward. London: Routledge, 1999.

Ricoeur, P. *Time and Narrative. Volume 1.* Translated by K. McLaughlin and D. Pellauer. Chicago: University of Chicago Press, 1983.

Rowland, T. *Culture and the Thomist Tradition: After Vatican II.* London: Routledge, 2003.

Santmire, H. P. "A Review of *A Religion Against It Itself.*" *dialog* 7 (1968) 224–29.

Sayers, D. "Towards a Christian Aesthetic." In *Christian Letters to a Post-Christian World,* edited by R. Jellema, 69–79. Grand Rapids: Eerdmans, 1969.

Schmidt, P. F. *Religious Knowledge.* Westport: Greenwood, 1981.

Shepherd, V. "Review of *Theology, Music and Time.*" *International Journal of Systematic Theology* 5.2 (2003) 241–47.

Sherrard, P. *The Sacred in Life and Art.* Ipswich: Golgonooza, 1990.

Steiner, G. *Real Presences: Is There Anything in What We Say?* London: Faber, 1989.

Tanner, K. *Economy of Grace.* Minneapolis, MN: Fortress, 2005.

——. *Jesus, Humanity and the Trinity: A Brief Systematic Theology.* Minneapolis, MN: Fortress, 2001.

——. *Theories of Culture: A New Agenda for Theology.* Minneapolis, MN: Fortress, 1997.

Tanner, K., D. Brown, and S. Greeve Davaney. *Converging on Culture Theologians in Dialogue with Cultural Analysis and Criticism.* New York: Oxford University Press, 2001.

Tillich, P. *On Art and Architecture.* Edited by J. Dillenberger and J. Dillenberger. New York: Crossroad, 1989.

——. *The Protestant Era: What is Wrong with Christian Civilization? Does Protestantism Need a Reformation?* Chicago: University of Chicago Press, 1938.

——. *Systematic Theology.* 3 vols. London: SCM, 1978.

——. *Theology of Culture.* Edited by R. C. Kimball. New York: Oxford University Press, 1959.

——. *What is Religion?* Edited by J. L. Adams. New York: Harper and Row, 1969.

Torrance, T. F. *Space, Time and Incarnation.* Oxford: Oxford University Press, 1969.

——. *Theological Science.* London: Oxford University Press 1969.

Ward, G. *Cities of God.* London: Routledge, 2000.

Watson, Francis. "'America's Theologian': An Appreciation of Robert Jenson's *Systematic Theology.*" *Scottish Journal of Theology* 55.2 (2002) 201–23.

Weber, W. *Essays in Sociology.* Edited and translated by H. Gerth and C. Wright Mills. London: Kegan Paul, 1947.

Williams, R. "Postmodern Theology and the Judgement of the World." In *Postmodern Theology: Christian Faith in a Pluralist World,* edited by F. B. Burnham, 92–112. New York: Harper Collins, 1989.

Wittgenstein, L. *Culture and Value*. Edited by G. H. von Wright. Translated by P. Winch. Oxford: Blackwell, 1980.

———. *Lectures and Conversation on Aesthetics, Psychology and Religious Belief.* Edited by C. Barrett. Oxford: Blackwell, 1966.

———. *Ludwig Wittgenstein: Cambridge Letters*. Edited by B. McGuinness and G. H. von Wright. Oxford: Blackwell, 1995.

———. *Notebooks 1914–1916*. Edited by G. H. von Wright and G. E. M. Anscombe. Oxford: Blackwell, 1961.

——— *Philosophical Investigations*. Translated by G. E. M. Anscombe. Oxford: Blackwell, 1958.

———. *Remarks on Frazer's Golden Bough*. Translated by A. C. Miles and R. Rhees. Retford: Brynmill, 1979.

———. *Tractatus Logico-Philosophicus*. Translated by D. F. Pears and B. F. McGuinness. London: Routledge, 1974.

———. *Wittgenstein's Lectures: Cambridge, 1930–1932*. Edited by A. Ambrose. Oxford: Blackwell, 1979.

Wolterstorff, N. *Art in Action: Toward a Christian Aesthetic*. Carlisle: Paternoster, 1997.

———. "The Theological Significance of Going to Church and Leaving." Unpublished paper.

———. *Works and Worlds of Art*. New York: Oxford University Press, 1980.

Yerkes, J. *The Christology of Hegel*. New York: State University of New York Press, 1983.

Zuckerkandl, V. *The Sense of Music*. Princeton: Princeton University Press, 1959.

———. *Sound and Symbol: Music and the External World*. London: Routledge, 1956.

Lightning Source UK Ltd.
Milton Keynes UK
UKOW04f1446020614

232700UK00001B/108/P